Got Milked?

GOT MILKED?

What You Don't Know About Dairy,
the Truth About Calcium, and Why
You'll Thrive Without Milk

Alissa Hamilton

 Collins

Got Milked?
Copyright © 2015 by Alissa Hamilton.
All rights reserved.

Published by Collins, an imprint of HarperCollins Publishers Ltd

First Canadian edition

No part of this book may be used or reproduced in any manner
whatsoever without the prior written permission of the publisher,
except in the case of brief quotations embodied in reviews.

HarperCollins books may be purchased for educational, business, or
sales promotional use through our Special Markets Department.

HarperCollins Publishers Ltd
2 Bloor Street East, 20th Floor
Toronto, Ontario, Canada
M4W 1A8

www.harpercollins.ca

Library and Archives Canada Cataloguing in Publication
information is available upon request

ISBN 978-1-44342-127-0

Designed by Lisa Stokes

Printed and bound in the United States
RRD 9 8 7 6 5 4 3 2 1

For Oscar, keep piling your plate high with broccoli and maybe one day you'll be a world-class athlete just like your grandfather

CONTENTS

Milk Matters: Me, Maxine, and America's First Fast Food, Milk

"I haven't given Oscar milk. He's two now. What do I do???"

That was Maxine's burning question when she, her mother Tina, her firstborn, Oscar, and her soon-to-be-second-born, Tobias, paid me a visit in August 2012.

Maxine was my best friend growing up. But it had been a while. After high school she followed Tina back to Amsterdam, where Tina was born. The August visit was a kind of reunion. The three and three-quarters of them, and my big sister, Kara, came over to my place for dinner, where Maxine's quandary started the memories rolling.

When I was little, "drink your milk" was a common refrain in most of my friends' homes. I was always turning down glasses of milk when I went over to play with the kids down the street. But Maxine's house was different. Her mother, Tina, who lived on tulip bulbs as a child in Amsterdam during World War II, had grown plenty strong without milk. Maybe that's why she didn't treat milk the same way that the parents of my other friends did: as an essential part of breakfast, lunch, dinner, and every "kid snack" in between. And yet here was Maxine wondering "Milk?" and Tina, curious, "If not cow's milk, then what?"

Substitute any nutritious, calcium-packed food for milk and Maxine's question sounds silly:

"I haven't given Oscar kale. He's two now. What do I do???"

You and I both know that Oscar will survive without kale, or salmon, or even broccoli, for that matter. Maybe he'll learn to like kale later. If he doesn't, all is not lost. There are plenty of other nutrient-dense vegetables to choose from.

As it turns out, Oscar was already loving broccoli when I met him. Broccoli is pretty much all he had for dinner. Maybe his body instinctively knew what many parents don't: broccoli is calcium rich. Maybe his bones were telling him: "I want calcium, give me broccoli." Or maybe he just liked the familiar, slightly sweet taste and super green color. For whatever reason, he wanted seconds, and then thirds. I'm pretty sure if Maxine had conditioned him to drink milk with his dinner, he wouldn't have had room for all the greens he playfully fingered before devouring.

While we all know that Oscar will be just fine if, by the age of two, he hasn't had tofu, the same is not true if we know he hasn't had an ounce of cow's milk, or the products made from it. Cow's milk has been promoted as a food without substitute, as being necessary and not interchangeable with foods outside the dairy group. Many of us sense that all is right when we pour milk on our cereal for breakfast. When I got to talking with Michelle, my college friend from Minnesota, about milk, she mentioned straight off that her grandmother thinks a meal without milk is incomplete. So does Michelle. Years of nudging from our elders, combined with government dairy recommendations and dairy-industry advertisements have implanted in our minds a way of thinking about milk that is hard to supplant. Milk is on our minds and tables.

Upon closer examination, the North American preoccupation with milk as vital betrays something more worrisome than a mere buy-in to dairy industry advertising. It signals a nationwide surrendering to fuzzy logic. The erroneous reasoning that has (mis)guided North Americans for decades runs as follows: calcium is essential for growing strong bones; milk is high in calcium; therefore, if we don't drink milk, our bones will lack the calcium they need to be strong, and we will suffer the broken health consequences. Spelled out this way, the leap in logic that every prospective law student tries to avoid when taking the standardized Law School Admissions Test (LSAT) is unmistakable: while milk is high in calcium, milk is not the only source of calcium; therefore, just because milk is high in calcium and calcium is essential for strong bones and good health does *not* mean *milk* is essential for strong bones and good health.

Descriptions by the National Dairy Council and other dairy promoters of milk's "unique nutrient package" as comprising "nine essential nutrients" have only reinforced the popular misconception that milk is an essential part of a healthy lifestyle. To harried parents who are half-listening and chasing after toddlers or juggling tween routines, multitasking means eliminating the unnecessary and sometimes, mistakenly, the essence: milk has "nine essential nutrients" gets clipped to "milk is essential." The USDA defines an "essential nutrient" as "a dietary substance required for healthy body functioning." Milk, which many healthy, functioning bodies live without, doesn't meet this fundamental definition of an "essential nutrient."

Milk's status as the ultimate health food is too embedded in the national psyche for logic and cautious reading to budge conventional thinking. Not even the research and resulting recommendations of Harvard physicians have been enough to move the North American mindset outside of the milk box. For years Dr. David S. Ludwig, professor of pediatrics at the Harvard Medical School (HMS) and professor of nutrition at the Harvard School of Public Health (HSPH), and his colleague, Dr. Walter C. Willett, chair of the Department of Nutrition at HSPH and a professor of medicine at HMS, have been challenging the U.S. Department of Agriculture's (USDA) dietary recommendations regarding milk, which have remained relatively consistent since World War II, when the USDA started getting serious about telling Americans how to eat.

These recommendations can be found at ChooseMyPlate.gov, an interactive government website designed to illuminate its MyPlate icon, which the USDA introduced in 2011 to replace its less intuitive Food Guide Pyramid. The icon illustrates five food groups: Fruits; Vegetables; Grains; Protein; and Dairy. Depicted as a blue circle just touching the plate where you'd find a glass, the Dairy category reads visually, if not literally, as "milk." Whether you conflate the two or not, Dairy is the only food group that is made up entirely of one food, milk. If the USDA has its way, you will obtain a substantial portion of your daily calories from this single food and the products made from it. Click on "Dairy," and then on "How Much is Needed" and you'll find that the answer is a lot. According to the guidelines at the time of this book's publication, children two to three years old should be consuming two cups of dairy per day; children four to eight, two and a half cups per day; and everyone else, three cups per day.

Doing the math shows that's not just a lot of milk; it's also a lot of sugar and, depending on how you take your milk, a lot of fat. You might want to have a pencil and paper, or at least a calculator, handy here. I'm going to assume that you are older than eight and among the majority who, according to the USDA, should be consuming three cups of dairy every day. Now let's say you choose to meet your daily dairy quota with a low-calorie product such as skim milk. You're still allocating a hefty 240 calories every day to one food, which is more than 10 percent of the daily calories of an average diet. And that's the conservative scenario. The reality is that not too many people enjoy skim milk. If you and your family are like most, you probably can't bear the watery stuff without added sugar and flavor. Moving to the more likely case, we'll start with you and consider the kids later.

Despite the dairy industry's repeated attempts to convince us that milk isn't only a kid's drink—witness, for one example, the GetEnough campaign created by the Dairy Farmers of Canada in association with the

Colorectal Cancer Association of Canada that features a calf-eyed girl in pink beckoning her mom to drink the large glass of milk she offers up with a smile while the facing page brings home the core message that milk "contains 16 essential nutrients" and *"two out of three adults just don't get enough milk products every day"* [emphasis *not* added]—I don't know many adults who fill their milk prescription by chugging it straight up. So while the book centers on milk, it is impossible to talk about milk without talking about dairy, the group of milk products high in calcium that the USDA has gathered together under one umbrella. Maybe you, like so many, compensate for your aversion to drinking a plain glass of milk by replacing it with a low-fat fruit yogurt for lunch. Sounds healthy, until you read the Nutrition Facts on the back. As it turns out, your average 6-ounce serving of flavored yogurt contains 170 calories and 26 grams of sugar. That's the equivalent of 6.5 teaspoons of sugar, which is a fair amount considering that the American Heart Association recommends no more than 6 teaspoons per day for women and no more than 9 for men. Whether you make the small container the center of your meal, or add it to your sandwich and chips because you feel neglectful for not setting a glass of milk beside your lunch, even yogurt, which Governor Cuomo has made the official snack of New York State through legislation he signed in October, 2014, ought to be approached with eyes wide open to what the nutrition label says.

Now for the children nine years and older, let's say they choose low-fat chocolate milk to fill the USDA's definition of their daily dairy needs. Three glasses of this ubiquitous milk product will provide them with 480 calories, or almost a quarter of their daily caloric needs. Since almost all the calories in low-fat flavored milk come from sugar, that's like apportioning a quarter of your child's daily calories to sugar. Looking at the numbers, there are almost 75 grams, or 18 teaspoons of sugar in one daily dose of dairy in the form of low-fat flavored milk. That approaches the 78 grams of sugar in three 8-ounce glasses of Coca-Cola. Yet while the USDA works to ban sugary foods, and specifically soft drinks, from school cafeterias, it stands by flavored milk as a healthy addition to your child's diet and school lunch programs. It doesn't take a Harvard doctor to see that there's something wrong with this picture.

I have already acknowledged that logic will not suffice to change our deeply rooted patterns of thinking about milk. Calcium is essential. Milk is high in calcium. It does *not* follow that milk is essential. No matter how many times I repeat that, you will probably still get an "I'm doing my body good" kick when you pour milk over your cereal in the morning. Not even the research, reports, and advice handed down to us from the most haloed institutions and reputable individuals have managed to reverse the three glasses of milk per day hang-up that decades of messaging has made dietary dogma in North America. You can't have apple pie without milk without feeling guilty about it.

The stand that Dr. Ludwig and others have taken that milk is not essential for health and wellness is indisputable. The best response that a spokesperson for the American Dairy Association and the National Dairy Council has offered to Doctors Ludwig's and Willett's position is that "it is difficult to get recommended levels of calcium by consuming non-dairy sources." In its defense, the dairy industry highlights the one attribute that milk has going for it: it's a convenient source of calcium, as well as "eight other essential nutrients in the diet including vitamins A, D, B_{12} and protein."

True, milk is convenient. It's everywhere. You won't find bushels of kale or broccoli at the corner Stop n' Go. You are guaranteed to find cartons of milk, from nonfat to full fat, from strawberry to chocolate flavored, from single-serve chugs to gallon-size jugs. True, milk is high in calcium. But it's also high in sugar, cholesterol, calories, and saturated fat. Just because milk is readily available, just because you can get it anywhere, doesn't mean you should. What we don't hear so much about is that milk is one of the most allergenic foods; the majority of American adults can't digest it; animal studies have shown that the major type of protein in milk, casein, also promotes cancer; and lactose, the sugar in milk, breaks down during digestion into the highly inflammatory sugar, D-galactose, which has been proven to promote aging and disease in mice. Even milk's high calcium content, a seeming incontrovertible good, may not in fact be doing our bodies good. We are told to drink milk for strong bones. However, comparative studies show that countries that don't habitually consume milk tend to have lower bone-fracture rates than those that do. These are just a few of the hazards of milk that you will read about in the following chapters.

We weren't always so milk obsessed. As Ron Schmid explains in the introduction to his book *The Untold Story of Milk,* up until the mid-1800s Americans mostly consumed milk, if at all, either in its fermented form—whether as yogurt, buttermilk (also known as "clabbered milk," or cheese)—or churned into butter. Even then such products would have been a luxury for nineteenth-century city-dwellers. It wasn't until the mid-nineteenth century, when Americans began to move en masse to cities, that fluid cow's milk grew in popularity. At the outset it was primarily used as a substitute for the breast milk of mothers who were now working long hours in factories away from their sucklings. That was the beginning. Then came pasteurization, the heat treatment that destroys pathogenic bacterial species such as tuberculosis that can and, prior to the widespread use of pasteurization technology, did creep into fresh milk, a medium that without proper handling is an ideal breeding ground for deadly microorganisms.

Pasteurization made the industrial scale production and distribution of fresh milk from farm to city possible. As you will read in the chapters to come, twentieth-century wartime exigencies more than civilian health needs made it desirable. But there's another twist to the story. In her history, *Nature's Perfect Food: How Milk Became America's Drink,* Melanie Dupuis, PhD, fills in one more piece of the puzzle of how fresh milk rapidly rose to become, by the 1940s, a North American staple: advertising. Dupuis tracks how patent medicine companies began developing infant formulas based on cow's milk in the nineteenth century. By the 1880s these companies were advertising such milk products in women's magazines alongside promotions for their patent medicines. The link between milk and medicine was thus forged right out of the gate, helping to transform cow's milk from America's first fast food into a mainstay.

One of the earliest foods to be the subject of mass advertising, milk was primed for what Dupuis calls the "consumerist ideology" that over-took America in the 1950s. She observes that during this golden age of food advertising, the focus shifted from agrarian images of production to urban scenes of consumption. For milk, ads that once depicted milkmaids at the teats of cows now featured happy, healthy infants. The idea of milk as an elixir carrying the secret to a robust future took hold. The discomfort that mothers like Maxine feel when they allow their toddlers to go without milk is proof that milk's grip on our thoughts about health and well-being is as strong as ever. Even skeptics such as Maxine can't escape the fact that when it comes down to it, she is stuck on milk.

In *Got Milked*, I take Maxine's question about her son Oscar, which resonates with so many parents, and the dairy industry's defense of dairy as convenient, as a summons to change our relationship with milk in North America. Why? Because our relationship with milk, which is based on false notions of its goodness, is not a healthy one. Milk is far from perfect, which begs the question: why does milk continue to occupy such a privileged place in the North American diet?

My hope in writing this book is that it will provide you with not only some answers but also the tools to get by easily, deliciously, and health-fully without milk and milk products. Read on and you may find your and your family's meals becoming more colorful, with green especially plenti-ful. Read on and you may find yourself slimming down and your children growing tall and strong *without* cajoling them to down a glass of milk at every meal. Read on—you only have pounds to lose and much, including soundness and vigor of body and mind, to gain.

CHAPTER 1

The Dairy Landscape: Mapping the Major Players Promoting Dairy in America

The cow's milk in the refrigerators and lining the shelves of big-box supermarkets today is not the milk your grandmother got. Nor is it anything most of us fully comprehend even if we get it. Recalling the days when orange juice was orange juice, Don, a consumer fraud lawyer who is a friend of mine, contrasted twenty-first-century commercial orange juice to milk. He knows that most of what is sold in cartons today is so far from the tree that flavor engineers rather than the oranges squeezed give the juice its familiar taste. But thank goodness "milk is milk," he stated, before retreating with a sheepish "isn't it?" Don believed that no matter where you are, no matter what supermarket you go to, you can count on milk being milk. I apologized for having to burst his bubble. Milk is no longer one clear and straightforward thing.

MODERN MASS-PRODUCED MILK

The incessant marketing of milk as essential has transformed it from a product with a single identity to one with many enigmatic personalities. There are the variations on the same theme—skim, with a fat content ranging between 0 and 0.5 percent and averaging 0.1 percent; low fat, with a fat content of 1 percent; the popular semi-skim, with a fat content of about 1.7 percent; reduced fat, with a fat content of 2 percent; standardized whole milk, with a fat content of 3.5 percent; natural whole milk, with a fat content of 4 percent; and flavored—that are less familiar than they might first seem. 3.5 percent "whole milk," for instance, is a misnomer. Although it started "whole," by the time it gets to you in the store it has had its fat removed and added back to make it "full" fat.

There are almost as many ways of processing milk as there are choices of fat levels and flavors. To be called "milk," the Federal Food and Drug Administration (FDA) requires that it be pasteurized. This is usually the first step milk undergoes once it leaves the farm. However, pasteurization is no longer one procedure. There are three major methods: the high-temperature–short-time (HTST) method; the batch-holding method; and the ultra-high-temperature (UHT) method. The first heats milk to just over 160 degrees Farenheit, or 72 degrees Celsius, for at least sixteen seconds. In the batch-holding method the temperature is lower, just over 143 degrees Farenheit, or 62 degrees Celsius, but the time is longer, thirty minutes. Finally UHT pasteurization is what it says: milk is subjected to super high temperatures, from 280.4 to 316.4 degrees Farenheit, or 138 to 158 degrees Celsius, for a couple of seconds.

Once milk has been pasteurized, most of the time it is homogenized, though the label on the milk carton doesn't have to say so. This means the milk is agitated and then passed through small filters under high pressure so that the fat globules break down in size. Dairy processors like the technology for a couple of reasons: it makes it easy to mix large batches of milk from different farms and still end up with a uniform product, in consistency and in fat content; and it prolongs the shelf life. Some researchers, such as the late Mary Enig, PhD, of the Weston A. Price Foundation's Campaign for Real Milk, also believe that the process has negative impacts. The two major criticisms are that it makes the milk more prone to oxidation and, due to the tendency of the fat globules to pick up fragments of milk protein once broken down, allergic reactions. Although others, such as editorial board member of the UC Berkeley *Wellness Letter* Dr. John Swartzberg, say these theories are unfounded, the issue of whether homogenized milk is unhealthy remains live and an ongoing area of investigation.

Sure you can buy naturally whole, unhomogenzied, unpasteurized milk, but not everywhere. In some states and all of Canada, the commercial sale of unpasteurized milk is illegal. This book is not about such contraband, which is a whole different story. It's about the milk that the USDA and the dairy industry are urging you to set down alongside your plate. The fact that modern processing technologies have made the link between milk and nature's medicine more tenuous has not stopped these milk advocates from continuing to use the health hook to convince us that milk is a fundamental food.

THE ROOTS AND SHOOTS OF MILK MARKETING

The USDA's nutrition guidelines are only one of many hurdles to weaning the world of America and beyond off of milk. The web of dairy institutions that spans the globe is anything but threadbare. In the United States alone the dairy network is vast and strong, with the National Dairy Council (NDC) at its center. Born in 1915 to, according to one dairy-industry history, "protect the public's good image of dairy in light of a foot-and-mouth disease outbreak," the NDC led the way in the early days in supporting dairy ad and education campaigns and research into the goodness of milk and dairy. At the same time, it cultivated close ties with the USDA, the federal agency that President Lincoln organized in 1862 to promote the production and consumption of US agricultural commodities. The strategy worked superbly, ensuring the government's endorsement of milk for every occasion. MyPlate illustrates the singular partnership between dairy and the USDA well. Dairy is the only agricultural commodity to receive its own color and undivided representation. Yes, there's a slice of green for vegetables, but who's gone on a broccoli run? Who hasn't gone on a milk run?

Other national organizations that have contributed to milk's "must-have" status include the National Fluid Milk Processor Promotion Board and the National Dairy Promotion and Research Board. The first oversees the National Fluid Milk Processor Promotion Program. The Fluid Milk Promotion Act of 1990 authorizes the program, which fluid milk processors fund through an assessment charged on all commercially processed and marketed fluid milk. The Fluid Milk Processor Promotion Board uses the assessments to finance generic advertising to expand the market for fluid milk products in the United States. The second, the National Dairy Promotion and Research Board, is responsible for administering the dairy-farmer–funded Dairy Promotion Program. The Dairy Production Stabilization Act of 1983 authorizes this program, the purpose of which is to increase milk and dairy consumption and decrease surpluses through product promotion, research, and education.

The spate of national dairy promotion statutes and organizations doesn't end there. Add to the roster Dairy Management Inc. (DMI), which is affiliated with the National Milk Producers Federation (NMPF). DMI, which incorporated in 1995, manages the National Dairy Council and the American Dairy Association, and founded the Innovation Center for U.S. Dairy. Funded by dairy importers, and check-off fees collected from America's almost 49,000 dairy farmers through the check-off program administered by the National Dairy Promotion and Research Board, DMI describes its purpose: "Created to help increase sales and demand for dairy products, DMI and its related organizations work to increase demand for dairy through research, education and innovation, and to maintain confidence in dairy foods, farms and businesses."

The Commodity, Promotion, Research, and Information Act of 1996 authorizes the USDA to oversee check-off organizations for various agricultural commodities, such as DMI for dairy. DMI consists of members of the National Dairy Promotion and Research Board and the United Dairy Industry Association, a self-described "federation of state and regional dairy producer-funded promotion organizations that provides marketing programs that are developed and implemented in coordination with its members."

Besides these national-level organizations, various state dairy councils and boards have contributed more than their share of time and money to shaping milk into a perceived perfect and essential food. California, which produces more milk than any other state, has been at the forefront of efforts to keep dairy a complete circle on MyPlate and milk in the refrigerators of North America. You've seen the billboards featuring Bill Clinton before he became a vegan, Harrison Ford, Martha Stewart, the Williams all-star tennis sisters, Glenn Close, Jennifer Hudson, all in TV's *Modern Family*, and recent inductee Miranda Lambert sporting milk mustaches. The California Milk Processor Board (CMPB), which the California Department of Food and Agriculture established in 1993, is the magician behind it all. Funded by California dairy processors, the CMPB attempted to reverse declining milk sales in 1993 by asking "Got Milk?" In 1994 milk sales in California increased for the first time in over a decade. With a 90 percent recognition rate, the curious, in-your-face campaign, the brainchild of the advertising agency Goodby, Silverstein & Partners, is considered by some to be one of the most successful in history. "Got Milk?" was registered as a federal trademark in 1995 and has since been co-opted by dairy boards across the United States. It knows no borders. Even Canadians get "Got Milk?"

In addition to the outward-reaching CMPB, there's the inward-looking Dairy Council of California. Established in 1919, its original priority was to ensure that the state's children were receiving adequate amounts of milk. The Mobile Dairy Classroom that first rolled out in the 1930s is still roaming the state teaching schoolchildren about the who, what, where, and how behind dairy production. The council's programs, funded by California's dairy producers and processors, have served to secure milk in California's classrooms and California as the nation's most prolific milk producer.

The list of agricultural commodities that have benefited from USDA authorized check-off organizations is long: almonds, beef, eggs, honey, lamb, mushrooms, peanuts, potatoes, pork, and soybeans, to name a few. There is even a Popcorn Board and a Highbush Blueberry Council. You may be familiar with "Beef: It's What's for Dinner," or "Pork. The Other White Meat." They are the chorus lines sung by the check-off organizations for beef and pork, respectively. No promotion, however, has proven as appealing or eye-catching as "Got Milk?" with its pantheon of mustached celebrities. If making it into the league of chicken is the best that pork can say for itself, it isn't saying much. If beef is what's for dinner, forget it. The slogan is prosaic, didactic, and makes the free-spirited want something different. "Got Milk?" on the other hand is engaging. The question, which has been linked to Girl Scouts selling their cookies, is at once waggish and lighthearted. Or it was for a long run. The fun and games are over. With everyone from the military to Michelle Obama to the National Institutes of Health (NIH) urging Americans to slim down, milk and cookies is no longer an easy sell. The CMPB is heeding the signs that milk has to be more than face paint and dessert drink to earn its stay. New videos depict break-dancing, basketball-playing, fast-swimming youth literally bursting with milk's energy. A glass of milk has 8 grams of protein, and the CMPB wants to show it: "What 8 grams of protein looks like when you unleash your inner rock star" is the caption that follows a woman playing the electric guitar. "Milk Life" is the new header.

While the CMPB, and with it the entire dairy establishment, are intent on emphasizing the punch that milk brings to the table, you don't have to take the blow sitting down.

CHAPTER 2

Ironed Out: Milk Is Making
Our Young Sick and Tired

The fact that my friend Maxine had never given her two-year-old son Oscar cow's milk haunted her. Her plea "what should I do?" surprised me at first. I had thought that when she moved from Toronto to Amsterdam after high school, she would shed the trappings of her North American upbringing. She did, for the most part, except for her continued devotion to the Harvey's hamburger (Harvey's is a fast-food chain in Canada that Maxine has long maintained outdoes its competitors when it comes to burgers), McDonald's French fries, and, as I learned when she came to Toronto and introduced me to Oscar, that central tenet of North American food culture: milk is essential. On second thought, maybe none of these are exceptions. Maybe the latter has become as universal as the meat and potatoes of fast-food chains. The notion certainly isn't foreign to countries on the other side of the world. When milk prices soared in November 2014 in New Zealand, making milk unaffordable for many families, a representative of the Child Poverty Action Group warned about the consequences for children of milk becoming inaccessible: "Their bones won't grow so well, and their bodies won't grow so well, and they can end up being a bit undernourished and get infections." There, as here, milk is considered a "basic necessity."

Whether Maxine's question was a hangover from her Canadian upbringing or not, it sent me on a quest to provide her a proper response. I needed to get to the bottom of it, to unpack the premise, and that would require more time than we had for our brief visit.

WHO KNOWS?

Sensing the uncharacteristic urgency of Maxine's ask, I got moving, only to hit a brick wall almost instantly. I brought up the cow's milk issue with Michelle, my friend from college who is now a family doctor, during our biennial reunion. Curious about what she tells her patients, I didn't expect her to say "nothing." Michelle explained that since she has no training in nutrition, she doesn't tell parents what to feed their children.

My first thought was that's crazy. As primary care providers, family doctors are ideally positioned to educate moms and dads about diet and health.

My second thought was good for Michelle. She only gives advice about what she is expert in. Since most medical schools don't provide more than one, if that, course in nutrition, food as medicine, disease prevention, and health promotion is not her area, nor that of most MDs unless it's an interest they pursue on their own. Some physicians' offices post charts and diagrams detailing model dietary practices. Luckily they're laminated to last a lifetime because they never change: eat more whole grains, low-fat dairy, fruits, and vegetables; limit saturated fats, sodium, and added sugars. Said gynecologist took it upon herself to go one further. Every visit she'd ask whether I drink tea, coffee, or alcohol. She was always happy when I said no. If I didn't know better, I might have believed that the key to leading a healthy life was simply avoiding caffeine and alcohol.

My third thought was, if not her doctor, then who will be there to help Maxine figure out whether she needs to give her children cow's milk? Certainly not the Internet. Ask Google whether parents should give their children cow's milk, and you'll find any answer you want, which is unhelpful if you know and more so if you don't. As with all issues significant or not, the Internet is a black hole of opinions that requires X-ray vision to sort out.

If neither her doctor nor her iPhone has the answer, who, I wondered, is Maxine going to call? Not a nutritionist. They are too expensive, both in terms of time and money, for the majority of parents teeter-tottering between day job and domestic life. Besides, most nutritionists are trained to spew the same tame stuff that you can read for free in the healthy-eating pamphlets that doctors' offices receive from government and interested parties, including the dairy industry. One nutrition student, Andy Bellatti, who was studying for his exams, blogged about his frustration with the field he was preparing to enter. This is what the Internet is great for, individual stories that shed light on some small bite of life. After identifying some of the threats to the integrity of his chosen profession that he'd written about in the past—big-brand advertising budgets, deceptive packaging, agricultural policies that effectively subsidize unhealthy foods, and the politics of the government-approval process for new food substances—Bellatti announces it's time to look inward. Rather than write about the external forces tearing up the field of nutrition, he decides to examine the precepts that he has to digest and regurgitate to become a registered dietitian. In his July 18, 2011, post he singles out five "unquestioned concepts" that he finds problematic. Number three, "Healthy Eater = Red Flag," is especially relevant. It explains the guilt in Maxine's voice when she told me, as if admitting to a parental crime, that she hadn't given then-two-year-old Oscar cow's milk. Her confession is made up of the same ingredients as the nutrition-school-preaching that Bellatti paraphrases: " 'meat = protein and iron' and 'milk = calcium and vitamin D,' and if you don't eat either of those two things, well, you've got your work cut out for you." One overarching idea reverberates in the institutions of higher health and nutrition education: "vegans must plan their diets adequately or else!" This is the battle cry that Bellatti and his fellow students are conditioned to repeat upon graduation to us, their connected, worldwide web audience.

As an art curator Maxine is an expert in tracking down, capturing, and showcasing the shape-shifting dialogue between truth and beauty. If she applied her cutting vision and overall discerning perception to the slogans that beckon her surrender, she would discover that many emanate from misty places that have remained impenetrable to modern-day light. Bellatti's blog helps to lift the fog by displaying the contents of the nutrition books he is obliged to study in great detail. If you don't drink milk "you've got your work cut out for you" is one of many dated lessons that are requisite learning for the aspiring nutritionist. Reviewing his notes and previous registered dietitian (RD) entrance exams, Bellatti bemoans the fact that he has to know how to make a cake that isn't spongy; how much ground meat he would need to make 300 3-ounce hamburger patties given a 20 percent shrinkage rate; and that to get the answer right to a question about how best to lower sodium intake, he should say "use low sodium instead of regular margarine." What he doesn't need to know is equally troubling to him. There is nothing on the exam about the implications of diets low in omega-3 fatty acids. Nor is there anything about the health benefits of, and differences among, super foods such as chia, hemp, and flaxseeds.

The picture is looking bleak. No doctor to guide Maxine, no way to trust the Internet to inform her, no nonconformist nutritionist to count on. The more I see and read, the more motivated I become to figure out the answer to the question that nags Maxine and so many new parents: what to do about cow's milk.

If physicians generally leave diet for other professionals to deliberate over, there is one situation when the expertise of MD and RD dovetail: when what we eat makes us sick with a diagnosable disease. On the one hand, most heart surgeons wouldn't be able to tell you the first thing about the nutrients in turnip tops. No need for a heart surgeon to know this, so the specialist school of thinking goes, because nobody's going to develop heart disease from eating too many leafy greens. On the other hand, almost any heart surgeon can tell you that cheese is high in cholesterol and cholesterol-producing saturated fat. Cholesterol and saturated fat have been linked to heart disease, so foods that are full of them are at the top of the heart surgeon's mind. Similarly, every emergency physician knows that dairy products contain proteins that are highly allergic and can cause anaphylactic reactions among a chunk of their inpatients. Knowledge about these potentially deadly nutrients in dairy is a necessary part of their job to keep their patients breathing. Then there's what any endocrinologist knows: even plain milk contains too much sugar for a diabetic to swallow.

What's new is that pediatricians are beginning to recognize that milk is making kids, even those who are not allergic, intolerant, or diabetic, sick. In answering the question "Is too much milk bad for my kid?" for the "Ask a Health Expert" column of one of Canada's national newspapers, the *Globe and Mail*, Dr. Michael Dickinson writes: "In fact, drinking too much milk is the most common nutritional problem that I encounter in my clinic." When I read this, I felt vindicated. You see, over the years my family has "diagnosed" countless classmates, people on the street, and even movie stars with what I will call "Got Milked Syndrome," although we didn't have a name for it then.

THE MILK COMPLEXION

My kindergarten classmate, whom I'll call June, looked as if she drank too much milk. So did a boy whose name I'll say is Dean. In our house, the milk complexion meant something different than that of the robust, rosy-cheeked farm girl or star athlete that the California Milk Processor Board represents in its "Got Milk?" ad campaigns. In June's case it meant a frail, thin-boned five-year-old with sunken cheeks. In Dean's it meant greenish skin and raccoon eyes. Brothers Sam and Noah, more real people with made-up names, also looked as if they drank too much milk. They always seemed to have yellowish ooze running down their noses or encrusted on their upper lips when the river ran dry.

Although for the most part my family's picture of a milkoholic wasn't pretty, it could be. Merchant Ivory built an empire trading in the majestic wan faces and corseted bodies of the nineteenth-century British aristocracy. There are modern examples, too. Although my dad wasn't a big fan of romantic comedies, unfortunately for him he lived with three girls. Fortunately for all of us, there was Uma Thurman. He was game to see anything she was in. She was a good actor, yes. But that was only part of the attraction. He liked her gangly, ashen looks.

If genes determine what our eye beholds as beauty, I didn't inherit them from my dad. While our family was at our neighbors' for dinner one evening, their daughter Gabby, who is almost ten years my senior, was talking excitedly about seeing *Titanic*. Not usually one to run to see the latest Hollywood extravaganza, she was smitten with the star actor. Imagine, serious lawyer, partner in a large firm, gushing over Leonardo DiCaprio. On our way home, puzzled, I said to my sister, Kara: "He looks like he drinks too much milk."

I don't know who was the first in the family to coin this way of describing people with a complexion that we—my mum, Kara, and I, if not always my dad—thought sickly. Whoever it was, it stuck, becoming part of our inside vocabulary. Back then, people knew what it meant to look like a smoker, or an alcoholic, but not a heavy milk drinker. Only recently are parents learning, and pediatricians recognizing, that kids can, and many do, drink too much milk.

Enter little Miss Martin, whose anecdotal story made the news one December day in 2012. According to her mom, Nancy, this young girl liked milk so much she would drink six child-size glasses every day. Nancy let her, as most moms would, because milk, she was taught, is all good. Then one day Nancy took her daughter in for a checkup, and the doctor noticed something was off: Miss Martin was pale. Based on looks alone, he suspected she was drinking too much milk. The doctor followed his visual examination with a question for Nancy: "She's quite pale and you're saying she's drinking a lot of milk, she's a picky eater. Does she sleep a lot?"

Nancy nodded her head, yes. The doctor concluded without so much as a blood test: "Oh, it sounds like she could be anemic." No need for needles or fancy procedures. When someone is suffering from milk-induced anemia, you can see it. Look around. Even I, at the age of five, could tell who were the heavy users.

If Nancy had known sooner that milk could be hazardous in high volumes, she would have answered the seminal parenting question, what to do about cow's milk, differently. Had she been properly informed, she wouldn't have enabled her toddler's six-glasses-per-day habit. It wouldn't have taken much for Nancy to prevent her daughter from spiraling into pallid lethargy and fussy food fits. Had her health-care providers told her from day one about the milk-anemia connection, she could have taken the proper dietary precautions to keep her child rosy-cheeked, bright-eyed, and energized through her terrible twos and beyond.

Instead, when Nancy gave birth, there was one predominant opinion regarding cow's milk: all low-fat milk products are healthy for children two years old and up. You have likely read or heard some version of the following: "Just one 8-ounce serving of milk is a good or excellent source of calcium, vitamin D, protein, and other key nutrients." Whether voiced by the dairy industry, a registered dietitian, or a government official, the general word on milk is consistent: milk is filled with essential nutrients. The warning from Miss Martin's pediatrician is one among a million more exaltations of cow's milk as only beneficial for those who have graduated from their first food and are not allergic.

THE SENSELESS HUNT: THE ORIGINS OF THE USDA'S DAIRY RECOMMENDATIONS

Although regrettable, it is not surprising that Nancy didn't receive better advice when her daughter arrived. In the United States, the Department of Agriculture (USDA) has been on a milk kick for at least a century. If old habits die hard, imagine how difficult it will be to put the centenarian milk habit to rest. Caroline Hunt, a nutritionist for the USDA, helped make milk a national hero with her 1916 guide *Food for Young Children*. The nutrition handbook begins judiciously: "Food for children between three and six years of age should be chosen with reference to their bodily needs, as described in the following pages." It does not continue that way. It proceeds with a hymn to milk that begins: "Milk is such an important food for children that it is desirable to speak of it by itself." Next: "Milk is the natural food of babies and the most important food for young children." The crescendo: "*A quart of milk a day* [emphasis added] is a good allowance for a child."

A quart is the equivalent of thirty-two ounces, or four eight-ounce glasses. It's hard to fathom even in today's dairy-devout culture how Hunt, after considering the "bodily needs" of three- to six-year-olds, could come up with a recommended 500 calories per day of milk for children as young as three. The USDA and its nutritionists have since revised the amount downward, both in terms of quantity, and, with the growing number of low-fat milk options, calories. However, the formative idea that milk should be the centerpiece of a child's meal has endured. The USDA, together with dietitians and the dairy industry, has effectively turned Hunt's ruling that "milk is the most important food for young children" into household doctrine.

Further along, the guide reiterates the importance of milk for "young children" in an ode that adds bread and cereal to the mix: "Well-baked bread and thoroughly cooked breakfast cereals are both good for children and with milk should make up a large part of the diet." Herein lies a clue to the mystery of that chicken and egg question, which came first, cereal or milk? Until now I assumed Kellogg's was responsible for the cereal and milk diet that so many children and bachelors live on today. Now I'm not so sure. According to one dairy industry estimate, almost one-fifth of milk is used for cereal. On its website, Kellogg's answers the question "Why cereal?" by referencing a scientific study that it summarizes: "Cereal helps incorporate milk into the diet. About 95 percent of ready-to-eat cereal in developed markets is eaten with milk, thereby providing calcium and protein for consumers." Clearly what's good for cereal is good for milk. No wonder Hunt and her predecessors at the USDA have been so keen on cereal. Whether cooked or not, the dried flakes that quickly transform into a meal serve as chauffeur to celebrity milk.

TOO MUCH

And yet for the past few years it seems as if opinions on milk may be changing. At least some parents are finally asking, "Is too much milk bad for my kid?" The *Globe and Mail* thought the question sufficiently prevalent and relevant to its Canadian readership to solicit the likes of Dr. Dickinson to address it. Having read that more than two glasses per day of milk can be bad for children, and "even lower the iron in their bodies," a parent of a four-year-old wrote in to the paper's "Ask a Health Expert" wondering whether it was safe to continue giving milk to the child. Dr. Dickinson unequivocally responds "certainly," milk is safe for the tot to drink. However, at the same time he concedes, "You are correct that milk is a poor source of iron and that ingesting too much cow's milk can lead to iron deficiency." Then follows the eye-opener that I quoted earlier: "In fact, drinking too much milk is the most common nutritional problem that I encounter in my clinic in toddlers between twelve months and three years of age." To Dr. Dickinson, "too much" is more than 24 ounces, or three glasses of milk per day. Although his advice is therefore not inconsistent with the two-cup-per-day government recommendation for toddlers that Health Canada and the USDA endorse, it does conflict with how parents are interpreting the guideline, which, gauging by Dr. Dickinson's patients, is as a baseline. Many still find it hard to believe that an abundance of milk could be anything but good for their child.

Given the way in which state, provincial, and federal governments in North America continue to talk about milk and dairy more generally, it's natural that pediatricians such as Dr. Dickinson are seeing so many toddlers suffering from what, for want of a medical term, I will continue to call "Got Milked syndrome." The USDA's ChooseMyPlate.gov site contains a plethora of information about the Dairy category. Clicking on Dairy brings up instructions on "how much is needed," its "health benefits and nutrients," and "tips for making wise choices." Although the site advises against consuming too many high-fat dairy products because of the calories and saturated fat, it has nothing negative to say about milk products on the low-fat side of the scale. There is certainly no warning that exceeding the recommended daily intakes for dairy could run down your iron stores. Visitors therefore can't be blamed if they leave the dairy site with the impression that more is better. But that's not what the doctors, even those who are staunch supporters of including milk in children's diets, are saying. Dr. Dickinson thinks milk is good to a point. But if you surpass that limit, your child runs the risk of becoming iron deficient.

EXACTLY HOW MUCH IS TOO MUCH?

Dr. Dickinson isn't the only pediatrician counseling moderation when it comes to kids and milk consumption. An article in the journal *Pediatrics* entitled, "The Relationship between Cow's Milk and Stores of Vitamin D and Iron in Early Childhood," received a lot of publicity for presenting the results of a December 2012 study funded by the Canadian Institutes of Health Research and St. Michael's Hospital Foundation. Dr. Jonathon Maguire, a pediatrician at St. Michael's Hospital and the Hospital for Sick Children in Toronto, led the study with one goal in mind. He and his team set out to answer the question that is throwing parents into a tailspin: "How much milk should I be giving my children?"

In an interview for the University of Toronto, where he is also a professor in the Department of Pediatrics, Dr. Maguire elaborates on the why behind the study: "We started to research the question because professional recommendations around milk intake were unclear and doctors and parents were seeking answers." The results, which suggest children should be drinking less milk than health experts in the United States and Canada have been advising, are turning heads. While the USDA says four-to-eight-year-olds should consume two and a half cups per day of milk or dairy, and Dr. Dickinson recommends two to three cups per day for the four-year-old subject of his column, Dr. Maguire's research reveals that children who drink more than two cups per day experience benefits, but also risks.

Dr. Maguire and his team discovered two diverging trends. On the one hand, for the 1,311 two-to-five-year-olds whose blood samples and milk consumption were tracked over two years, each cup of milk, on average, increased vitamin D levels by 6.5 percent. Vitamin D, which is essential for calcium absorption and healthy bones, is added to milk in the United States and Canada. The fact that children who drank more milk had higher blood levels of the vitamin therefore makes sense. Score one for milk.

On the other hand, each cup of milk decreased the children's iron stores by an average of 3.6 percent. This strike against milk made the study noteworthy. While a 3.6 percent drop in iron may seem small, Dr. Maguire underscores that, especially for children who are susceptible to iron deficiency, "that little bit is actually very important." Pediatricians don't take iron deficiency and its big sister anemia, the fatigued state of being that is most often triggered by low iron stores and that ultimately results from insufficient levels of red blood cells to transport oxygen through the body, lightly. Iron is critical to brain development. The lack of it has been linked to delayed motor function among infants.

Although the precise reason for the drop in iron that the researchers observed remains to be determined, one fact is certain: milk is low in iron. The researchers speculate that the children were substituting milk for more iron-rich foods. Another theory, based on evidence that milk inhibits iron absorption, is that the milk the children drank actively blocked iron uptake from the iron-rich foods they were eating. To illustrate, say you're making breakfast for your daughter. On Monday you give her half a glass of milk with a scrambled egg. On Tuesday she has soccer so you give her a full glass of milk with the egg. On both days she's consuming just over one milligram of iron from the egg. However, it's possible that on Tuesday, when she needs the egg's iron even more for her game, she absorbs less of it due to the half glass more of milk she drinks with it. More research is needed to know for sure, but this seems to be a plausible theory.

In the meantime, Dr. Maguire has arrived at an answer to the "How much milk should I be giving my children?" inspiration of his research. He concludes that *no more than* two cups per day of milk is the right amount for young children in order for them to maintain adequate vitamin D and iron levels. I don't think it would be wise to interpret this advisory as meaning two cups of milk *in addition to* yogurt for breakfast, cheese and crackers for lunch, and ice cream for dessert. Considering that not only milk but also milk products are low in iron, it is reasonable to read the upper limit as meaning two servings of dairy, period, whether that be measured as 1.5 ounces of hard cheese—which counts as one serving, or the equivalent of one cup of milk, according to the USDA—and one cup of yogurt; or as a third of a cup of shredded cheese atop a piece of lasagna stuffed with half a cup of ricotta cheese; or as simply two 8-ounce glasses of milk.

Although Dr. Maguire acknowledges that children who do not spend a lot of time in the sun or who have darker skin color may need more than the 200 international units (IU) of vitamin D that two glasses of vitamin D–fortified milk provides for these children, more milk is not the solution. Rather, he suggests that parents consider a vitamin D supplement. Since milk is fortified with vitamin D, taking it in milk is much the same as taking it separately anyway. There are plenty of kid-friendly sources of vitamin D on the market, from naturally flavored fish oils that contain essential fatty acids that are critical to brain development, to inoffensive, inexpensive drops, flavored or not. Milk is one, but by no means the only, way for children and adults to obtain vitamin D.

Now that Dr. Maguire has an evidence-based answer to his research question, the next challenge is to figure out how to communicate it to the parents who are asking. The USDA's dietary guidelines still say that children between the ages of four and eight should be drinking two and a half cups per day, or 25 percent more than Dr. Maguire's suggested two cups per day *maximum*. That's a significant difference, especially for small stomachs. The gap is more worrisome, and the need to reach parents more pressing, in light of a study published in September 2014 in the *New Zealand Medical Journal* that found that even pregnant women who drink a lot of milk risk giving birth to babies who are iron deficient. Of the 131 baby subjects examined in the study, those whose mothers consumed three or more servings of milk per day during pregnancy had lower iron stores than those whose mothers consumed less milk.

All this evidence linking high milk intakes of infants and mothers to widespread iron deficiency among the young makes the presentation of any recommendations regarding milk critical. Dr. Maguire's two-cup-per-day limit for milk is just that, an upper limit. However, against the backdrop of both the USDA's enthusiasm over the benefits of low-fat milk products and its ChooseMyPlate.gov website that is bereft of signals to steer parents away from thinking that more must be better and toward the understanding that high doses of milk will run children down, the USDA's two-and-a-half cups per day recommendation reads as a minimum.

DON'T GET MILKED

Freshly weaned from her mother's milk, Miss Martin got cow's milk and got milked. Fortunately, Nancy's pediatrician pointed out her daughter's unhealthy love of milk in time for Nancy to help her toddler recover with an iron-rich diet consisting of plenty of legumes. The government's dairy cheerleading is partly to blame for Nancy's ignorance that milk could sap her child of vitality and make her sick and grumpy. Dr. Dickinson can attest to the fact that Nancy isn't alone. She is one of many mothers who has struggled, thanks to confusing milk messaging, to return her child to normal. Both Dr. Maguire and Dr. Dickinson recognize that milk is a staple of the Western diet and have no desire to change that. They simply want to prevent children from getting sick on it.

Government agencies in the United States and Canada tell us everything about what milk has to offer and nothing about what it takes away. Until they act on peer-reviewed research demonstrating the existence of a negative correlation between milk consumption and iron levels in young children, stories such as that of the Martins will continue to proliferate.

CHAPTER 3

A Date with MyPlate: A Taste of the USDA's 3-a-Day Dairy Recommendation

If you ever wondered what the USDA's MyPlate looks like for real, it isn't as colorful as the icon appears. When Joe Satran, food writer and self-described twenty-something New Yorker, put MyPlate to the test by sampling its contents for a week, he discovered MyPlate is in fact mostly brown and white. I tailed Satran one frosty February week as he wrote about his experiment for the *Huffington Post*. He couldn't have picked a more appropriate time of year. In February much of the United States is blanketed in snow. That February was no exception. White was here, there, and everywhere. Fitting that it should also cover Satran's plate. Regrettable too. I don't know about you but during the deep dark depths of February I long for color more than ever. The red, green, orange, purple, and blue that represent the five food groups on the USDA's MyPlate are a welcome reminder of the virtues of a diverse, rainbow-colored diet. This picture of the perfect plate signals the warmth and radiance that a well-balanced meal can deliver. Too bad MyPlate's looks are deceiving.

BREAKFAST AS BROUGHT TO YOU BY THE USDA

I don't think Satran realized what he was getting into when he committed to follow the USDA's eating orders cup for cup and ounce for ounce for a week. I commend him for his courage. As much as I want to know what's behind the USDA's glossy image of the model diet, I crave color too much when it's cold and icy outside to do what Satran did for a day, let alone seven snow-white ones. So while I scrolled through the photos of Satran's toneless USDA-approved meals, I continued, you might say heartlessly, to prepare resplendent dinners of pink (lentils), purple (dried juniper berries), green, yellow, orange, red, and black (pepper). Indulgent as charged. In my defense, this routine is my primary winter source of light. If I were to sacrifice it for the dim mess that MyPlate was serving up to Satran, my sanity would go with it.

If Satran were as much of a lover of plants and their natural-born pigmentation as I am, my habit of gorging on the color spectrum while viewing his posts would have bordered on sadistic. But he admitted up front that he thought the hardest part about helping himself to MyPlate would be finishing all the fruits and vegetables on it. Like so many New York bachelors, he was used to working long hours, going to the gym, and then ordering in. And like most takeout, his was not heavy on fruits and vegetables. Breakfast and lunch tended to be no greener than his late-night dinners. He launches his weeklong blog about MyPlate by describing a typical day in the life: Greek yogurt and jam for breakfast, a smoked meat sandwich for lunch, beer at happy hour, topped by what sounds, from his account, like the meat-sandwich equivalent of Elaine's "big salad" on *Seinfeld*. Evidently he was coming to the Plate with a uniform diet of mostly brown and white. The surprising part is that wouldn't change much when he matched his plate with MyPlate.

While Day One introduced Satran to his kitchen and the corner store, neither of which he knew well, Day Two confronted him with a bigger challenge: in his words, "The Dairy Problem." It turns out the half plate of fruits and vegetables that MyPlate depicts in red and green and that seemed imposing to him at the start was no big deal after all: "The serving sizes for vegetables in the USDA guidelines are pretty small; it turns out two cups of steamed broccoli is less than half a $1.49 bunch sold at my local bodega. And fruit is so easy to snack on that it's a cinch to incorporate two cups (really, two pieces) into my day." He didn't need to go too far out of his way to add some red, green, and yellow to his dreary February days. Drawing the color out of his plate, which incredibly he needed to do to meet the USDA's dairy recommendations, was another matter.

On a normal day, before his MyPlate foray, milk products were a part of Satran's weekly meal plan: "I eat yogurt for breakfast maybe three times a week, I eat ice cream or frozen yogurt for dessert maybe once a week or once every other week, I sometimes add milk to my coffee and I occasionally grate Parmagiano into my scrambled eggs or atop my sautéed spinach." Sounds like a good deal of dairy to me. Not, apparently, to the USDA. After plugging his age, body size, and activity level into the USDA's calculator, Satran found he was falling way short of the three cups per day of dairy that the screen said he was supposed to be getting. He had to make up for the shortfall somehow so he says he incorporated "extra milk and yogurt whenever possible." He began by translating MyPlate's one-dimensional blue circle into a three-dimensional glass of milk. He editorializes: "I literally can't remember the last time I did that." MyPlate was returning him to juvenile patterns of eating, to a time when a glass of milk with breakfast and dinner wouldn't have been noteworthy. He took a photo of his first breakfast and it looked awfully white: Greek yogurt with blueberries, a plate of plain toast, and the aforementioned glass of milk. He comments in the margins: "A little large and heavy on the dairy, but yummy overall." "Large and heavy on the dairy" is not my idea of "yummy," but some people have iron tummies.

Putting aside the subjective question of how Satran's milked-up breakfast scores on the taste index, objectively speaking, his morning meal leaves much to be desired. Start with what he might have had instead of the add-on glass of milk. Say he drank water instead. He would have had about one hundred calories to spend on something else. The photo shows that even without the glass of milk, he had four food groups covered with his bowl of Greek yogurt and blueberries and two slices of toast. Dairy: one cup of Greek yogurt, check. Fruit: one cup of blueberries, check. Grains: two slices of toast, or two ounce-equivalents in USDA speak, check. Protein: I'm going to give it a check, even though the USDA hasn't yet. Greek yogurt contains twice the amount of protein as regular yogurt. This fact has led Greek yogurt makers and a senator from New York State, where much Greek yogurt is made, to urge the USDA to recognize Greek yogurt as a member of the protein family. At the time of this publication, the USDA was still on the fence. In the summer of 2013, the USDA agreed to launch a pilot program to offer Greek yogurt as part of the protein portion of school lunch programs in four states. In early 2014 it decided to expand the program to four more states. Regardless of how the USDA ultimately chooses to classify Greek yogurt for the purposes of MyPlate, the numbers speak for themselves. Satran's one cup of Greek yogurt contains about twenty-five grams of protein, outperforming that leading protein provider in North America, the quarter-pound hamburger, by a good 7 grams. That's enough to qualify Greek yogurt as a protein source in any apolitical books.

ASSESSING SATRAN'S MEAL WITHOUT MILK

Before considering what to do with the one-hundred-calorie surplus that Satran would have had had he divested himself of the Monday morning glass of milk, first the rundown. To precisely understand how his breakfast, sans milk, stacks up against his daily requirements as the government defines them, the 2010 Dietary Guidelines for Americans (2010 Guidelines) come in handy. It estimates that a moderately active man in his mid-twenties should daily consume: 2,600 calories; two cups of fruit; three and a half cups of vegetables; nine ounce-equivalents of grains; six and one-half ounce-equivalents of protein foods, for fifty-six grams of protein; and three cups of dairy.

According to this prototypical regimen, Satran was off to a good start without the glass of milk. Before the day was barely underway, he had eaten half the fruit, almost half the protein, one third of the dairy, and just under a quarter of the grains that the 2010 Guidelines say he needs. The only group he was missing was vegetables, which isn't unusual considering that North Americans don't tend to welcome vegetables at the breakfast table. They may creep into an omelet or a muffin, but generally they're considered off-limits in the morning hours. The danger in saving vegetables for later is that later turns into never, which is exactly what seems to be happening in America. According to the 2010 Guidelines, Americans are not eating the recommended amounts of fruits and vegetables and are, partly because of this, deficient in four nutrients: potassium, dietary fiber, calcium, and vitamin D. The Guidelines conclude that intake of these nutrients is low enough to be "of concern in American diets." The Guidelines also blame under-consumption of whole grains, milk and milk products, and seafood for the nutrient shortfall. This latter message has been publicized enough to convince a smart man like Satran that what he must do to improve his breakfast is first and foremost add more dairy and toast to his dairy and toast.

By Wednesday, perhaps taking the cue from down below, he had ditched the milk. But his breakfast of fruit, yogurt, and toast was still dragging him down: "A solid breakfast, though I'm getting a little tired of all this toast." At the same time that he was feeling compelled by MyPlate to up his intake of milk and bread, Satran was learning that the guidelines weren't helping him find balance or satisfaction. There's only so much milk and toast one person can comfortably eat in a sitting.

MYPLATE'S RECIPE FOR BLAND CUISINE

All Satran's talk about MyPlate won't make you hungry. But it may make you curious enough to visit, or revisit as the case may be, the icon. Although in theory the dairy group, coded blue, adds color to MyPlate, in practice it does the opposite, drowning plates, and by extension palates, in white. MyPlate's home site, ChooseMyPlate.gov, confirms the dairy group's lack of true colors. This may not surprise you, but it did me. I knew that the group included calcium-fortified soymilk, so I thought that other calcium-rich foods might receive proxy status. Wrong. Not even other soy-derived, high-calcium foods such as tofu are accepted into the club. With the exception of calcium-fortified soymilk, the group consists solely of cow's milk products. Click on "What's in the Dairy Group?" and you'll find an exhaustive list of its contents: "All fluid milk products and many foods made from milk are considered part of this food group. Most Dairy Group choices should be fat-free or low-fat. Foods made from milk that retain their calcium content are part of the group. Foods made from milk that have little to no calcium, such as cream cheese, cream, and butter, are not. Calcium-fortified soymilk (soy beverage) is also part of the Dairy Group." Even if you choose to fill your recommended dose of dairy with colored products such as strawberry or chocolate flavored milk, the dairy group is white at its core.

Paradoxically, while the USDA's MyPlate would have us whitewash our meals with milk products, the USDA keeps telling us we need to eat more fruits and vegetables. Part of what differentiates the USDA's MyPlate icon from its former Food Pyramid is a greater emphasis on fruits and vegetables. As the icon shows, fruits and vegetables make up half of the USDA's vision of the ideal All-American plate, with grains and protein comprising the remainder. However, while the icon's generous portion sizes for fruits and vegetables intimidated Satran at first, he found the proportionally smaller blue circle representing dairy and the brown triangle representing grains to be the unsuspecting giants of the USDA's five food groups. One comment succinctly summarizes Satran's experience with MyPlate: "There are a couple food groups that the USDA wants you to eat an insane quantity of: dairy and grains, above all." His weeklong date with MyPlate and accompanying photos accentuate the gap between the USDA's diagram and reality. One the one hand, MyPlate is a medley of colors surrounding a small slice of brown. On the other hand, Satran's plates are the reverse: brown and white, lightly peppered with specs of color. Humdrum monochrome rather than multihued vibrancy dominates his every bite.

A GREENER, SCIENTIFICALLY SOUND WAY
TO START YOUR DAY

Since the USDA continues to push dairy and grains to the point that fruits and vegetables inevitably get shortchanged, someone has to stand up for the marginalized. Rather than forcing himself to drink a glass of milk with the first breakfast of his MyPlate experiment, Satran could have invested those roughly one hundred liquid calories in one tablespoon of nut butter divided between two stalks of celery. If it's never too late to start increasing your vegetable intake, it's also never too early. The morning is a great time to add crispy fresh greens to a meal that in America is so often boxed and lackluster. It doesn't always have to be greener on the other side.

I'm not alone in thinking that a glass of water would have been more sensible a choice than milk to go with Satran's already dairy-strong breakfast bowl of yogurt and berries. The Harvard School of Public Health has set out to correct what it has concluded is the mistaken, unsubstantiated dietary advice of MyPlate. Months after the USDA drew up its MyPlate icon in the summer of 2011, HSPH introduced the Healthy Eating Plate in order to, the Healthy Eating Plate's home site says, "fix the flaws" of MyPlate. In a press release following the launch of the Healthy Eating Plate, HSPH's Department of Nutrition chair, Dr. Walter Willet, lamented: "Unfortunately, like the earlier U.S. Department of Agriculture Pyramids, MyPlate mixes science with the influence of powerful agricultural interests, which is not the recipe for healthy eating." The Healthy Eating Plate, he went on to say: ". . . is based on the best available scientific evidence and provides consumers with the information they need to make choices that can profoundly affect our health and well being." One remarkable difference between MyPlate and Harvard's Plate is the absence of dairy from the table setting. In comparing its Plate to MyPlate, an HSPH webpage explains that the latter "recommends dairy at every meal, even though there is little evidence that high dairy intake protects against osteoporosis but substantial evidence that high intake can be harmful." On the Healthy Eating Plate, a glass of blue liquid labeled "water" therefore replaces MyPlate's blue dairy circle.

Satran completes his MyPlate food journal with the entry: "My MyPlate Experiment Made Me a Little Neurotic, But Not That Healthy." If Satran chose to live by Harvard's Healthy Eating Plate instead of the USDA's MyPlate for a week I suspect his table would have been turned: at the end of the final day he would have felt free from neurosis and full of a sense of well-being.

MyPlate's daily dairy quotas are worse than a prescription for uninspired eating. As the HSPH's Healthy Eating Plate website says, and doctors David Ludwig and Walter Willett emphasize in their 2013 *JAMA Pediatrics* commentary "Three Daily Servings of Reduced-Fat Milk: An Evidence Based Recommendation?", they are unscientific. For a brief period in July 2013, Dr. Ludwig's words spread from the *Boston Globe* to Canada's *Globe and Mail*, from Yahoo to the *Huffington Post* to the UK's *Daily Mail*. Maybe you read somewhere that Dr. David Ludwig thinks "the recommendation for virtually everyone to drink three cups a day is excessive and not evidence based."

Or maybe you heard him opine on the fact that milk is not the best source of calcium: "On a gram for gram basis, cooked kale has more calcium than milk. Sardines, nuts, seeds, beans, green leafy vegetables are all sources of calcium." His message that milk is not essential could not be clearer: "We can satisfy all our calcium and other nutrient requirements from a high-quality diet, including green leafy vegetables, beans, nuts, seeds and perhaps fish. . . . But the marketing of milk has been enormously successful, based on milk sales. And the USDA aims to promote commodities, such as milk. The marketing arm of kale or sardine producers, for example, hasn't been able to compete."

Then again maybe you, like my good friend Ghada, missed the flurry of media activity that doctors Ludwig and Willett were stirring up. Ghada, who is among the majority of adults who cannot digest lactose, is especially attuned to news about milk and whether or not to drink it. I figured Ghada would be all ears if experts came along with something to say other than how milk's supernatural powers will make you as strong and invincible as tennis champions Venus and Serena Williams, or for Canadian patriots, the equally dazzling team of sisters, the Dufour-Lapointe Olympian skiers. An ad blitz brought to Canadians by one of Canada's largest dairy processors shows the trio—Justine took gold and Chloe silver in women's moguls in Sochi in 2014—drinking "A Champion's Choice," Milk 2 Go Sport, a milk product portrayed as fuel for a winning edge.

Months after I sent her links to some of the coverage of Willett's and Ludwig's article, Ghada saw an episode of the *Dr. Oz Show* that referred to a Harvard study saying nobody needs milk. She reached out to me and asked if I had seen it, as if she were hearing everything that was said on the show for the first time. There's so much health advice competing for our attention that it takes the wizardry of Oz to hold it for a second. I realized that spreading the word beyond the converted that milk is not necessary for health and wellness was not going to be easy.

CHAPTER 4

Science Fact or Science Fiction? Making Sense of the Conflicting Claims about Milk

Researching milk pulls up a long list of contradictions: milk builds strong bones, milk weakens bones; milk gives you a healthy complexion, milk triggers acne and eczema; milk helps you lose weight, milk makes you gain weight; milk fights cancer, milk causes cancer. This is just a small sampling of the conflicting "scientific" claims that circulate about milk. Although irreconcilable, the assertions do have one thing in common: they all carry the authority of science. How is this possible?

If you aren't already a seasoned listener, allow me to introduce you to *Quirks and Quarks*, a shining jewel in the highly decorated crown of Canadian Broadcasting Corporation (CBC) radio. If you ever wondered how dinosaurs got to be so big or Monarch butterflies keep to their course, *Quirks and Quarks* is for you. The unassuming host, Bob McDonald, is a master of communicating hard science to a lay audience. Each week he selects a handful of scientists, from PhD students and professors, to astronomers and physicists, to chat about their latest research. At some point during his guests' often long and complex explanations of the phenomena preoccupying them, Bob politely chimes in with his trademark "Oh, I see, so. . . ." In a few seconds, and not many more words, he jumps lithely to the heart of the matter and clarifies it for the listener.

Bob's inquisitive nature and upbeat character make for great listening. So does the show's periodic feature, "Science Fact or Science Fiction?" The segment pairs the question of a listener with the answer of an expert. For instance, Andrew Hurdle of Midland Ontario wonders, science fact or science fiction, squinting can improve your eyesight? Dr. Stephanie Baxter, from the Department of Ophthalmology at Queen's University in Kingston, Ontario, gives a brief explanation before delivering the final answer: science fact. *Quirks and Quarks* holds the promise that there is an A-list of people in the know. These wise men and women don't live secluded in caves or at the tops of tall mountains. They can be reached by picking up the phone.

SLEEP ESCAPES

"Science fact or science fiction?" is the question that doesn't get asked enough when it comes to everything that's said about milk. Drink milk for sound sleep, science fact or science fiction? I don't have the sleep-expert equivalent of a Dr. Baxter to turn to for the correct answer, but I have found some leads. Dr. Nina Shapiro of the Geffen School of Medicine and Sleep Center at the University of California, Los Angeles, is not one. She has partnered with the California Milk Processor Board in its "Got Milk? Milk-ZZZ" campaign, which means it's her job to lend credibility to the series of ads launched by the CMPB during the first half of 2013 that spin tales about what you get if you don't drink milk before hitting the sack: broken dreams. In one ad a man is flying freely with some birds when he abruptly starts crashing to earth. Another ad begins with an Italian beauty swimming in a pool, beckoning the viewer, presumably the dreamer, to join her. Then, surprise, a bald man pops out of the water in place of the Mediterranean goddess. In both cases the dreamers are rudely awakened, the ads suggest, because they didn't drink their milk before bed. As part of the CMPB's larger goal of making milk the go-to for a sleep-deprived nation, it recruited Dr. Shapiro to educate Americans that a glass of milk before bed is an effective part of a deep-sleep-inducing nighttime routine. Smart marketing. Dr. Shapiro serves to ground the CMPB's whimsical ad campaign with her weighty credentials and stash of seeming facts: "Milk is high in protein, vitamins, calcium, and the amino acid tryptophan which all have a positive impact on sleep quality." Sounds convincing until you go deeper.

Arthur Spielman, PhD, an insomnia expert and professor of psychology at the City University of New York, reveals the fiction of the supposed fact. He acknowledges that milk contains tryptophan, an amino acid that produces serotonin, which is a known mood enhancer and relaxant. But he cautions that studies testing milk have failed to show any effect on sleep patterns. He explains: "Tryptophan-containing foods don't produce the hypnotic effects pure tryptophan does, because other amino acids in those foods compete to get into the brain."

Doctors at the University of Arkansas side with Spielman: the milk-sleep connection is science fiction. On the website of the University of Arkansas for Medical Sciences (UAMS), a short paragraph under "Medical Myths" challenges the premise that "Got Milk?, Milk-ZZZ" builds on. Beneath the query "Will drinking warm milk make you sleepy?" the entry reads: "The 'milk myth' may have persisted because milk has small amounts of tryptophan." "Small amounts" is the key. The post continues, "There is not enough tryptophan in a normal serving of milk to cause any real drowsiness." What's more, low-fat milk contains about half the amount as whole milk. CMPB spokesdoctor Nina Shapiro says milk is high in tryptophan. Strictly speaking, she is not incorrect. "High" is relative. Milk is high in tryptophan compared to my late great-aunt's favorite before-bedtime snack, an apple, which contains barely any. Still, that doesn't mean it will make you sleepy.

In honor of Mother's Day, the *Toronto Star* newspaper decided to put some of "Mothers' best health advice" to the test. "Drinking warm milk will make you fall asleep" failed to make it into the "best advice" category.

Sleep specialist Dr. Atul Khullar, medical director of the Northern Alberta Sleep Clinic, speaks truth to lore: there isn't enough tryptophan in milk to make you fall asleep. If there's any merit to the notion, it has nothing to do with milk per se. As Dr. Khullar notes, any warm liquid is calming and therefore potentially sleep inducing. In other words, a hot cup of chamomile tea is just as likely as warm milk to lull you to sleep.

Tip for the sleep challenged: before trying anything else, light and soundproof your sleeping quarters. That means removing any and all digital clocks with numbers that glow in the dark, as well as wristwatches with their mini lights that are so tempting to turn on when sleep isn't cooperating. Next, try blindfolding. Years ago my sister gave me an eye mask with silky eye pouches filled with lavender. Highly recommended. The mask manages to block out even those stubbornly bright street rays that cut through nightshades like heavy metal to disrupt the gentle lullaby of circadian rhythms. Add a set of earplugs to silence the sounds of a world that never sleeps and feel yourself tune out completely.

I keep to the routine tirelessly: first the mask, then the plugs, then, as the bustle of life fades away, a vision of falling into a soft cloud of slumber. I don't usually get there for at least an hour or two, but that's half the time it used to take. Bonus: no spilled milk or middle-of-the-night bathroom trips as the warm liquid inside you follows gravity. My routine is easy and economical. Even my first-class mask, which is almost five years old, didn't cost more than fifteen dollars. Although the lavender smell has faded, it returns when I wash or wet it. As for the earplugs, you can buy a pack of the inexpensive mini sleep preservers at your local pharmacy. With persistence and a bit of training, short-circuiting yourself is bound to bring you to a night full of reverie. Long flights of fancy, unlike the interrupted one in the CMPB's ad, may even await you on the other side.

The more steeped I become in milk, the more *Quirks and Quarks* and its host serve as reassurance that not all science is fiction. Not all scientists will sacrifice the long and arduous search for science fact for instant gratification. I return, buoyed by Bob McDonald's enthusiasm, to the battleground of clashing theories about milk and whether or not it's a virtue.

TO DRINK OR NOT TO DRINK MILK

Drink lots of milk, milk is high in calcium and therefore builds strong bones. That's the premise of the two-to-three-glasses-of-milk-per-day government recommendation and the California Milk Advisory Board's "Milk Does A Body Good" campaign. Until recently research has focused on the question of whether *calcium* builds strong bones (see chapters 8 and 9). However, a new study, as well as previous research from Harvard, merit mention here because they speak to the question as to whether milk specifically benefits bones. They start the wheels of second thought turning.

The first, a study published in the *British Medical Journal* in October 2014, was immediately picked up by the *New Scientist* with the justifiably alarming headline: "Guzzling milk might boost your risk of breaking bones." The study, which tracked over one hundred thousand Swedish women and men for a mean twenty years in the case of the women and eleven in the case of the men, indicates that the women who drank three or more glasses of milk per day were almost twice as likely to die, mostly from cancer or cardiovascular disease, during the study period than the women who only drank one glass of milk per day. They were also 60 percent more likely to suffer a hip fracture. The authors conclude: "High milk intake was associated with higher mortality in one cohort of women and in another cohort of men, and with higher fracture incidence in women." However, the authors recommend exercising caution in interpreting the results due to the observational nature of the study and consequent confounding factors possibly at play.

That's not to say the researchers were confounded by their findings. They point to the high levels of lactose in milk, which breaks down during digestion into D-galactose, a sugar that has been found to be an agent of inflammation in animals. More specifically, the researchers write that low doses of D-galactose have been shown to mimic the effects of aging in animals exposed to it, causing everything from "oxidative stress damage" to "chronic inflammation, neurodegeneration, decreased immune response, and gene transcriptional changes." These findings support their basic hypothesis that: "high consumption of milk may increase oxidative stress, which in turn affects the risk of mortality and fracture." The theory that D-galactose is the mischief-maker would explain another of the study's results: high consumption of yogurt and cheese, which are both low in D-galactose's precursor, lactose, was not associated with greater morbidity and incidence of bone fractures among the women surveyed but rather the reverse: the women who consumed more of these fermented dairy products had a slightly lower risk of dying or suffering a bone fracture during the study than those who consumed lower amounts.

Nor were the researchers necessarily surprised by the strong positive association between the women who were the heaviest milk-drinkers and their susceptibility to bone fractures. Dr. Karl Michaëlsson, an MD and professor at Sweden's Uppsala University who led the team of researchers, has said, "I've looked at fractures during the last 25 years. I've been puzzled by the question because there has again and again been a tendency of a higher risk of fracture with a higher intake of milk." However, he doesn't pretend that the study delivers the final word on the relationship between milk consumption and bone and overall health. He admits that the study only shows a correlation between milk and the noted effects. A randomized controlled trial would be required to prove whether milk is the cause. This fact has led C Mary Schooling, PhD, a professor and epidemiologist at the City University of New York's School of Public Health, to write in an editorial about the study: "As milk consumption may rise globally with economic development and increasing consumption of animal source foods, the role of milk in mortality needs to be established definitively now." Let the trials begin.

The Harvard School of Public Health offers a second piece of relevant, not widely discussed, information to mull over when considering milk's impact on bone strength. A page of its website dedicated to the question "Calcium and Milk: What's Best for Your Bones and Health?" explains that "too much preformed vitamin A (also known as retinol) can promote fractures." It points out that: "Many multivitamin manufacturers have already reduced the amount of preformed vitamin A in their products." It therefore suggests that you: "Choose a multivitamin supplement that has all or the majority of its vitamin A in the form of beta-carotene, a vitamin A precursor, since beta-carotene does not increase one's fracture risk." Because vitamin A is added to fat-reduced milk in the United States and Canada, the logical takeaway is that to ensure maximum bone health, you should approach vitamin A fortified milk with moderation if not caution.

Why else are we told to drink milk? Because it's a good source of protein. Hence the CMPB's decision to sideline the old "Got Milk?" for the tagline "Milk Life."

But wait, not so fast. Some leaders in the field of nutrition science say we might want to avoid milk precisely because it's a bad source of protein. In their book *The China Study,* which helped convince Bill Clinton to turn vegan, T. Colin Campbell, PhD, professor emeritus of nutritional biochemistry at Cornell University, and his son Dr. Thomas M. Campbell, a family physician, document the link between casein, the dominant type of protein in milk, and cancer. In a laboratory program that Dr. Colin Campbell initiated and that ran for twenty-seven years with funding from the National Institutes of Health (NIH), the American Cancer Society, and the American Institute for Cancer Research, Campbell and his team found "dietary protein proved to be so powerful in its effect that we could turn on and turn off cancer growth simply by changing the level consumed." They also discovered that not all protein is created equal. "What protein consistently and strongly promoted cancer?" Campbell asks. "Casein, which makes up 87 percent of cow's milk protein, promoted all stages of the cancer process."

Makes you think twice about turning up the volume on milk as the CMPB is urging us to do with its makeover of milk into a protein blast.

The list of reasons to drink milk goes on. Drink milk because it contains high concentrations of insulin-like growth factor (IGF), which builds strong muscles and aids athletes in recovering from strenuous workouts. Then again, we hear from other quarters that we shouldn't drink milk for just that reason: it contains naturally high levels of IGF and unnaturally higher levels in milk from cows injected with the genetically engineered recombinant bovine growth hormone, rBGH, which has been approved in the United States for use by dairy farmers to boost milk production. IGF is such a powerful growth promoter, say physicians such as Dr. Mark Hyman, that it is "like Miracle-Gro for cancer cells." Dr. Hyman singles out ovarian and prostate cancer cells as especially responsive to the hormone he likens to cancer fertilizer.

On the subject of hormones, one study widely reported in October 2014 concludes that if you're over 35 and want to become pregnant, you should drink milk and eat ice cream because the hormones in milk will make you more fertile. However, other research has identified fertility-related hormones such as estrogen in milk as the trigger of concerning health repercussions. Even if IGF is, contrary to what Dr. Hyman and others say, safe to consume for sustained periods at the levels found in conventionally produced milk, a study from Harvard's School of Public Health has linked the recommended three servings a day of dairy to poor sperm quality. Scientists in Japan have found that reproductive hormones spike in the milk of pregnant cows, which is the state of the majority of cows milked for our fast-paced commercial market. Putting two and two together, Myriam Afeiche, PhD, the Harvard study's leader, speculates that the association between dairy consumption and compromised sperm quality "could be attributed to the high levels of naturally occurring reproductive hormones [notably, estrogen] in commercial dairy products."

The debate about whether or not to drink milk continues. Drink milk, some say, it is the perfect solution for a healthy complexion: its amino acids moisturize, its enzymes smooth, and its antioxidants protect the skin against damage from environmental toxins. Don't drink milk, say others, it causes acne. The latter is the CliffsNotes version of a review of fifty years of research, including a 2007 Harvard School of Public Health study that found a strong link between regular milk drinking and acne flare-ups. You may have been led to believe that the fat in milk is responsible for the oily eruptions. But it seems that's another myth. The Harvard study found that skim milk was associated with the worst breakouts. Researchers suspect that the increased processing that skim milk undergoes results in increased levels of hormones in the milk, which in turn explains why skim milk was associated with more severe skin inflammations than milk that hasn't been stripped of its fat.

LOW-FAT DAIRY: DIET FOOD OR FAD?

Trying to lose weight? Drink milk. Or maybe not. There are at least three diverging theories about whether milk should be part of a weight-loss program. Between 2003 and 2005 the US National Dairy Council spent 200 million dollars to promote milk as a food that would help dieters shed pounds. Big food corporations such as General Mills followed the NDC's lead with ads telling consumers that three servings per day of its Yoplait Light Yogurt would slip them into that "itsy bitsy, teeny weenie, yellow polka dot bikini." The message was followed by criticism, most vocally by the Physicians Committee for Responsible Medicine (PCRM), which filed petitions with the United States Federal Trade Commission (FTC) and Food and Drug Administration (FDA) for false and misleading advertising. The PCRM noted that the two clinical studies that General Mills and the NDC cited were led by one Michael B. Zemel. Zemel did not dispute receiving $1,680,000 in research grants from the NDC, as well as $275,000 from General Mills for researching yogurt and calcium-fortified cereals. He also admitted to receiving royalties from General Mills and the dairy farmer trade group, Dairy Management Inc., for the license to use his patented findings linking dairy consumption and weight control.

If the dairy industry was essentially saying, "Drink milk and lose weight," and the PCRM was saying, "No, wait," a 2005 study out of Harvard Medical School and Brigham and Women's Hospital in Boston has introduced evidence that drinking milk contributes to weight *gain*. The study, involving over 12,000 children, found that those who drank more than three servings of milk per day were 35 percent more likely to become overweight than children who drank one to two servings. The study's lead researcher, Catherine Berkey, ScD, concludes that "children should not be drinking milk as a means of losing weight or trying to control weight." The bulletin to the spring-break beach-bound college student: rethink Yoplait as a slim fast pass into a "teeny weenie" bikini. Needless to say, the dairy industry has given up on the weight-loss angle for other hooks to catch consumers.

The foregoing reveals three different theories regarding the milk-weight connection: milk promotes weight loss; there's no solid proof that milk has a slimming effect; and milk may contribute to weight gain. Before deciding which two messengers to kill, consider research out of the University of Virginia School of Medicine (UVSM) that challenges the USDA's suggestion that to prevent toddlers from becoming obese, they should be given skim or low-fat rather than full-fat milk. Admittedly, the research, which focuses narrowly on toddlers, is not directly relevant to the target audience of the dairy industry's late weight-loss–focused ad campaign. Still, for anyone wanting to lose weight and wondering whether milk should be part of the strategy, the study's findings are of interest.

Since 2005 the American Academy of Pediatrics (AAP) and the American Heart Association (AHA) have been saying that to avoid unwanted weight gain children should switch from drinking full-fat to low-fat or skim milk once they reach the age of two. Outside of the United States, opinions vary. While the Irish Heart Foundation has sided with the American guidelines, in the United Kingdom the balance of the advice is different. There the health experts generally don't advise parents to give their children skim milk before the age of five because they believe growing young bodies need the calories. With the aim of clarifying whether low-fat milk helps children maintain lower body weights, Dr. Mark DeBoer, associate professor of pediatric endocrinology and chair-elect of the AAP's Committee on Nutrition, and his colleagues decided to investigate further how, if at all, the milk that young children drink affects their body weight. Toward this end, DeBoer and his team sat down with the Early Childhood Longitudinal Survey, Birth Cohort, which tracks, among other factors, the Body Mass Indices (BMI) and milk-drinking habits of 10,700 children born in 2001. Parents participating in the survey recorded the type of milk—skim, one percent, two percent, full-fat, or soy—they gave their children at the age of two and then again at the age of four. The complementary data collected on the children's BMIs showed that one in three of the survey's subjects were either overweight or obese at both ages. Although troublesome, these statistics are consistent with what we already know: North America is suffering from an obesity epidemic. More startling to DeBoer and his team was that a higher percentage of the heavy-set two- and four-year-olds were drinking low-fat or skim milk as compared to the normal-weight two- and four-year-olds. Their principal finding is that the two percent milk drinkers had lower BMIs than the one percenters.

When these study results were released in March 2013, AAP members responded with skepticism. Pediatricians standing by the low-fat milk recommendations of the AAP and AHA maintained that the correlation could be explained away by the fact that parents of overweight toddlers would be more likely to give their children skim versus full-fat milk. Their essential contention is that skim milk drinking is not the cause but rather the effect of higher BMIs.

These pediatricians who adhere to the status quo AAP low-fat milk recommendations ignore one of the study's critical and perhaps most alarming findings: children who were drinking low-fat or skim milk at the age of two were 57 percent more likely to *become* overweight by the age of four. The trend from normal weight at age two to overweight by age four that the researchers observed among the low-fat and skim-milk drinkers directly challenges the premise of the AAP's low-fat milk advisory. The logic behind the recommendation is that low-fat milk contains fewer calories, and fewer calories translate to lower body weights. False, says DeBoer's study; it isn't that simple.

DeBoer doesn't profess to have figured it all out. Perhaps the fat in milk curbs children's appetites, making them less inclined to gorge on calorific, sugary snacks throughout the day. With no definitive answer as to the mechanisms at play, the questions persist: Does skim or low-fat milk positively contribute to weight gain? Does full-fat milk help to maintain a normal body weight? Even after DeBoer's analysis of it, the information amassed in the Early Childhood Survey is insufficient to resolve these questions as they relate to the survey's young subjects, let alone the adult population. Instead of guessing what's best, DeBoer suggests sticking to what everybody knows is good for children: cut down their time sitting in front of the TV and drinking sugary drinks, load them up with fruits and vegetables, and take them outside for some good old fresh air and sunshine.

Two studies published subsequent to DeBoer's research suggest children are not the only ones who may not benefit from listening to the USDA's "Key Consumer Message": "Switch to fat-free or low-fat (one percent) milk." The first, a meta-analysis of sixteen studies published in the *European Journal of Nutrition* in February 2013, "The Relationship between High-fat Dairy Consumption and Obesity, Cardiovascular, and Metabolic Disease," corroborates an earlier Swedish study that found a correlation between full-fat dairy products and a lower risk of excessive weight gain around the abdomen. The authors conclude from their meta-analysis that "high-fat dairy consumption within typical dietary patterns is inversely associated with obesity risk."

With so many contradictory conclusions about milk in its many forms, you would be justified in throwing up your hands in despair. The best scientists don't fully get it. When, in February 2014, a reporter from the *New Scientist* asked Dr. Walter Willett what to make of the "dairy fat paradox" Dr. Willett offered a few ideas: "One likely explanation is that the full-fat version provides more satiety, but it is also possible that some of the fatty acids in milk products have an additional effect on weight regulation." However, he ended the interview inconclusively: "The picture of dairy foods and health is complicated and deserves further study."

KNOWN UNKNOWNS

So, is milk healthy? Scientific uncertainty, especially of the combative kind that surrounds milk, can be exasperating. But it need not be that way. It can be stimulating, as it is for scientists such as Dr. Willett who continue to search for the truth, all the while knowing that reaching it is a bonus that is rarely if ever attainable. Physicist Ursula Franklin said it elegantly and more generally when the host of a CBC radio show on the subject of Wisdom wondered whether the nonagenarian was optimistic about the future. Recognizing that humans have marvelous yet limited receivers, she waxed philosophical: "The universe has more content than we will know. The fact that it is intrinsically unknowable makes me an optimist." Real scientists accept that the universe is "intrinsically unknowable," yet forge on with optimism.

CHAPTER 5

Know Your Weights and Measures:
Decoding the Riddle of the Daily Value

M ilk, dietitians, dairy associations, and physicians repeatedly say, provides "eight essential nutrients" in addition to calcium. The phrase in praise of milk as more than a good source of calcium is so commonplace that perhaps you accept it on faith. Breaking down the claim, however, reveals an assertion that is as enigmatic and problematic as it is unquestioned.

The critical eight, in addition to calcium, that milk advocates agree are ad worthy are vitamin D, protein, potassium, vitamin A, vitamin B_{12}, riboflavin, niacin, and phosphorus. Each of these nutrients falls into one of seven groups that together the USDA defines as "the major nutrients:" carbohydrates, proteins, fats, vitamins, macrominerals, microminerals, and water. The "vitamin" group is thirteen-strong; the "microminerals" group is made up of eight; and the "macrominerals" group has a membership of six. The nutrients in milk that dairy proponents highlight cross four of the seven categories. Vitamins D, A, B_{12}, riboflavin and niacin are "vitamins"; calcium and potassium are "macrominerals"; phosphorus is a "micromineral"; and protein is, well, "protein."

You may have noticed that milk contains more "major nutrients" than the calcium plus eight nutrients that we hear about all the time. It also contains carbohydrates, in the form of sugar; fats, mostly of the saturated kind; and the micromineral sodium. Those in the business of propping up milk do not spotlight these rogue protagonists of the North American diet. Just because they aren't spoken about doesn't mean they are insignificant or inconspicuous. A cup of milk contains a substantial 13 grams of sugar, a little more than the amount of sugar in half a Hershey's Milk Chocolate Bar. It also carries four times the Daily Value (DV) for sodium than it does for niacin, one of the nutrients that milk promotional material highlights. That may not mean much to you because the DV continues to be something of a mystery decades after its induction onto the packaged food label. Here's a quick primer.

UNPACKING THE UBIQUITOUS YET LITTLE UNDERSTOOD DAILY VALUE (DV)

Although the Daily Values are the most recognizable way of quantifying the nutrients we need each day, the DVs are actually a spin-off of the more authoritative, if less well-known, Dietary Reference Intakes (DRIs). The DRIs are the catchphrase for a collective of four age- and gender-based reference values: the Recommended Dietary Allowance (RDA) , or "average daily level of intake sufficient to meet the nutrient requirements of nearly all (ninety-seven to ninety-eight percent) healthy individuals"; Adequate Intake (AI), which is "established when evidence is insufficient to develop an RDA and is set at a level assumed to ensure nutritional adequacy"; Estimated Average Requirement (EAR), which is primarily used for assessing the adequacy of nutrient intakes of populations rather than individuals and defined as the "average daily level of intake estimated to meet the requirements of fifty percent of healthy individuals"; and finally the Tolerable Upper Intake Level (UL), which, as the longhand suggests, is the "maximum daily intake unlikely to cause adverse health effects." Who sets the DRIs? The Food and Nutrition Board of the Institute of Medicine (IOM), the nongovernmental, nonprofit health arm of the National Academies with the mandate to provide unbiased advice to decision makers and the public.

To understand how the DRIs work in practice, consider calcium. There are no calcium RDAs for infants zero to twelve months old. Instead, there is an AI of 200 milligrams for infants zero to six months old, and an AI of 260 milligrams for infants seven to twelve months. After that there are RDAs, from a low of 700 milligrams for boys and girls one to three years old, to a high of 1,300 milligrams for boys and girls nine to eighteen years old. The calcium RDA for men and women between nineteen and fifty years old is the middle ground, 1,000 milligrams.

With this guide to the DRIs at your fingertips you can begin to decipher the DVs, which are both less specific and more convoluted. Jointly regulated by the United States Food and Drug Administration and Health Canada and designed for the Nutrition Facts label on packaged food products, they are built on the Reference Daily Intakes (RDIs) and the Daily Reference Values (DRVs). On the one hand, the RDIs apply to vitamins and minerals. They are an offshoot of the RDAs of the late 1990s that have since been revised by the Food and Nutrition Board of the IOM. On the other hand, the DRVs relate to nutrients that produce energy, namely fat, saturated fatty acids, cholesterol, carbohydrates, fiber, sodium, potassium, and protein. In summary, the DVs are the FDA's and Health Canada's interpretation of the Food and Nutrition Board's outdated nutrient recommendations.

To further confuse matters, the DVs are usually expressed as a percentage. The next time you see a carton of milk, check out the Nutrition Facts box on it. It says that a serving—which is one cup, or eight ounces, or 244 grams, depending on what country you're in and whether it has adopted the metric system—provides 30 percent of the DV for calcium. To know exactly what this means, you need to know more than the label tells you.

Unlike the RDA, AI, EAR, and UL, the DV for a particular nutrient does not vary according to age or gender. Rather it is one figure based on a standard diet of 2,000 calories for everyone over the age of four. Because nutrient needs vary according to age and gender, the DV is therefore somewhat arbitrary. In the case of calcium, the FDA has decided on 1,000 milligrams as the magic number. The RDAs, which *are* gender and age-based, may say you need more or less. However, the DV isn't designed for you specifically.

At least now you know how to figure out, from the DV, how much calcium and other nutrients are in the foods you buy. Returning to that carton of milk that says each 8-ounce serving contains 30 percent of the DV for calcium, that means one serving delivers 300 milligrams of calcium, which may not be 30 percent of *your* recommended daily intake for calcium.

The fact that the Nutrition Facts box isn't as neat and clean as it looks is something to keep in mind as you read my following analysis of the National Dairy Council's circular entitled "Milk's Unique Nutrient Package: Benefits for Bones and Beyond." The one-pager brazenly begins: "Milk contains nine essential nutrients, making it one of the most nutrient-rich beverages you can enjoy." As ground zero for the "milk contains nine essential nutrients" claim, the publication merits fact-checking.

DON'T BELIEVE EVERY DV YOU READ: THE NIACIN MIX-UP

The NDC's tribute to niacin, the penultimate nutrient on its top-nine list, introduces fiction into its fact sheet with the heading "Niacin (Niacin Equivalents) 10% Daily Value." What comes first is fact: "Niacin is important for the normal function of many enzymes in the body, and is involved in the metabolism of sugars and fatty acids." Then the fiction: "A glass of milk contains 10% of the Daily Value for niacin."

A note at the bottom of the page explains the 10 percent statistic: "All percent Daily Values in this handout are based on nutrient values for one cup of fat-free white milk. Source: USDA National Nutrient Database for Standard Release 21 (2008)." The DV for niacin is 20 milligrams. If one cup of nonfat milk provides 10 percent of the DV for niacin, as the NDC claims, one cup must contain 2 milligrams of niacin. It doesn't. One cup of milk contains ten times less, or two-tenths of a milligram of niacin. Just to be sure, I followed the NDC's USDA lead to double check. The "USDA National Nutrient Database for Standard Release 25," ("Release 25") a more recent version of the twenty-first release ("Release 21") that the NDC cites, says the niacin content for one cup of "Milk, nonfat, fluid, with added vitamin A and vitamin D" is 0.23 milligrams.

Note that 0.23 milligrams of niacin per cup of nonfat milk is one, *not* ten percent of the 20-milligram DV for niacin. Giving the NDC the benefit of the doubt, I thought maybe a USDA update and not the NDC's mistake accounted for the NDC's inflated 10 percent statistic. So I looked up the earlier Release 21 that the NDC references. It lists nonfat milk as containing 0.094 mg of niacin per 100 grams. Performing a little arithmetic shows that the USDA has not changed its calculation of the amount of niacin in one cup of nonfat milk. One cup of milk weighs about 244 grams. If there are 0.094 milligrams of niacin in 100 grams of milk, there are 0.22 milligrams in a cup.

Settled. One cup of milk contains one percent of the DV for niacin. The NDC misplaced the decimal. The repercussions aren't so subtle. Its false calculation has been accepted as fact by dairy organizations and manufacturers everywhere. Thus, as of 2104, the website of the Washington Dairy Products Commission, which represents the dairy farmers of Washington State, claims that every 8-ounce serving of milk provides 10 percent of the DV for niacin. If you have milk in your fridge, check the label. The Nutrition Facts box on a carton of the Canadian brand Natrel says one cup of its organic skim milk contains 10 percent of the DV for niacin. Look around and you'll see how far and wide this piece of misinformation has spread.

The amount of niacin in one cup of milk is so microscopic that not even the USDA identifies milk as a good source of it. In its fact-providing appendix about the "Major Nutrients," how they contribute to good health, and in what foods they can be found, the USDA's Food and Nutrition Service (FNS) explains that niacin "helps cells use oxygen to release energy from food; and maintains health of skin, tongue, digestive tract, and nervous system." A lengthy list of food sources follows: "liver, meat, poultry, and fish, peanuts and peanut butter, dried beans and dried peas, and enriched and whole-grain breads and cereals." No mention of milk. While the FNS lists milk as a food source for a handful of other nutrients that the NDC does not spotlight, it clearly does not consider milk a good way to fill your niacin needs.

According to the FNS, in addition to calcium, milk *will* deliver vitamin K, which it says is "necessary for proper blood clotting"; magnesium, which "helps regulate body temperature, muscle contractions, and the nervous system and helps cells utilize carbohydrates, fats, and proteins"; iodine, which is "needed by [the] thyroid gland to produce thyroxine, which is essential for the oxidation rates of cells"; pantothenic acid, which "aids in the metabolism of fat . . . and the formation of cholesterol and hormones"; and finally, vitamin B_6, which is "needed to help nervous tissues function normally, helps to maintain the health of the skin and red blood cells, [and] assists in metabolism of proteins, carbohydrates, and fats."

I suspect these five nutrients—vitamin K, magnesium, iodine, pantothenic acid, and vitamin B_6—don't appear in the NDC's, or anyone else's, description of milk's "unique nutrient package" because they are found in many other foods at higher levels. Eat a broccoli spear for 65 percent of the DV for vitamin K and seventy times more vitamin K than you'll down in a glass of whole milk (fat-reduced milk contains even less vitamin K); eat an ounce, about a handful, of shelled pumpkin seeds for five times more magnesium than you'll get in a cup of milk; sprinkle a teaspoon of seaweed—I like dulse flakes—on your dinner instead of salt for over 100 percent of the DV for iodine; toast one ounce of shelled sunflower seeds and while they're still warm dust with your seasoning of choice—cocoa powder and cinnamon, or curry powder and a little salt are two of my favorites—for a quick snack and 20 percent of the DV for pantothenic acid, which is more than twice the amount of pantothenic acid in a cup of milk; finally, add just one tablespoon of chili powder to your favorite dish for three times more vitamin B$_6$ than one cup of milk provides.

So far not so good for the NDC's exaltation of milk as a superior food. Opening up its "unique package" reveals the first disappointment: niacin, one of the nine nutrients that the NDC and others shine a light on, exists in barely detectable quantities in milk. At 0.23 milligrams per cup of nonfat milk, consuming the recommended three servings per day of dairy provides only 3 percent of the DV for niacin. Counting niacin as part of milk's "unique package" is misleading. What's more, highlighting niacin to the exclusion of magnesium, iodine, pantothenic acid, or vitamin B$_6$, all of which exist in milk at higher levels than does niacin, is illogical and unhelpful. That's not to say the dairy industry should focus on these latter nutrients instead. Milk is not the best source for any of them. Eat your greens, seeds, and spices, and you'll be leaps and bounds ahead of anyone who drinks milk instead.

CHAPTER 6

Overrated: Tall Tales about Milk's Short List of Essential Nutrients

Niacin is only the beginning of what's wrong with the National Dairy Council's list of milk's singular package of nine nutrients. The eight others—in order of their appearance, calcium, vitamin D, protein, potassium, vitamin A, vitamin B_{12}, riboflavin, and phosphorus—also warrant close consideration. Leaving aside the big "C" calcium for now, which needs, and coming up receives its own set of chapters, let's start from the top and work our way down.

VITAMIN D

Exposing skin to sun stimulates the body's production of vitamin D. We can also obtain this "sunshine vitamin" from select foods, notably fatty fish and mushrooms that have been exposed to ultraviolet light. It is not, however, present, unless through fortification, in the fat-free pasteurized milk that is the subject of the NDC's "Milk's Unique Nutrient Package" leaflet. Advertising milk as a good source of vitamin D is like holding up Kellogg's Froot Loops cereal as a good source of vitamin C, iron, niacin, folate, and B_{12}. (A one-cup serving of Fruit Loops contains just under 25 percent of the

DV for each of these nutrients). When a food has been topped up with nutrients, when, say, vitamin D is added to nonfat milk and multiple vitamins are added to processed cereals, a lab, not the "food," is the source of nutrition.

No health expert would argue that there is a difference between taking vitamin C in a pill or in a bowl of Froot Loops on the one hand, and eating a kiwi or red bell pepper on the other. The vitamins that come from nature's lab are always preferable to those fabricated by humans in white coats. Presumably that's why the USDA does not include "fortified cereals," which are often high in vitamin C, as "food sources" of the nutrient. There are too many foods that are naturally high in vitamin C for the USDA to have to rely on second bests.

Although the USDA implicitly recognizes that fortified foods are inferior sources of the nutrients that are added to them, I would go further: fortified foods are not "food" sources of their added nutrients, period. Sunlight, fatty fish, and ultraviolet-light-exposed mushrooms, in that order, are the best sources of vitamin D. Milk, if tinkered with, may be a source of vitamin D, but it is a less than ideal source and not any more a food source of it than is the olive oil that is mixed with vitamin D and sold as a supplement in dropper bottles.

Even the dairy industry trades on the notion that fortification generates a lesser, suspect product. You can watch it do so by viewing California Milk Processor Board ads that poke fun at the contents of what the ads refer to as "imitation" milk. One ad derides long-winded ingredients such as riboflavin, zinc gluconate, and calcium carbonate that are commonly added to soy-based milk. Riboflavin. Sound familiar? It is one of the nutrients the NDC highlights in milk. Zinc gluconate and calcium carbonate are also nutrients. They are added to soy milk in the same way and for the same reason that vitamin D is added to cow's milk: to enhance the healthfulness of the final product. The dairy industry at once peddles milk under the sun as being high in vitamin D and at the same time casts a shadow on soy-based milks for being fortified with equally essential nutrients.

Leaving ethics and the hypocrisy of dairy-industry advertising aside, there is a science-based reason to stop selling vitamin D as part of low-fat milk's "unique nutrient package." Vitamin D is fat soluble. Ask yourself how much benefit you derive from a fat-soluble nutrient that is suspended in the relatively fat-free environment of the low-fat and nonfat milk that the government recommends.

After the link was made in the early 1900s between rickets and vitamin D deficiency, public health officials in the United States began advocating for vitamin D fortification of milk. Since the 1930s, fortifying milk with vitamin D has become the norm in the United States. Similarly, the Canadian government mandated that milk and margarine be fortified with vitamin D in the 1970s. At the same time, wary of overconsumption, it prohibited vitamin D fortification of other foods. Although singling out milk as a food high in vitamin D may thus have made some sense decades ago, times have changed. First, even though one 8-ounce glass of milk contains, as the NDC says, a respectable 25 percent of the DV for vitamin D—which translates to 100 international units (IU)—that amount no longer looks like a lot considering many health experts are recommending vitamin D intakes of over 1000 IU. Second, vitamin D fortification of breakfast cereal is now voluntary in the United States and is gaining acceptance in Canada. The government's loosening of restrictions on supplementing foods with vitamin D in Canada and the United States means that even if you concede that fat-reduced milk is a source of vitamin D, it is certainly no longer a "unique" source of it. Vitamin D has moved beyond milk and margarine into the recipes of popular processed foods. Championing it as part of milk's special grouping of nutrients stretches the definition of exceptional.

VITAMIN A

Vitamin A is another fat-soluble vitamin that has made it onto the NDC's list of low-fat milk's noteworthy nutrients. Vitamin A is a natural component of whole milk. But because vitamin A likes fat, when the fat is removed, the vitamin A goes with it. Any vitamin A that exists in fat-reduced milk is necessarily lab-made and added back to it. If you see vitamin A on the label of your carton of low-fat milk, you may be paying for it, but whether you can absorb it is another question. Introducing a fat-soluble vitamin into an almost fatless product defies food sense. If you don't drink whole milk and you're concerned that you're not getting enough vitamin A, look for it elsewhere. There are plenty of natural sources of it. A tablespoon of paprika, which makes every meal prettier and zestier, adds not only a tantalizing deep red color but also 3691 international units (IU) of vitamin A, or 74 percent of the 5,000 IU DV. For an appetizer add a baby carrot—a misnomer since these bite-sized carrots are really adult carrots cut and molded into Cheezie imposters—and you just upped your vitamin A intake by 2,069 IU. You read right, one small piece of carrot contains 42 percent of the DV for vitamin A. Other significant sources of vitamin A include liver, of the turkey in particular, one of which contains 1,250 percent of the DV for vitamin A; sweet potatoes, with 438 percent of the DV in one medium-size potato; butternut squash, with 457 percent of the DV per cup cooked; and kale, at 354 percent of the DV per cup cooked. There is clearly no shortage of vitamin A in the North American food supply.

Milk's "unique package" of nine has shrunk by three. First, the amount of niacin in milk is negligible and much less than the score that the NDC gives it. Second, vitamin D is slipped into milk much the same way that it is added to a capsule or that Kellogg's mixes it into its cereals. Any way you look at it, it's a supplement, not a natural constituent of milk. Third, the NDC says a glass of nonfat milk "provides" 10 percent of the DV for vitamin A. But just because your glass of fat-reduced milk contains vitamin A doesn't mean it "provides" it to you. If the original fat-soluble vitamin can't stand fat-free milk it's hard to believe that the synthetic version that is put back into it could do your body much good.

Eliminating niacin, vitamin D, and vitamin A from the nine nutrients that the NDC and its allies attribute to milk leaves six to consider.

PROTEIN

Protein is unquestionably an essential nutrient. However, it's not scarce in North America. If there is a protein problem, it's that Americans are consuming too much of it. While the World Health Organization (WHO) recommends that women and men need 48 and 56 grams of protein per day, respectively, average protein intake in the United States far exceeds those levels, and is increasing. In the 1990s Americans were consuming about 109 grams of protein per person per day. By 2007 protein intake had reached 114 grams. According to these figures, Americans are thus consuming, on average, more than twice as much protein as the WHO says we need.

A 2012 Food and Health Survey conducted by the International Food Information Council found that only fiber and whole grains ranked higher than protein in nutrients that people said they are trying to consume. Supermarket aisles display North America's protein fixation in three dimensions. The big-name food manufacturers are inventing sundry ways of satisfying Americans' protein craving, from Kellogg's Eggo Protein Waffles, to Post Foods' Great Grains Protein Blend Whole Grain Cereal, to Coca-Cola's Core Power high-protein milk shakes, to Greek yogurt. No longer aimed solely at athletes, high-protein products are making it into the cereal bowls, lunchboxes, and briefcases of adults and children across the country.

Although protein is all the rage, there is growing evidence that North Americans' attraction to protein may be fatal. A study published in March 2014 in the journal *Cell Metabolism*, "Low Protein Intake Is Associated with a Major Reduction in IGF-1, Cancer, and Overall Mortality in the 65 and Younger but Not Older Population" concludes that middle-aged adults who consume a diet high in animal-based proteins such as meat and milk have a greater risk of dying from cancer and diabetes. The study's authors found that of the thousands of adults whom they tracked for more than two decades, those who consumed 20 percent or more of their calories from protein, defined as a "high protein" diet, were four times as likely to die from cancer as their low-protein–consuming cohorts, who obtained less than 10 percent of their calories from protein. The Atkins "high protein" diet continues to generate controversy, but for different reasons. The focus has been on whether all the saturated fat that it sanctions can really be healthy in the long run for your heart and waistline. This newer research regarding the effects of eating high amounts of protein suggests something more troubling: eating a high-protein diet appears to be as malignant, the study's authors say, as smoking twenty cigarettes a day.

According to one of the study's authors, Valter Longo, PhD, a University of Southern California professor of gerontology and director of USC's Longevity Institute, many in America and elsewhere are eating two to three times more protein than they should be. The USDA is partly to blame for Americans' insatiable appetite for protein. Although "protein" and "fruits" are sized equally and slightly less generously than "grains" and "vegetables" on MyPlate, upon closer examination, the USDA's guidelines are not so balanced. The exact amount of protein that the USDA says we need is measured in "ounce equivalents" and depends on age. For everyone older than nine, the portion size ranges from five "ounce equivalents" to 6.5 "ounce equivalents." Although the MyPlate icon is intuitive—fill your plate with slightly more vegetables and grains than protein—the "ounce equivalent" is not.

The USDA explains, "In general, one ounce of meat, poultry or fish, one quarter cup cooked beans, one egg, one tablespoon of peanut butter, or a half ounce of nuts or seeds can be considered as one ounce equivalent from the Protein Foods Group." Note that while meat translates ounce for ounce, if you choose nuts and seeds to meet your protein needs, one ounce of these legumes equates to two "ounce equivalents" for the purposes of the USDA's protein recommendations. When broken down, eggs aren't on a one to one basis either: three eggs whites are, according to the USDA, the same as two "ounce equivalents" of protein; and three egg yolks are the same as one "ounce equivalent" of protein. To further complicate matters, the USDA inserts the caveat that its protein guidelines are designed for people who "get less than thirty minutes per day of moderate physical activity, beyond normal daily activities." It advises that the more active may "be able to consume more while staying within calorie needs."

For an example of what the USDA's guidelines look like in grams of protein, say you're a thirty-year-old man and thus advised to consume 6.5 "ounce equivalents" of protein per day. A 6.5-ounce steak will do it which, at about 8 grams per ounce, translates to 52 grams of protein. That sounds like a reasonable amount of protein until you factor in the protein that you'll get from the dairy foods that the USDA recommends you consume *in addition to* protein foods. Remember, when the USDA says you need 6.5-ounce equivalents of protein per day, dairy doesn't count.

Time to revisit the dairy section of ChooseMyPlate.gov to understand the effect on Americans' recommended protein intake of maintaining dairy as a food group separate from protein. The two groups of the population who are advised to consume the most protein, nineteen-to-thirty-year-old men and fourteen-to-eighteen-year-old boys, are also advised to take in the most dairy: three cups per day. Since one cup of low-fat milk has approximately 8 grams of protein, multiplied by three, that's another 24 grams of protein to add to the roughly 52 grams that these two groups would be eating if they choose to meet their USDA-defined protein needs with a steak. Combined, the 6.5 ounces of steak and three servings of milk equal 76 grams of protein per day, well above the WHO's prudent 56 grams for men. Evidently, the USDA and WHO protein recommendations are not in sync. Having established dairy as a group unto itself, the USDA has effectively given the average American the green light to consume excessive amounts of protein.

It's clear that Americans have no intention of putting the brakes on their protein intake, and dairy processors are taking note. Although the USDA doesn't classify dairy as a protein source, dairy advertisements position it that way. In partnership with Kellogg's, the Milk Processor Education Program (MilkPEP), a program funded by milk processors to increase fluid milk consumption, has created the Share Breakfast program to provide one million breakfasts to children who would otherwise go without. Of course, the program supports the sharing of a particular kind of breakfast, and it's not bacon and eggs, or my favorite, chia pudding (see recipe for Pudding of Champions in chapter 14). It's all about cereal and milk, or in Share Breakfast's terms, fiber and protein.

In 2013 actor Taye Diggs and his three-year-old son, Walker, posed for the camera wearing milk mustaches and sharing a bowl of cereal and milk. Diggs's message: "Starting every day with milk and cereal is an important part of my daily routine. It helps me start the day right with protein and other nutrients and gives me the energy I need to manage my hectic schedule, whether I'm playing with my son or on set." The caption embedded in the little-Diggs-big-Diggs photo reinforces the milk-protein connection: "A breakfast of cereal and milk delivers powerful nutrients, including high-quality protein, that your family needs to start every day. A fact worth sharing." The literature major in me compels me to parse the photo's footer. As with many milk ads, this one emphasizes the singularity of milk's nutrients. Milk doesn't deliver just any kind of protein. Milk's protein is "high-quality." Sounds as if milk's protein is special. However, against the myriad of plant- and animal-based foods that the USDA identifies as "Protein Foods," milk doesn't look so remarkable. "Meats; Poultry; Seafood; Eggs; Nuts and Seeds; Beans and Peas," all necessarily contain "high-quality" protein, hence the USDA's designation of them as "Protein Foods."

I don't know what the "low-quality" protein is that the Diggs's ad implicitly offsets against milk. Perhaps the ad is taking a dig at certain plant-based proteins, such as nuts and seeds and grains and some legumes that require each other to provide the full complement of amino acids that animal-based proteins supply. I do know that there is no shortage of ways to obtain "high-quality" protein for breakfast. If you don't like eggs, scramble some tofu, onions, and tomato; or mix some peanut, almond, or cashew butter into oatmeal; or try beans and rice, which needn't be reserved for dinner. Even better, go for the Guatemalan staple of boiled black beans and plantains with a side of corn tortillas. You can use canned beans for convenience, and substitute bananas if your corner store doesn't carry the banana's large and starchy relative. If all that sounds like too much fuss, on the weekend, when you have some time, take a trip to the bulk section of your supermarket where you'll find bins of nuts, seeds, the nibs of cocoa beans and dry roasted soybeans. Combine and keep refrigerated for a perfect "high-quality" protein and fiber-rich fast and easy breakfast. There are way too many "high-quality" affordable protein foods around, from bare-bone plant foods such as quinoa, to canned fish, to single-ingredient nut and seed butters, for milk to top the list when you're out shopping for a protein hit.

The next part of the Diggs's ad to zero in on is the "fact" that the ad says is "worth sharing." What is this fact worth sharing? It is, in fact, three-pronged: (1) "cereal and milk deliver powerful nutrients"; (2) one of these nutrients is "high-quality protein"; and (3) your family needs these nutrients "to start every day." Rebuttal: (1) "powerful nutrients" is redundant; (2) just as the nutrients that cereal and milk deliver are not unusually powerful, neither is the protein in milk uniquely "high-quality"; (3) nobody needs to "start" every day with the nutrients in cereal and milk. If you choose to have oatmeal and peanut butter for breakfast, for instance, calcium may not be a significant part of breaking your fast. That's okay, as long as you have some later in the day, maybe stir-fried tofu and broccoli for lunch or salmon for dinner.

When "Milk Life," that campaign that aims to transform milk from a breakfast drink to a protein life force for any time of day, was set in motion in early 2014, it created a splash. Milk's got a good deal of protein, no doubt about it. The question raised by the USC study linking high animal protein intake to an increased risk of cancer is whether all that animal protein makes milk life or death.

Longo and his co-authors aren't the only ones cautioning that the amount of animal protein we consume in America is overkill. The World Health Organization, which has made a point of clarifying that protein deficiency was eradicated from the European Union after World War II, is blaming protein for a new Western-centric condition: weak bones. WHO hypothesizes: "To date, the accumulated data indicate that the adverse effect of protein, in particular animal (but not vegetable) protein, might outweigh the positive effect of calcium intake on calcium balance." The Food and Agriculture Organization (FAO) of the United Nations also addresses this so-called calcium paradox—the fact that nations in which calcium intake is the highest also have the highest rates of bone fractures—in its report on Human Vitamin and Mineral Requirements. Its take is similar. The report's calcium chapter states: it is "possible that hip fracture rates may be related to protein intake, vitamin D status, or both, and that either of these factors could explain the calcium paradox." According to the report, it has been known since the 1960s that dietary protein, animal protein in particular, positively affects the amount of calcium that is lost in the urine. The FAO describes the relationship as a one-milligram to one-gram ratio: one milligram of calcium is lost in the urine for every one-gram rise in protein intake. Animal protein lovers take heed: the more protein you take in, the more calcium you excrete.

Although this authoritative and widely available news doesn't seem to be reaching protein-crazed North Americans, at least one dietitian down under is trying to spread the word. In a 2013 *New Zealand Herald* article, "Factors That Could Be Bad for Your Bones," performance nutritionist and clinical dietitian Dave Shaw outlines six menaces to bone health. "Too much protein" is in the bone-rotting company of soft drinks, caffeine, alcohol, salt, and inactivity. Most of us are familiar with the latter five bad actors. But many of us are still oblivious to the basics that make protein a leading contributor to brittle bones: "Protein's important for building strong healthy bones, but too much can cause calcium to be excreted in the urine. A diet high in protein and low in fruit and vegetables makes an acidic environment that draws calcium from the bone to act as a buffering agent." We in the West have come full circle. Before World War II, protein was the center of a public health crisis; we didn't have enough of it. More than half a century later protein has returned with a vengeance, its abundance proving to be a serious menace.

POTASSIUM

With four down—niacin, vitamin D, vitamin A, and protein—and five to go, we arrive at potassium. According to the NDC, one cup of milk contains a modest 11 percent of potassium's DV. If you are curious about why the NDC still highlights potassium as part of milk's "unique nutrient package," it may have something to do with the fact that the IOM has identified potassium, along with calcium and vitamin D, as "nutrients of concern." Even before the 2010 Dietary Guidelines for Americans singled out potassium as a nutrient that Americans tend to be low in, the NDC was cautioning, in its "Potassium Recommendation Fact Sheet," that "No single age group of Americans is meeting" the IOM's Dietary Reference Intake for Potassium. The NDC "Fact Sheet" proceeds: "According to nationwide food consumption surveys, milk is the number one food source of potassium for Americans in all age groups."

If this is true, if Americans are obtaining most of their potassium from milk, it could be the reason Americans are not getting enough of the mineral that is critical to regulating the flow of bodily fluids and maintaining electrolyte balance and muscle function. Back in 1989, when American tennis great Michael Chang was overcome with muscle cramps in his legs during the fourth set of a grueling French Open final against Ivan Lendl, I watched him as he attempted in agony to replenish his potassium stores. He didn't drink milk. He ate bananas. Miraculously, he recovered and went on to win the match, making him, at seventeen, the youngest male ever to win a Grand Slam event. Looking on as a young tennis competitor myself, I made a point from then on of keeping a banana or two close at hand when faced with the potential of a long match on a hot day.

There are so many fruits and vegetables that pack more potassium than milk. One banana has 422 milligrams of potassium, compared to the 360 in a cup of low-fat milk. Even better, one cup of cooked beans (adzukis are particularly heavy potassium hitters) contains 35 percent of the 3,500-milligram DV for potassium. That's over three times the potassium than what's in one cup of milk. Couple the beans with one cup of cooked Swiss chard, which pairs well, for another 27 percent of the DV for potassium. And don't forget potatoes. An average-size potato contains 926 milligrams of potassium, for 26 percent of the DV for potassium. Even one 3-ounce serving of salmon contains more potassium than a glass of milk: 534 milligrams, or 15 percent of the DV. If milk "is the number one food source of potassium for Americans," as the NDC claims, Americans aren't taking advantage of all the colorful whole foods available in farmers' markets and supermarkets.

VITAMIN B_{12}

Moving past potassium brings us to vitamin B_{12}. B_{12}'s reputation for being heat sensitive makes it a peculiar inclusion. No one denies that B_{12} breaks down under the high temperatures of milk pasteurization, not even those whose livelihoods depend on milk. The website of the Dairy Farmers of Ontario discusses pasteurization and its effects on milk's makeup. While it reassures us "studies have shown that calcium absorption remains unaltered through pasteurization," it doesn't say the same about vitamin B_{12}, thiamin, and vitamin C. It admits: "Pasteurization does involve a minor loss of ten percent of thiamin and vitamin B_{12} content, as well as a twenty percent loss of vitamin C content." However, it downplays these losses: "Because losses are small, in comparison to the large amount of these two B vitamins present, milk continues to provide significant amounts of thiamin and vitamin B_{12}."

This is what the Dairy Farmers of Ontario website has to say in full about the benefits of pasteurized milk: "Pasteurized milk is an excellent source of calcium, protein, riboflavin, vitamins A and D, phosphorous, and a good source of thiamin and B_{12}." It doesn't even mention potassium, an NDC favorite that the Ontario organization seems to recognize is unfitting to list. Yet it spotlights thiamin, which does not make it onto the NDC's top nine. And while the Dairy Farmers of Ontario website says that milk is an "excellent" source of vitamin A at only 11 percent of the DV per cup, it goes on to say it is only a "good" source of vitamin B_{12} at 22 percent of the DV per cup.

As a Canadian I feel compelled to apologize for the confusion. We do that here—say sorry when someone else walks into us. I don't know the criteria that the Dairy Farmers of Ontario are using to determine whether milk is an excellent versus a good source of a particular nutrient. I suspect the fact that thiamin and B_{12} are heat sensitive has something to do with the organization's lower rating of them despite the fact that they are found in higher concentrations than vitamins that make it into the "excellent" group. The organization's creation of a hierarchy between B_{12} and thiamin on the one hand and milk's other nutrients on the other brings back the question: how much of these B vitamins can you really count on getting in a glass of heat-treated milk? The NDC's answer for B_{12} is 22 percent of the DV. However, the legitimacy of providing such a blanket value for the amount of B_{12} in a serving of pasteurized milk is questionable. Since not all pasteurized milk is heated or treated the same way, it follows that not all glasses of pasteurized milk should have equal amounts of B_{12}.

Take Ultra High Temperature (UHT) pasteurized milk. In 2012 the food packaging and processing company Tetra Pak let loose its "Milk Unleashed" campaign to educate "active moms" about its milk in juice-box–type containers that doesn't need to be refrigerated. Its milkunleashed .com website features drop-down headings such as "Nutrition" and "Protects What's Good" that bring up descriptions of UHT milk's composition: "A carton (eight ounces) of shelf stable milk has eight grams of protein and nine essential nutrients—calcium, Vitamins A, D and B_{12}, potassium, phosphorus, magnesium, riboflavin, niacin and zinc—nearly half of the daily recommended vitamins intake." Leaving aside the fact that there are ten, not nine, nutrients on this list, there is a more fundamental reason to look askance at Tetra Pak's plug for its product. The concluding statement that a serving of UHT milk supplies "nearly half of the daily recommended vitamins intake," is abstruse at best and easily misinterpreted at worst. Dietitians who know that the FDA has set daily consumption values for nineteen "vitamins" and eight "energy producing" nutrients including potassium, have the expertise to correctly read the claim to mean a glass of UHT milk contains almost half the number of vitamins for which the FDA has set recommended intakes. However, your average "active mom" to whom the claim is addressed is bound to read things differently. The ad leaves the impression that a serving of UHT milk contains nearly half the *amount* of each of the listed vitamins that she and her family need each day. It doesn't. Remember that an 8-ounce serving of milk contains only one percent of the DV for niacin.

Regardless of how you look at it, the sentence that Tetra Pak has scripted to answer consumer questions about the nutrition of UHT milk is too vague to be of value. Wondering whether the extra high heat that UHT milk undergoes impacts its vitamin content in ways that differ from other methods of pasteurization, I returned to the site. By focusing on the number of vitamins in UHT milk rather than amounts of the vitamins, the "Nutrition" drop-down leaves viewers in the dark. So I kept looking. Under "UHT Milk FAQs," one question, "Is shelf safe milk just as nutritious as refrigerated milk?" seemed promising. I was wrong: "Shelf safe milk is real milk. It tastes great and provides the same nutritional values of conventional refrigerated milk. . . . More UHT milk nutritional information is available here." "Here" brought me back to the "Nutrition" section that only refers to the numbers of nutrients in UHT milk and not the absolute quantities of each.

In a last-ditch effort, I scrolled down the "What Is Shelf Safe Milk?" menu to "Protects What's Good," hoping to find the "good" that UHT pasteurization preserves in milk, only to be disappointed yet again. All I learned was how Tetra Pak technology is helping to protect the environment. That's when I gave up. Since the website that Tetra Pak dedicates to educating consumers about UHT milk doesn't provide concrete details about UHT milk's nutritional profile, I'm guessing that the heat-degradable vitamins such as B_{12} don't survive UHT treatment in amounts worth bragging about. Broadly speaking, it would be wise to consider how your milk has been processed before buying dairy industry claims about milk's superior nutritional content.

Delving into each of the nutrients that the dairy industry parades in its hard sell to convince Americans to drink more milk is essential to assessing whether milk deserves to be a staple of our protein-saturated, saturated-fat–laden diets. Having established that niacin, vitamin D, vitamin A, protein, potassium, and vitamin B_{12} are not nutrients that pasteurized, fat-reduced milk can legitimately grandstand, three remain for examination: riboflavin, phosphorus, and finally the subject of the next three chapters, the lead of all milk PR, calcium.

RIBOFLAVIN

Some nutrients attract all the attention: calcium, vitamin D, and vitamin C come to mind. Not riboflavin. You don't often hear people talking about riboflavin, not when buying your multivitamin, not even when reviewing the blood work from your annual physical. But it is essential. According to the USDA, riboflavin, otherwise known as vitamin B_2, enables cells to "use oxygen to release energy from food," helps to "keep eyes healthy and vision clear" and "skin around mouth and nose healthy." Maybe that's why in the 1980s Men at Work hit song "Down Under," the man in Brussels who gives the traveling protagonist a Vegemite sandwich is "six-foot-four and full of muscles." Vegemite, a spread commonly consumed in the Land Down Under, is made from yeast extract, which is full of riboflavin. One teaspoon of it, also known as Marmite, contains 50 percent of the 1.7 milligram DV for riboflavin. Two teaspoons and you're on your way to metabolizing the energy you need to grow as tall and strong as the man in Brussels. If Vegemite is not your thing, the Kiwis have a hold on another store of B_2 abundance: the livers of the lambs for which they're famous. Although all liver is high in B_2, lamb liver contains the most, delivering 230 percent of the DV for B_2 in one 3-ounce piece. A bit of potentially useful trivia if you ever find yourself in the country of the lambs.

Like most of you, I never eat Vegemite, or Marmite, or brewer's yeast, which when concentrated is called "yeast extract." Vegemite and Marmite, which are made from beer-brewing residue, are not so popular in North America. As for liver, I like it every once in a while. However, I don't buy it and would never make it a daily habit. Mackerel, on the other hand, which is widely available in cans, is easy to keep around. One fillet contains about 56 percent of the DV for riboflavin, as well as a large amount of the healthy omega-3 fatty acids. Wild Atlantic salmon is another strong contender, with three raw ounces providing 19 percent of the DV for B_2. B_2 is also a good reason to make trout part of a weekly fish rotation: three raw ounces contains 17 percent of B_2's DV. Sprinkle a tablespoon of paprika on top before broiling and you just added another 7 percent of B_2's DV to the fish meal. While mackerel, salmon, and trout make for good breakfast, lunch, and dinner options to fill your B_2 needs, snacktime can also be the right time to jump-start the energy-metabolizer. An ounce of almonds provides

17 percent of B_2's DV, and a half cup of dry-roasted soybeans will give you about 20 percent of the DV.

The FDA allows foods that contain between 10 to 19 percent of the DV for a nutrient per serving to be called a "good source" of that nutrient. If a food contains 20 percent or more of the nutrient, it can be labeled as "high," or "rich" in, or an "excellent" or "great" source of the nutrient. According to these guidelines, milk, at 26 percent of the DV for B_2 per cup, is, as the NDC says, an "excellent source" of B_2. So riboflavin, unlike the other nutrients considered so far, deserves to stay on the list. Still, the abundance of nutrient-dense and common foods that come with B_2 included makes milk redundant. The fact that B_2 is essential doesn't mean milk is.

PHOSPHORUS

Boasting 25 percent of the 1,000-milligram DV for phosphorus in every cup, milk is an "excellent source" of phosphorus and therefore another deserving entry. But do you know what else is an excellent source of phosphorus? Soft drinks, specifically colas, which everybody agrees are unhealthy in part because they are full of phosphorus in the form of phosphate additives such as phosphoric acid. Although the right amount of phosphorus is essential for metabolizing calcium and is therefore critical to bone health, too much of the mineral interferes with calcium absorption. In North America, where soft drinks continue to be a popular thirst quencher, we arguably don't need another "excellent source" of phosphorus. Perhaps that's why phosphorus tends to appear last on lists of milk's assets despite the fact that milk is higher in phosphorus than almost any other essential nutrient. Maybe even the dairy industry is unsure about whether milk's high phosphorus content is a strike for or against it.

Even if you eschew soft drinks as we're continually advised to do, phosphorous isn't in short supply. It is in everything from the base of the food chain to prized foods such as bacon. Watermelon seeds, for example, are a wellspring of nutrients. One ounce contains almost 8 grams of protein, the same amount as in a cup of low-fat milk, and 21 percent of the DV for phosphorus. And that's not all. Wrapped up in one ounce of the seeds is 36 percent of the DV for magnesium; 23 percent of the DV for manganese; 19 percent of the DV for zinc; 11 percent of the DV for iron; 10 percent of the DV for copper; 5 percent of the DV for niacin; and 4 percent of the DV for thiamin and folate. That makes watermelon seeds an "excellent source" of three essential nutrients—magnesium, manganese, and phosphorus—and a "good source" of three more—zinc, iron, and copper. As soon as we're old enough to drink from a glass, we're told to finish our milk. We're never told to eat up our watermelon seeds. Think of all the life essentials wasted.

Rice bran is another nutritional match for milk when it comes to phosphorus and more. A third of a cup contains roughly 66 percent of the DV for phosphorus, or more than two and one-half times the amount of phosphorus that a cup of milk serves up. It also contains roughly 279 percent of the DV for manganese; 80 percent of the DV for B_6; 77 percent of the DV for magnesium; 72 percent of the DV for thiamin; 67 percent of the DV for niacin; 41 percent of the DV for iron; 29 percent of the DV for pantothenic acid, which I have already mentioned helps to metabolize fat; 33 percent of the DV for dietary fiber; and five grams of protein. Rice bran is therefore an "excellent source" of eight essential nutrients, and a "good source" of many more. Compared to milk, which is an "excellent source" of only three, rice bran is a top performer.

With about 232 milligrams of phosphorus in one cup of low-fat milk, milk is an "excellent source" of the strong-teeth- and bone-building mineral. But so are so many other foods: an ounce of pumpkin seeds has 328 milligrams; an ounce of sunflower seeds, 324 milligrams; an ounce of wheat germ, 321 milligrams; an ounce of sesame seed paste (aka tahini), 221 milligrams; and an ounce of Brazil nuts (about six nuts), 203 milligrams. If nothing on that list piques your interest, there's also the aforementioned rice bran, which provides almost all the phosphorus you need in one serving; oat bran, which provides 23 percent of the DV per one-third cup serving; and my new favorite, watermelon seeds. No, you're not going to eat watermelon seeds every day. The idea is not to identify substitutes for milk but to illustrate that milk needs no substitute.

Can calcium make up for the unimpressive showing of the eight other nutrients on milk's list of nine essentials? Can calcium pull milk from the pack of nutrient-dense foods and turn it into the indispensable food for all of North America that the dairy industry wants us to believe it is? We'll dig into this question and try to find answers in the next three chapters.

CHAPTER 7

The Seeds of Strong Bones: Breaking Up with Milk Is Easier Than You Think

Dairy advertising that equates milk with calcium and vice versa has pushed calcium into the nutritional spotlight. An 8-ounce serving of milk contains 300 milligrams of calcium, or 30 percent of the Daily Value. That makes milk an "excellent source" of calcium, as the National Dairy Council claims. But calcium isn't the only nutrient that counts. There is no hierarchy of essential nutrients. The motley crew that keep us alive interact in ways that we still don't fully understand. In the intricate, mysterious nutrient dance that our bodies stage twenty-four hours a day, every actor is as vital as the next. If you listen to dairy defenders, however, you'd think calcium choreographs the whole show. "Be sure to get your three servings of dairy per day," dairy processors, dietitians, physicians, and government officials say. The upshot, as Dr. David S. Ludwig of Harvard observes, is: "Americans are consuming billions of gallons of milk a year, presumably under the assumption that their bones would crumble without them." His colleague, Dr. Walter Willett, knows better: "In current US guidelines, the need for high intake of dairy products is overstated, in part because the requirements for calcium have been overstated. I think one or two servings a day (about two hundred and fifty to five hundred grams of milk) will provide adequate calcium, and with this level it is fine to be full fat."

HOLY BASIL

Our bones need calcium, we can all agree on that. They also need a host of other vitamins and minerals. Vitamins D and K, magnesium, manganese, and phosphorus are some of the most critical. Milk is high in calcium and phosphorus and is supplemented with vitamin D. However it lacks manganese and is not a significant source of vitamin K or magnesium, providing a minuscule 0.73 micrograms, or just under one percent of vitamin K's DV of 80 micrograms, and only 7 percent of the DV for magnesium per cup.

Not only is calcium not the king of bone-building nutrients but milk is not the best source of calcium in our food supply. You probably never considered the dried herbs in your cupboard to be a match for milk. And yet dried basil is an excellent source of three bone-building nutrients—vitamin K, manganese, and calcium—and a good source of one more, magnesium. When I say "excellent," I mean it. Two tablespoons of dried ground basil contains 107 percent of the DV for vitamin K; 50 percent of the DV for manganese; and 22 percent of the DV for calcium. Add to that 18 percent of the DV for magnesium and there is no denying that dried basil is a bone-building superfood. It also beats milk on two other counts: (1) economy—two tablespoons of dried ground basil only costs about 90 cents at my bulk foods' shop; and (2) complete goodness—it shares none of milk's flaws, which include but are not limited to its sugar, saturated fat and cholesterol content, its allergenic proteins, and its iron-depleting tendencies. Given all we now know about what our bones require and the varied number of foods that contribute to the roster, milk's position of privilege is no longer supportable.

The American dream is that no matter who you are or where you come from you can succeed. America is supposed to be the place where the cream can rise to the top. It's the place where dried basil should have a fair chance at knocking dairy off the table. However, unless a critical mass of minds change, multicolored bone-building foods will continue to be unwelcome in the blue food group that caps MyPlate. Barring a nutritional revolution, minerals such as manganese that are essential for normal bone development will continue to be treated as lower-class nutrients in comparison to calcium. Under the current dietary regime, the basils, pumpkin seeds, and sardines of the world have no hope of rising to the top of bone-healthy foods because in the realm of diet and nutrition, in our vision of the ingredients that make up a strong constitution, we accept a homogenized, white-dominant food kingdom.

We've all heard the various reasons dairy defenders give for guarding milk's hegemony and keeping the "milk run" a part of our daily vocabulary. Calcium is in a class of its own, they say, because, for one, the 2010 Dietary Guidelines for Americans have identified calcium as a nutrient "of concern." They maintain that Americans aren't consuming enough calcium and that upping our milk intake is the most obvious and convenient solution. They point to statistics that say that milk is the most significant source of calcium in our food supply.

The American Dairy Association and the National Dairy Council jointly made these arguments in response to Doctors David Ludwig and Walter Willett's July 1, 2013, *JAMA Pediatrics* Commentary, "Three Daily Servings of Reduced-Fat Milk: An Evidence Based Recommendation?" A spokesperson for the dairy organizations countered the physicians' criticism of the government's zealous milk recommendations with sweeping claims about milk's deliverables: "Because 73 percent of the calcium available in the food supply is provided by milk and milk products . . . it is difficult to get recommended levels of calcium by consuming non-dairy sources." Although decisive sounding, the statistic, which comes from the website of the International Dairy Foods Association (IDFA), falls apart under scrutiny. It is impossible to back up because in order to determine how much calcium is "available in the food supply," you'd have to test each and every one of its constituents. The endeavor would be hard enough without having to take into account the reality that our food supply is in a permanent state of flux.

BRANCHING OUT FROM MILK

My friend Roger grows most of the perishables for his family of four on the small patch of land that surrounds his Maine house. He's not the only one who is planting plenty of calcium-dense plants such as kale, turnips—with their tops drooping in calcium—and broccoli. As founder of the nonprofit Kitchen Gardeners International, he helped persuade the Obamas to plant a kitchen garden at the White House. Urban gardens are growing in number across North America. Does the IDFA count these calcium oases as part of "the food supply"? Does the IDFA include the even greater number of calcium-dense herbs that sprout in backyard planters and the windows of apartment buildings from North Dakota to California? I think not because it cannot. Although these small plots grow in the light of day, they evade standard accountings of the "food supply." Thank goodness we don't live in a *Lord of the Flies*–type island environment in which we have to source all of our food from one clearly defined stockpile. We don't all rely, as the IDFA's statistic suggests, on one discrete food supply. We eat on and off the grid. We grow our own and purchase food from suppliers that are far away and nearby. Provided that you have access to more foods than you'll find in your typical convenience store, where cigarettes, milk, and candy are best sellers, you won't have a problem meeting your calcium needs without milk or milk products.

With urban farms cropping up in and around towns and the traffic in supermarkets moving to the perimeter where the produce chills out, a trend is emerging. Americans are learning about the goodness contained in the vegetables that once accompanied meals only as garnish. Today my grandfather would have a hard time defending his conviction, which he made known during Sunday extended-family dinners, that carrots, spinach, and seeds are for rabbits and chickens. In 1990, the year my grandfather died, former Olympian Carl Lewis became a vegan. Lewis has made a point of telling the world that the first year he converted was his best year of track competition. Muscleman Mac Danzig, a star US mixed martial arts fighter, avoids dairy and won't eat a Big Mac either. Since 2004 he has been 100 percent vegan. Even testosterone-pumped racecar drivers win without the milk and blood of other animals coursing through their veins. Three-time Rolex Grand Am Champion Andy Lally, who became a vegan in 2009, acknowledges that the crowds who watch him are meat-and-potatoes folk. He hasn't let that slow him down.

Weight lifters too are bulking up on plant-based foods. Bodybuilding champion Kenneth Williams, for one, has been a proud vegan since 2000. Then there are the retired warriors. Mike Tyson says he's staying out of trouble and living a healthy lifestyle by juicing the power from greens. No dairy and red meat for this former heavyweight fighter. These poster men for the foods that my World War II navy officer grandfather dismissed as not fit for the strong and mighty attest to a growing awareness of the fruits and vegetables that my grandfather pushed to the edge of his dinner plate. With so many brave hearts eating green, milk products can no longer bank on the consumers' calcium dollar in the future.

FOLLOW YOUR NOSE

I feel it in my bones. Farmers' markets are where the future nutrients, including but not limited to calcium, are growing: the protein-, iron-, and calcium-packed amaranth leaves that cook like spinach and are very nice steamed and dressed with lemon; the Brussels sprouts that, left on their stalks, resemble wands that can be used, if you have an active imagination, to charm your meals with their cruciferous magic; the tatsoi, the delicate-textured and slightly fiery Japanese green also known as "spinach mustard" that will wow you with 30 percent of the DV for calcium, 325 percent of the DV for vitamin C, 19 percent of the DV for potassium, 12 percent of the DV for iron, 5 percent of the DV for niacin, and 4 percent of the DV for phosphorus and magnesium in just one cup of raw greens; and the turnips with their calcium-dense leaves that don't survive the long and arduous routes that connect field to Walmart. Turnip greens, one cup of which cooked contains 20 percent of the DV for calcium, are a "great source" of not only calcium but also six other nutrients. One cup cooked turnip greens provides 662 percent of the DV for vitamin K; 220 percent of the DV for vitamin A; 66 percent of the DV for vitamin C; 42 percent of the DV for folate; 25 percent of the DV for manganese; and 20 percent of the DV for fiber. They are a "good source" of three more. One cup cooked has 18 percent of the DV for copper; 14 percent of the DV for vitamin E; and 13 percent of the DV for vitamin B_6. A trip to the farmers' market makes you realize just how much good food is wasted in conventional channels of distribution. When the person in front of me requests topless turnips, I don't complain about getting a twofer and lightening the load, if only by a few ounces, of the compost the farmers have to haul home. More turnip greens please!

When I visit the farmers' market, I happily do without a grocery list, anodyne play lists, clean floors, and grid-like layouts. I hold on to my autonomy and certainty that what I see and smell is what I get. If you have a sweet spot for peaches, you know the feeling, at once serene and intoxicating, that the promise of a basket full of perfectly ripe peaches arouses. My mum passed hers on to me. She'd only buy peaches when they were in season. From August to early September there wasn't a Sunday morning when she didn't set out a big glass bowl of them sliced with a squeeze of lemon to keep their flesh, a combination of sunshine and sunset, blazing. Peaches were the perfume of August mornings. Peaches were the start of deliciously long days outside in warm rays. Peaches seduce me forward when I dismount from my bike at the Dufferin Grove market on Thursdays in August.

As October falls into November, which skates into December, I get cold feet. The warm and well-lit grocery stores beckon. Their brick and mortar shelter is tempting for a second. Then I remember all their rules and regulations and turn my back on the grocery store's draconian convenience for the market's flexibility and nutrient-dense bounty. I prefer the slight discomfort as I take off my gloves and get my hands dirty with the radish, celery root (aka celeriac), and kohlrabi that are caked in the same rich soil that brought the roots to maturity. Nicole, who helps Ted move his truckload of veggies into the hands of the patrons who flock to him like birds after berries, always has a carrot for my dog, Dixi. Nicole bites off a chunk small enough for Dixi to chew while Dixi wags her tail knowingly.

I have followed Ted Thorpe from the small stand he set up on a side street in downtown Toronto twenty years ago to Dufferin Grove, which he helped turn into the bustling market that it is now. I have watched the market transform from a nugget in the park where the committed convened into a beehive of activity. Bakers, sheep's cheese and tofu makers, mushroom hunters, wild blueberry pickers, fishmongers, chocolatiers, and hickory nut gatherers share space with venison, beef, chicken, and fresh egg sellers and, of course, the noble fruit and vegetable growers. People from all walks of life stop to shop. Although the market officially runs Thursdays from three to seven, it extends after-hours. On Fridays, when the vendors have gone home, there is a seven-dollar donate-if-you-can dinner that the community organizes. Market ingredients make up the menu of soup, salad, main dish, and dessert offered each week for all comers.

"Because 73 percent of the calcium available in the food supply is provided by milk and milk products . . . it is difficult to get recommended levels of calcium by consuming non-dairy sources." Now that you have accompanied Dixi and me on our weekly journey to market, you can see the leaks in this dairy-industry defense of milk and milk products. Only an impossibly microscopically detailed inventory of "the food supply" could capture the calcium that is exchanged in the outdoor markets that are turning up everywhere. The scope of the dairy industry's definition of "the food supply" can't capture what the surveyors, whoever they may be, don't see: the purslane, also known as pig weed, that Ted harvests from the wild; the dandelion greens that I glean from the park and the corners of my house; and the cauliflower leaves that I rescue from farmer Amanda's compost. All of these dodge the dairy industry's detection and are thus left out of its conception of "the food supply." So do meals like that shared one Friday night in September among a gathering of diners at Dufferin Grove. The calcium-rich menu of baked tofu—from curd freshly made the day before by a market vendor—with barbecue sauce and cornmeal biscuit topping, black-eyed pea salad and coleslaw, is too grassroots for the dairy industry's radar to register.

Perhaps 73 percent of the calcium available in some food supplies comes from milk and milk products. Perhaps 73 percent of the calcium available in your corner convenience store is concentrated in milk and milk products. But shop and eat outside of the box and you quickly discover that calcium is all around you. It grows in the cracks in the concrete, kitchen gardens, the windows of high-rises, and on communal rooftops. All you have to do is look up and down.

BACK TO THE FUTURE FOR CALCIUM

Calcium is on its way to becoming even more available as ancient seeds are being revived and repackaged into the future of food in North America. Quinoa, the small grainlike seed that is in fact a member of the grass, not grain, family, is fueling a "super foods" revolution. Amaranth, a plant that produces an even smaller seed than quinoa, may be the next dinner-party sensation. One cup of cooked amaranth seeds delivers 9 grams of protein, 29 percent of the DV for iron and 12 percent of the DV for calcium. The purple leaves that grow like weeds from the seeds contain twice the calcium of Popeye's favorite. If you can't find amaranth in the produce section of your grocery store, the seeds, and flour made from them, are making their way into the products that line the shelves of even conventional supermarkets. Especially high in protein and fiber compared to common grains such as rice, amaranth flour and seeds are becoming a go-to for bakers of gluten-free goods in particular.

If calcium is what you're after, little can compete, ounce for ounce, with the chia seed. A derivative of the Mayan word for "strength," chia means what it says. Ask certified nutritionist Lindsey Duncan and he will say chia seeds contain calcium, delivering "eighteen percent of your Daily Value per ounce, which is three times more than skim milk." Full also of magnesium, phosphorous, iron, potassium, zinc, omega-3 fatty acids, protein, and fiber, the seeds beat milk in every health-significant way.

Back in the 1980s, when North Americans were more likely to grow chia pets than vegetable gardens, not too many thought to eat the seeds, which are a member of the mint and sage family. Today most health food stores sell the seeds, black or white, in bags or bulk for doing just that: adding them to smoothies, soaking them for a pudding-like breakfast cereal, or sprinkling them on salads.

If you're used to drinking your calcium, cow's milk and calcium-supplemented plant-based milks are no longer your only options. Chia seeds are going mainstream. One product marketed as a fruit smoothie started small but is riding the consumer interest wave into Kroger's, Target, and Costco, where the seeds are now sold in bulk and in some of the club store's bakery items. Juice companies too have begun churning out chia-based breakfast smoothies. The momentum behind the small but potent seeds is too strong for their popularity to turn south. According to Datamonitor Consumer, which tracks product innovation in consumer packaged goods, more than four-fifths of the ancient-food launches between January and October 2013 were chia and quinoa based, up from 55 percent in 2010.

Datamonitor's director of innovation insights, Tom Vierhile, believes chia seeds and quinoa have the most commercial potential of all the ancient foods that are finding their way into the cereals, energy bars, and beverages that inundate mainstream channels of trade. Vierhile reports, "The packaged food industry has coalesced behind these two ancient grains to the point that they now account for a dominant percentage of new product activity in the food industry." Nielsen reports that the chia category alone is growing at an astounding 239 percent and is projected to be worth over one billion dollars by 2020. I've witnessed chia's exponential growth in popularity. The seeds didn't even exist in the bulk foods section of my local health food store in 2010. I bought my first bag in the spring of 2013, and even then only as an experiment. And now they're a mainstay of national supermarket chains.

The evolution of chia from a staple of the Aztecs and Mayans, to a seed consumed mostly in South America, to a sprouted artifact of 1980s North America, to its twenty-first-century infiltration of markets from the United States and Canada to the Middle East, Europe, and Asia, is extraordinary when you think about it. Creating a new chain to supply a food that was foreign to most of the world until a few years ago is not as easy as one, two, three. The connections that have instantly been made to grow and move mountains of the calcium-saturated seeds across land, air, and water are proof that our food supply of calcium and other nutrients is moving away from being as plain and white as the dairy industry paints it.

Science fact: calcium is just one among a network of essential bone-building nutrients. Science fiction: dairy is the best, most available and accessible source of dietary calcium.

CHAPTER 8

Milking Calcium: The Dark Side of Our Excessively High Calcium Recommendations

W hat the dairy industry tells the media about milk's significance to the American diet is different from what industry insiders are saying to one another. To us they say milk is essential, especially for meeting our calcium needs. To each other, they say the opposite. In the words of Tom Gallagher, CEO of Dairy Management Inc., the US dairy-farmer-funded organization that promotes dairy products: "If we don't see fundamental changes in the milk business, and I don't mean incremental changes, then milk is going to become an irrelevant beverage at some point."

That "point" has arguably arrived. Chia seeds represent only one of many foods that are adding spice and life to bland milk-toast traditions. You don't have to search Mayan ruins, climb the Andes, or travel to Thailand to find strawberry-banana chia snacks, chocolate–sea salt quinoa clusters, or coconut-ginger cricket bars. The storm of plants and now insects that is flooding North America with calcium and other bone-friendly nutrients seems destined to drown out dairy-industry cries to keep milk alive.

Gallagher's announcement in October 2014—two years after sounding the alarm about milk's impending irrelevance—of DMI's partnerships with seven companies, including big names such as Coca-Cola, to boost fluid milk sales reveals that the dairy industry isn't prepared to sit idly by as fluid milk sales fall, which they have been doing at a rate of about 8 percent over the past decade. With the partners investing a total of over 500 million dollars over the next few years to build opportunities to increase the sale of fluid milk, and with 30 million coming from the USDA administered check-off program, Gallagher speaks confidently about reinvigorating a market in which one out of every two adults over the age of eighteen doesn't drink milk. He is hopeful that products such as Coca-Cola's lactose-free Fairlife, which boasts 50 percent more protein, 50 percent less sugar, and 30 percent more calcium than regular milk, will reintroduce milk into the dietary vocabulary of adults. He encapsulates the driving conviction behind DMI's multiparty venture in one sentence: "We have to have products that are relevant to consumers at every stage of life." However, the signs are saying that even milk on steroids will have trouble competing with the strength and now pervasiveness of plant power.

THE USDA'S FIXATION ON MILK FOR CALCIUM

As the dairy industry schemes ways to lure consumers chasing after the latest "superfood" innovation back to milk, the USDA continues to hold up milk as a food like no other, as the one and only food worthy of recognition as a "food group." Look at the other four groups with which milk shares space on MyPlate. There's the Vegetable Group. It consists of a group of foods from "dark green," to "starchy," to "red and orange" vegetables. There's the Grains Group. It too consists of multiple foods from whole cornmeal to brown rice and oatmeal. There's the Fruit Group, which similarly is not one food but many that are as incomparable as apples and oranges, prunes and melons. Finally there's the Protein Foods Group. Nuts and seeds, beans and peas, seafood and meats, eggs and poultry, and "processed soy products" are all members of this diverse group of plants and animals. The dairy group, in contrast, is, with the exception of "calcium-fortified soymilk (soy beverage)," a group of one: variously processed forms of cow's milk.

What makes cow's milk so special? Go to the dairy section of MyPlate's home site and scroll to the bottom where "Selection Tips" is starred for the USDA's answer. First you'll find some advice for the lactose intolerant. The gist is, don't let negative reactions to milk discourage you or your loved ones from consuming it—the lactose intolerant can still consume dairy by reducing portion sizes, choosing low-lactose products such as cheese, or adding enzymes to milk to breaJ235k down the sugar. Then the warning: "Calcium-fortified foods and beverages such as cereals, orange juice, or rice or almond beverages may provide calcium, but may not provide the other nutrients found in dairy products." Notice that the USDA only lists heavily processed, calcium-fortified products to make its case that you might lose out if you choose to venture outside of the Dairy Food Group to meet your calcium needs. But you got a taste of the Dufferin Grove farmers' market in the last chapter. Giving up dairy doesn't mean having to rely on fortified foods for calcium or any of the other nutrients that milk delivers.

The USDA does not stop there in its not-so-subtle objection to going milk-free. It has more not very wise words "For Those Who Choose Not to Consume Milk Products." The heading alone betrays the USDA's bias. It implies that avoiding cow's milk is always a choice, when for some it's not a matter of preference but of life or death. The two bullet points that follow the subheading "Calcium choices for those who do not consume dairy products include" are just that: shots at said "calcium choices." First up is the same inventory of calcium-fortified foods that the USDA signals on the main dairy page are not on a par with milk. Then—their placement suggesting they are second-best to the fortified foods that precede them—come the foods that naturally contain calcium: "Canned fish (sardines, salmon with bones), soybeans and other soy products (tofu made with calcium sulfate, soy yogurt, tempeh), some other beans, and some leafy greens (collard and turnip greens, kale, bok choy)." This catalog of calcium- and nutrient-dense foods is followed by yet another cautionary note: "The amount of calcium that can be absorbed from these foods varies." The seemingly inconspicuous sentence communicates the not-inconsequential idea that dairy is the only reliable source of calcium.

It is true that many plants contain naturally occurring compounds called oxalates that reduce the amount of calcium in the plants that your body can assimilate. However, some plants contain sufficiently high levels of calcium to compensate. Hence Dr. David Ludwig's pointed effort, which I have already noted, to address the misconception that milk is the best way to get your calcium: "On a gram for gram basis, cooked kale has more calcium than milk. Sardines, nuts, seeds, beans, green leafy vegetables are all sources of calcium." And his reassurance that: "We can satisfy all our calcium and other nutrient requirements from a high-quality diet, including green leafy vegetables, beans, nuts, seeds and perhaps fish." His words bear repeating because they redeem the beans and greens that the USDA characterizes as second-rate sources of calcium.

Even the dairy industry admits calcium from vegetables is just as, if not more, easily absorbed than calcium from dairy. As an article in the *Chicago Tribune*, "Not Milk? If You Can't Imagine Life without a Daily Dose of Dairy, Consider Research that Questions the Value—If Not the Safety—of This Dairy Staple" reports, as far back as 2006 when the article was published, the National Dairy Council's Calcium Counseling Resource indicated that "the calcium from some vegetables such as broccoli, bok choy and kale is absorbed as well as or better than calcium from milk and milk products." Finding this statement about the NDC's position hard to believe, I wanted to hear it from the horse's mouth, which I did once I opened the NDC's publication devoted to "Absorption/Utilization Issues" involving calcium. Page two contains a table, "Comparison of Food Sources of Absorbable Calcium." The middle column charts the "fractional absorption" of calcium in a list of milk and plant-based foods. According to the table, milk has a fractional absorption of 32.1 percent, while broccoli, bok choy and kale have fractional absorptions of 61.3 percent, 53.8 percent and 49.3 percent respectively. Wow, that broccoli is something.

CALCIUM'S UNDUE INFLUENCE

You may not know why you should bother to look beyond dairy for your calcium and "eight other essential nutrients." There's more to the untold story about calcium than that it's easy to find in foods outside the dairy group. When I was in Florida researching orange juice in 2004, I interviewed Allen Morris, a prominent figure in the industry who at one time or another had worked for the biggest orange-juice producers. When we got to talking about food labels, and misinformation about products and their contents, he perked up, so much so that I made a note to myself in the margins that he became "more chatty." His years of experience in the marketing and production of orange juice had convinced him that trying to inform consumers is a hopeless endeavor: "ninety percent of all the things consumers make decisions on are wrong and false." He used the example of fortifying foods with calcium. Calcium fortification of orange juice was creating a special problem for dairy farmers who feed their cattle pellets made from the compressed leftovers of orange juice processing plants. Morris explained that there are: "laws limiting how much citrus pulp pellets you can feed the cows because . . . it's high in calcium and it keeps them from absorbing calcium, makes them throw it off." He called attention to the inconsistency that while lawmakers have realized the necessity of regulating the calcium intake of cows, "there's no limit [of calcium] in the vitamin supplement you can sell pregnant women." He challenged me to "figure out why you can give pregnant women something that's not good for them but you can't give it to a dairy cow."

If I had known then what I know now about the risks of taking in too much calcium, I might have encouraged him to tell me more. Instead, although he said he could "go on and on," we switched subjects after he wrapped up his calcium rant with the observation that the "lack of understanding of orange juice is nothing compared to all the other misinformation that's out there, it's incredible." He was one step ahead of me. He grasped, before studies critical of calcium recommendations in the thousands of milligrams entered mainstream media, that we have been getting calcium all wrong. The most underreported story about calcium may turn out to be its overrepresentation in our diet.

The Recommended Dietary Allowances for calcium are the same in Canada and the United States. The RDA is highest, 1,300 milligrams, for children between the ages of nine and eighteen. It dips to 1,000 milligrams for men between the ages of nineteen and seventy and women between the ages of nineteen and fifty. After that, women older than fifty and everyone older than seventy are advised to up their intake to 1,200 milligrams per day. Health Canada's website states, "Over ninety-nine percent of the body's calcium supply is found in the bones and teeth where it supports their structure." Hence the calcium–strong bones connection that we have all internalized. We may not know offhand why we need magnesium, why the National Institutes of Health in the United States has set the RDA for magnesium for young men and women at 400 milligrams and 310 milligrams respectively. However, we all know why the RDA for calcium for that same age group of men and women is 1,000 milligrams. If there is one thing about our health that we all know, it's that we need adequate amounts of calcium in our diet for our bones. We trust government to set the precise number correctly. Yet physicians and researchers are beginning to question why the calcium RDAs in the United States and Canada are so high given the absence of evidence that so much calcium is beneficial and the existence of studies indicating that the recommended levels may actually be harmful.

In 2011 *Time* magazine's Health & Family section headlined an article, "Study: U.S. Calcium Guidelines May Be Too High," which reported the results of a Swedish study of 60,000 women whose calcium intake and bone-fracture rates were followed for nineteen years. The article begins with the question of whether there is such a thing as too much calcium. Eva Warensjo, PhD, a researcher at Uppsala University in Sweden who was behind the study and the article published in the *British Medical Journal* about it, confirms: "According to our study, yes, the U.S. recommendations might be set too high." Too much calcium, the study found, may actually increase the likelihood of fractures. She believes the appropriate range is between 700 and 800 milligrams of calcium per day. Dr. Julie Switzer, a member of the American Academy of Orthopedic Surgeons' Women's Health Issues Advisory Board, was persuaded. Referring to the study, she stated: "This may be opening the door to modifying our recommendations for calcium intake." That was back in 2011. There is no sign of change.

The Swedish study has not been the first to flag calcium RDAs of 1,000 milligrams and above as substandard. If Warensjo's study undermines the traditional thinking that our bones, especially those of postmenopausal women, need megadoses of calcium to form and stay strong over the long run, in *The China Study*, which the *New York Times* praised as the "the Grand Prix of Epidemiology," T. Colin Campbell, PhD, and his son Thomas M. Campbell II, MD, look at the effects of high dietary calcium on bone strength and other aspects of health such as cancer. For instance, they cite studies and reports connecting dairy consumption to prostate cancer. Specifically, they quote the findings of a 2001 review of the research on the link between the two: "In these studies, men with the highest dairy intakes had approximately double the risk of total prostate cancer, and up to a four-fold increase in risk of metastatic or fatal prostate cancer relative to low consumers." The authors of the review conclude, "This is one of the most consistent dietary predictors for prostate cancer in the published literature." The Campbells also refer to an earlier study that hypothesizes, "The consistent associations with dairy products [and prostate cancer] could result from, at least in part, their calcium and phosphorus content."

FINDING THE LIGHT

Why might high calcium intakes correlate with an increased risk of bone fractures? Calcium and vitamin D work together in constructing sturdy skeletons. As Dr. Neville Golden, a specialist in adolescent medicine at the Stanford University School of Medicine, told National Public Radio's Science Desk, "You can drink as much calcium as you like, but if you don't have enough vitamin D, you're not going to absorb it." In other words, when the balance between calcium and vitamin D intake is off, when calcium becomes too dominant, the partnership breaks down. The Campbells explain the process by first providing some background about vitamin D, the many benefits of which are widely touted. They remind us that we can make all the vitamin D we need by exposing our skin, sunscreen free, to sunlight for fifteen to thirty minutes a few times a week. Our body converts what our skin soaks in into what the Campbells call "supercharged" D. This "supercharged" D, otherwise known as 125 D, is responsible for all the good that we hear vitamin D does, preventing everything from cancer and autoimmune diseases to osteoporosis.

The Campbells rule out the possibility of one day being able to pop "supercharged" D in a pill. According to them, it is too powerful and dangerous for medical use. Only the body knows how to mete it out in proper doses. The complex system works with amazing precision until it doesn't. One culprit that has been found to throw the intricate operation out of whack is calcium. Excess calcium curbs the production of 125 D, which leaves the body susceptible to an untold number of diseases.

YOUR BONES HIGH ON CALCIUM

The Campbells note, "An avalanche of commentary warns that most of us are not meeting our calcium requirements." Ironically, at the same time that Dr. Golden raises awareness about the importance of vitamin D to strong bone formation, he adds to this "avalanche" when, in the NPR interview, he cautions that teenagers who shun milk risk calcium deficiency and therefore stunted bone growth. Faced with what they call a "calcium bonanza," the Campbells reproduce a chart, "Association of Rates of Hip Fractures with Calcium Intake for Different Countries," which graphs the data gathered by David Mark Hegsted, PhD, who was, among his many hats, a professor of nutrition at Harvard's School of Public Health from 1962 to 1978. Published in 1986, the chart shows a positive association between calcium consumption and bone-fracture rates. Of the ten countries studied, Hong Kong had the lowest calcium consumption. Averaging below 500 milligrams of calcium per day, it also had the second-lowest, after Singapore, incidence of hip fractures: 40 fractures per 100,000 people. The United States, with an average calcium consumption of 1,000 milligrams per day, tops the chart for frequency of hip fractures. At 100 fractures per 100,000 people, the hip-fracture rate was five times greater in the United States than in Singapore.

The USDA is delivering a different message: Americans aren't getting enough calcium. Dietitians like to remind us that the 2010 Dietary Guidelines for Americans have identified calcium as a nutrient "of concern" to scare us into consuming more milk and dairy. The USDA provides a generous amount of information on its website about calcium's critical role in bone formation. You won't read about the "calcium paradox" there. It leaves you thinking everybody could use more calcium. Yet even the World Health Organization recognizes there is a paradox that deserves attention. In its "Recommendations for Preventing Osteoporosis," which can be found in the nutrition section of its website, it defines osteoporosis as being "characterized by low bone mass and micro-architectural deterioration of bone tissue, leading to bone fragility and a consequent increase in risk of fracture." Unlike the USDA, which offers pat prevention measures such as consuming more dairy, WHO's recommendations are more nuanced. It acknowledges: "The paradox (that hip-fracture rates are higher in developed countries where calcium intake is higher than in developing countries where calcium intake is lower) clearly calls for explanation." In its "Disease-specific Recommendations" it states that for countries with a high fracture incidence, "a minimum of four hundred to five hundred milligrams of calcium intake is required to prevent osteoporosis." There is no talk of needing *more*.

WHO isn't alone in writing calcium recommendations that defy the USDA's expectations of what Americans should be consuming. The UK's recommendations are more in line with those of WHO. In the UK the "Estimated Average Requirement" (EAR) varies according to age, 525 milligrams being the baseline for everyone older than nineteen. The Reference Nutrient Intake (RNI), defined as "the amount of a nutrient that is sufficient, or more than sufficient to meet the nutritional requirements of practically all (97.5 percent) healthy people in the population," is slightly higher, at 700 milligrams for the nineteen and older age group. However, as Hannah Theobald, PhD, of the British Nutrition Foundation admits, "the RNI exceeds the needs of most individuals." Next to WHO's calcium recommendations—and recommendations such as those in the UK that are consistent with them—1,000 milligrams, the RDA for calcium for everyone between the ages of nineteen and fifty in the United States, appears awfully high.

The prudence of setting 1,000 milligrams as a baseline is especially questionable in light of three trends that WHO highlights. First, the age-adjusted rates for incidence of hip fractures "are many times higher in affluent developed countries than in sub-Saharan Africa and Asia." Second, "Hip-fracture rates are highest in Caucasian women living in temperate climates, are somewhat lower in women from Mediterranean and Asian countries, and are lowest in women in Africa." Third, "Countries in economic transition, such as Hong Kong Special Administrative Region (SAR) of China, have seen significant increases in age-adjusted fracture rates in recent decades." There are a couple of common threads running through these trends: the regions with the lowest calcium intakes tend to have the lowest hip-fracture rates; and in the regions where greater wealth has led to greater dairy, and therefore greater calcium, intakes, there has been a corresponding and "significant" increase in age-adjusted fracture rates. These regional currents signal a tipping point for calcium beyond which bones begin to fall apart.

According to the USDA's MyPlate, most of us are supposed to drink three glasses of milk per day, the equivalent of 90 percent of the 1,000 milligram DV for calcium. Besides being advised to consume more calcium than is the norm in populations with more resilient bones, we are therefore also told we ought to obtain almost all of that calcium from one source, milk.

The World Health Organization's take on the role that animal protein plays in explaining the calcium paradox provides helpful perspective on the USDA's calcium-dairy recommendations. Remember WHO's suggestion that "To date, the accumulated data indicate that the adverse effect of protein, in particular animal (but not vegetable) protein, might outweigh the positive effect of calcium intake on calcium balance." Milk and milk products are high in animal protein. If animal protein, as WHO states, "might outweigh the positive effect of calcium intake on calcium balance," then maybe the reason the rate of bone fractures in the United States is off the charts has more to do with the source rather than the amount of calcium that Americans consume. If MyPlate didn't have dairy on it, or a glass of milk next to it, if it were full of calcium-rich plant-based foods instead, then maybe the United States wouldn't have the misfortune of holding the world record, at least as of 1986, for hip fractures.

Not all doctor recommendations in the United States are consistent with those of the USDA. The Physicians Committee for Responsible Medicine has long challenged the DVs for calcium and the dietary guidelines for dairy. In 2005 a team of three—PCRM senior nutrition scientist Amy Joy Lanou, PhD; Neal Barnard, MD; and Susan Berkow, PhD—authored a review of all fifty-eight studies that had been published since 1966 with respect to the effects of dairy and calcium on the bone integrity of the young. The authors wondered: (1) whether there is sufficient evidence to support the calcium recommendations in the United States; and (2) whether the literature supports the claim that dairy is better than other calcium sources for promoting bone integrity. They conclude no and no. First, while they found that low calcium intakes of below 400 milligrams per day may impair bone development, increases in calcium intake above 400 to 500 milligrams per day did not correlate with or predict bone mineral density or fracture incidence in children and young adults. Second, they determined that the calcium in milk and milk products is not as well absorbed as the calcium in dark leafy greens, and that the sodium and protein in dairy increases urinary excretion of calcium. Ultimately, they counsel parents that their children need lots of sunshine, exercise, and at least 400 to 500 milligrams of calcium per day from plant-based foods. They also emphasize the importance of avoiding smoking and consuming high amounts of salt and caffeine, all of which interfere with calcium uptake.

Published in 2005, the PCRM-led literature review is old news. More recently, a study co-authored by Diane Feskanich, ScD, an assistant professor at Harvard Medical School, and published in the journal *JAMA Pediatrics* in November 2013, challenges the orthodoxy that drinking lots of milk at a young age builds bones that are more resilient in the future. Tracking the dietary patterns and numbers of hip fractures among a group of more than 61,000 women and 35,000 men over a period of twenty years, Feskanich and her co-authors found no correlation between milk consumption during teenage years and lower risk of hip fractures later in life. In fact, they found the reverse in the case of the men: men who drank more milk as teenagers had a higher risk of hip fractures. Although not sure how to explain the positive correlation between the amount of milk the men drank as teens and their risk of a hip fracture later on, Feskanich insists, "It does make you stop and ponder and want to see better evidence for our dietary recommendations."

Apparently Feskanich misjudged her audience. The closing exchange between one television news anchor and the journalist reporting on the story captures the more likely reaction of the rest of North America. Anchor: "Can't imagine not drink'n my milk." Reporter: "Neither can I." As long as the USDA remains steadfast that Americans need to consume more calcium, which has become code for more milk, the two newswomen can't be blamed for being unfazed by a story that milk's bone-building benefits may be overstated. If they only knew that Dr. Feskanich's study is not isolated but is one small chapter in an expanding volume of literature that is raising questions about whether milk really contributes to bone health. If they realized that, on the one hand, there are no good data to show that we need all the calcium and dairy that the government says we do, and, on the other hand, there is a growing body of evidence to indicate that we jeopardize our health by following the current recommendations, perhaps they too would stop "drink'n" their milk and ponder.

Of all the DVs that have been set, calcium's stands out as erring on the side of more rather than less. The DV for vitamin C, for instance, is only 60 milligrams. A single yellow pepper contains more than five times that amount, 340 milligrams to be exact. One orange has about 83 milligrams. I must consume, from fruits and vegetables alone, at least ten times the 60-milligram DV for vitamin C. If 60 milligrams is truly all we need, you too are probably consuming megadoses of vitamin C without even knowing or thinking about it.

Vitamin C isn't the only nutrient with a remarkably modest DV. The recommendations for vitamin D and other bone essentials are as alarmingly low as the recommendations for calcium and dairy are recklessly high. This discrepancy is enough to make even die-hard milk drinkers wonder what's really going on behind the closed doors where nutrition guidelines are set.

CHAPTER 9

"D" Is Not for Dairy: Think Daylight and Dried Herbs

Rickets is on the rise. The disease that tends to leave its victims, mostly the young who are vitamin D deficient, crippled by bowlegs and curved spines conjures images of the malnourished children of a Dickensian orphanage. Not the picture of perfection you expect to find in the cushy daycares of twenty-first-century North America. Although rickets all but disappeared from Britain around the 1950s when government-sponsored programs convinced parents to give their children cod liver oil, more than half a century later pediatricians in the United Kingdom and the United States are observing a resurgence of the disease among their patients. They blame the return in part on lifestyles sheltered from the sun. Whereas the children of Victorian England lived under the dark sooty skies of industrialization, children these days are spending all of their time inside, hidden away from the sun's enriching embrace.

GROWING VITAMIN D DEFICIENCY

When I was a kid, after school meant playing kickball in the lane, climbing fences, or transforming the neighborhood into a battleground for a heady game of capture the flag. In those days we used our feet rather than our index fingers to bring down our enemies. A few years later, above-freezing temperatures meant long hours training on outdoor tennis courts. I didn't need to take cod liver oil. One hour of exposure to the summer sun can generate between 10,000 and 20,000 international units of vitamin D, loads more than the DV for vitamin D, which when I last checked was 400 international units (IU).

Despite the capacity of our bodies to produce thousands of international units of vitamin D hourly, the Institute of Medicine sets the Tolerable Upper Intake Level, the "maximum daily intake unlikely to cause adverse health effects," for vitamin D at 4,000 IU for everyone older than nine. The IOM's RDAs for vitamin D are equally counterintuitive. Ranging, depending on age and life stage, from 600 to 800 IU they are a fraction of the amount we are wired to make from the sun's rays.

In the spring of 2009 *Scientific American* ran a story: "Vitamin D Deficiency Soars in the U.S., Study Says." The article summarized the research that was about to be released in the *Archives of Internal Medicine* documenting a huge drop in the vitamin D blood concentrations of Americans between the years 1994 and 2004. Whereas in the years spanning 1988 to 1994, 45 percent of the subjects of the National Health and Nutrition Examination Survey (NHNES) had blood levels of 30 nanograms per milliliter or more of vitamin D, by 2004, only 23 percent of those surveyed met this threshold.

The late Mary Frances Picciano, PhD, former senior nutrition scientist at the Office of Dietary Supplements at the National Institutes of Health, downplayed the results. She said that using the IOM's then threshold of 11 nanograms per milliliter, only 10 percent of Americans could be considered vitamin D deficient. As for the drop, she attributed much of it to changes in measuring methods. Dr. Adit Ginde, assistant professor at the University of Colorado Denver School of Medicine and co-author of the study, disagreed. He admitted that while methodology may have contributed to some of the drop, the decline was too steep not to be real. Given the existence of other research demonstrating a similar downward trend, he was confident that "this is the reality right now in the U.S." More recent reports of a rise in rickets corroborate the study's verdict that vitamin D deficiency is rampant and growing in the United States.

Soft bones and curved spines are not the only signs of lives lived concealed from the light of day. The Mayo Clinic's website once contained a catalog of diseases linked to inadequate intakes of vitamin D. The long list foreshadowed trouble for a nation that has been diagnosed as vitamin D deficient. In its section on "Patient Care and Health Info," a webpage about vitamin D dosing stated that not all of the vitamin D RDAs "have been found to be effective for conditions that have been studied." The "conditions" it proceeded to list included but were not limited to vitamin D deficiency; cardiovascular disease; diabetes; hypertension; mood disorders; multiple sclerosis; muscle weakness or pain; osteoporosis; respiratory infections; rheumatoid arthritis; tuberculosis; viral infections; and fall, fracture, and cancer prevention. It referred to studies showing that for each of these diseases vitamin D at levels well above the DV of 400 international units, in some cases such as multiple sclerosis as high as 10,000 international units, are advantageous.

The Mayo Clinic has since revised the website, removing wording implying that the RDAs may be inadequate and that higher levels may be beneficial. Instead the new site has substituted nonjudgmental language, stating the fact that higher doses have "been taken" for each of the conditions. However, at least one blogger, Rachel Feldman, cites passages from the Mayo Clinic's site before it was modified. In her post "Benefits of Vitamin D," Feldman highlights in bold italics the Mayo Clinic's original statement that followed its reference to the IOM's vitamin D RDAs: "Not all doses have been found to be effective for conditions that have been studied." Keep reading her restoration of the Mayo Clinic's old webpage and you will see that if your only condition is that you want to prevent cancer, the studies suggest that 600 international units of vitamin D, which is the RDA for everyone between the ages of one and seventy, is insufficient.

The IOM's take on vitamin D is disconcerting in the face of evidence of dropping blood concentrations of it and the grave repercussions for our health. It's also baffling considering its position on calcium. On the one hand, we are advised to consume more than double the amount of calcium than is typically found in the mostly nondairy diets of populations with the lowest bone-fracture rates. On the other hand, we are told to avoid vitamin D in amounts that we naturally make when we're doing what we're supposed to be doing when the sun is shining: letting ourselves out.

ALL IN FAVOR OF RAISING THE VITAMIN D RDAS

Some physicians are seeing the light. In 2005 Dr. Andrew Weil upped his recommendations for vitamin D from 400 to 1,000 international units per day. In 2013 he went public with the announcement that he's going higher. After reviewing meta-analyses indicating that Americans are low in vitamin D and that a daily intake of 2,000 international units prevents breast and colorectal cancer, he has decided to advise we all get that much.

In 2005 David Mark Hegsted, whose research helped to expose the "calcium paradox," was already where Dr. Weil is today on the subject of vitamin D. In an interview with Marion Nestle, PhD, professor of nutrition, food studies, and public health at New York University, about the forces shaping the field of nutrition science, past, present, and future, Hegsted illuminated a bright spot. He was confident that those studying vitamin D were on to something: "You know, it's a hell of a lot more important than we thought it was. I gather now, the experts say between two thousand and four thousand units."

Hegsted's "now" is almost a decade ago. *Now* experts are going further and taking a stand against the IOM's conservative guidelines for vitamin D intakes and blood concentration levels. The website of the Harvard School of Public Health has posted a response, co-authored by Dr. Heike Bischoff-Ferrari, director of the Centre on Aging and Mobility at the University of

Zurich, and Dr. Walter Willett, to the IOM's 2010 revisions to its vitamin D and calcium recommendations. The Comment's subtitle says it all: "For Adult Bone Health, Too Low on Vitamin D—and Too Generous on Calcium."

Basically, the doctors were not impressed by the IOM's decision to elevate its recommended daily vitamin D intake from 400 to 600 IU for everyone between one and seventy years old, and from 600 to 800 IU for everyone older than seventy. Addressing the slight increase, the doctors accept that 600 to 800 IU of vitamin D per day will enable most adults to reach the IOM's current threshold blood concentration of 50 nanomoles per liter (20 nanograms per milliliter). However, they cite studies revealing that a blood concentration of 50 nanomoles per liter of vitamin D is too low to reduce falls and fractures and that concentrations well above this threshold may lead to increased bone density. The doctors point to the target levels issued by the International Osteoporosis Foundation (IOF) for support. To reduce falls and fracture, the IOF says everyone aged sixty and older should be taking in 800 to 1,000 IU of vitamin D per day, with the aim of maintaining 75 nanomoles per liter of vitamin D in the blood.

Although the doctors refer to the IOF's recommendations, they do not believe that bone health should be the only consideration in setting guidelines for vitamin D intake and blood concentration levels. Like the Mayo Clinic has done, they recognize that the benefits of vitamin D are more far-reaching. So while they are critical of the fact that the IOM's recommendations are "largely based on bone health," they are encouraged by one of its 2010 updates: the increase of the safe upper limit for vitamin D from 2,000 to 4,000 IU per day for adults and from 1,000 to 3,000 IU per day for children. This boost, they say, at least allows room for experts to research and recommend higher levels of vitamin D intake. When the Mayo Clinic posts links on its website to studies showing that 2,000 IU per day of vitamin D helps to prevent cancer and 600 IU is not enough to ward it off, when children are showing up in pediatric clinics with rickets, it is reasonable to infer that the DV of 400 IU for vitamin D is dangerously low.

CALCIUM CONTINUES TO CLOUD OVER THE LIGHT

Despite all the evidence that Americans are short in vitamin D, calcium remains the nutrient that consumes us. The authors of the Harvard School of Public Health Commentary are as disapproving of the IOM's zeal for calcium as they are of its restraint toward vitamin D. They invoke WHO's 500 milligrams of calcium per day benchmark to shore up their argument that the IOM's guidelines for calcium intake seem unreasonable. But the authors don't rely on appearances alone. They have proof. On the one hand, they note the lack of data showing a positive relationship between calcium intakes and hipbone density, except when blood concentrations of vitamin D fall below 50 nanomoles per liter. On the other hand, they refer to evidence that calcium supplementation of between 1,000 and 1,200 milligrams per day, which is within the range of what the IOM recommends for women and men over fifty years old, may adversely affect the risk for hip fracture. The absence of data showing a beneficial relationship between high calcium intakes and increased bone density or decreased fractures, combined with the existence of solid data linking calcium supplements to cardiovascular disease and kidney stones suggest that the IOM's safe upper limit of 2,000 to 3,000 milligrams of calcium per day for adults is not so safe.

The doctors end by questioning the decisions that the IOM doesn't make. In particular, they wonder why the IOM declined to make integrated recommendations regarding calcium and vitamin D intakes given that vitamin D has been shown to increase calcium absorption. They cite evidence indicating that there is no correlation between consuming high doses of calcium—above 800 milligrams per day—and bone health when serum concentrations of vitamin D or vitamin D intakes are adequate. All things considered, they regret that the IOM failed to consider that "calcium recommendations could be adjusted downward with vitamin D supplementation; they could also possibly be adjusted downward for safety reasons."

In its report on Human Vitamin and Mineral Requirements, the Food and Agriculture Organization acknowledges what we in North America have tended to ignore: we are remarkably adaptable. On the subject of calcium intake, the report explains that calcium balance is a function of not merely calcium intake but also calcium absorption and excretion. It diagrams calcium's circulation through our body: how it enters us through the foods we eat, is absorbed by our blood and bones, and is excreted through feces and urine. The report goes on to say, "A striking feature of the system is that relatively small changes in calcium absorption and excretion can neutralise a high intake or compensate for a low one."

Hegsted long recognized this amazing ability of our species to adjust to the particulars of our food environment. In a paper he wrote reviewing his career, he highlights the one discovery that recurs throughout his research: "Among the conclusions from studies on protein and calcium is that reasonably healthy people are adapted to their current diets." He uses the "calcium paradox" to illustrate: "People all over the world, for example, are raised on relatively low calcium intakes yet have less osteoporosis than those who consume western-style diets." To call the relationship a paradox, as has become the norm, presumes that because some calcium is critical for building bone, more should be better. The fact that the data do not support this finding is less a contradiction than a reality of life that most of us learn early on: you *can* have too much of a good thing. Balance is key.

MISSING SCIENCE

Vitamin D isn't the only bone essential that the science says the government is underestimating: magnesium is also underappreciated. Magnesium, like calcium, is critical in bone formation. It is also important for normal muscle, nerve, heart, and immune system functioning. Although the USDA has singled out calcium as a nutrient "of concern," magnesium is arguably more deserving of the designation. An article published in 2005 in the *Jour-*

nal of the American College of Nutrition and summarized on the US National Library of Medicine's website reported that 68 percent of American adults were consuming less than the RDA for magnesium and 19 percent were consuming less than 50 percent of the RDA. The findings are noteworthy given that the individuals who consumed less than the RDA for magnesium were also found to have elevated levels of C-reactive protein, a marker of inflammation that may contribute to an increased risk for cardiovascular disease.

I have already sung the praises of pumpkin seeds. Among their many wonders, they are one of the best sources of magnesium. A one-ounce serving contains 150 milligrams of magnesium, which, it's worth repeating, is 37 percent of the 400 milligram DV for magnesium. Yet the USDA hasn't created bulletins and websites and partnerships with pumpkin-seed producers to encourage Americans to eat three servings per day of pumpkin seeds to ward off cardiovascular disease, diabetes, high blood pressure, anxiety disorders and osteoporosis, all of which result from magnesium deficiency. Considering the effort it has exerted to make milk products a staple, pumpkin seeds, you might say, have been neglected.

Why aren't pumpkin seeds a food group? Why aren't they and magnesium in the spotlight? The better question is why milk and calcium have long received all the attention. I don't have a simple answer, but it doesn't lie in science. As Dr. David Ludwig states, "Indeed, the recommended levels of calcium intake in the United States, based predominately on balance studies of three weeks or less, likely overestimate actual requirements and greatly exceed recommended intakes in the United Kingdom. Throughout the world, bone fracture rates tend to be lower in countries that do not consume milk compared with those that do. Moreover, milk consumption does not protect against fracture in adults, according to a recent meta-analysis." Built on such brittle foundations, no wonder the USDA's calcium and dairy recommendations are jeopardizing the backbones of America.

The United States and Canada could learn from the United Kingdom, which speaks the same "drink your milk for calcium" language but with a more sophisticated accent. There, unlike in North America, doctors working with the government are open to discussing the negative impacts of high calcium intakes. In her briefing paper "Dietary Calcium and Health," the British Nutrition Foundation's Hannah Theobald devotes a section to "Guidance on High Intakes." She acknowledges that there is some evidence that "high intakes of calcium might potentially cause nutrient deficiencies via interference with the absorption of other minerals such as zinc, copper and magnesium." Although she is satisfied that when calcium is consumed under normal dietary conditions it will not interfere with these three nutrients, she is not prepared to say the same about calcium's effect on iron. Instead, she recognizes that calcium intakes of between 150 and 300 milligrams—an amount equal to or less than that in a single glass of milk—have been shown to interfere with iron absorption.

In the United States, the National Institutes of Health is more skeptical. Its website about calcium states that "high calcium intake" might "interfere with the absorption of iron and zinc, though this effect is not well established." Theobald's presentation of the literature thus departs from that of the NIH in two ways. First, Theobald distinguishes calcium's relationship with iron from its interaction with other minerals. She emphasizes that not only "high" but also low to moderate levels of calcium intake have been observed to interfere with iron absorption. Second, her conclusion that the studies "suggest" there is a short-term effect imparts her conviction that the evidence is worth considering. While she is not persuaded that iron absorption is detrimentally affected over the long run, she calls for more research to fully understand the nature of the relationship. The NIH, in contrast, is dismissive. It concludes that calcium's interference with iron absorption "is not well established"—full stop.

Comparing the two readings reveals one certainty: the small amount of data we have on our nutrient intakes and needs is wide open to interpretation. Whether or not and to what degree calcium blocks iron absorption depends on where you stand. If you're with Theobald, your perspective will be markedly different than if the NIH is your guide. The same holds true regarding the question of whether calcium intakes in a given population are adequate or "of concern." Theobald reports that mean intake of calcium from foods is 1,007 milligrams per day for men and 777 milligrams per day for women in the United Kingdom. The numbers in the United States are similar. Depending on life stage, they range from 871 to 1,266 milligrams per day for males and 748 to 968 milligrams per day for females. Yet while Theobald maintains that "average intakes [of calcium] are more than adequate," the NIH infers the opposite from comparable averages in the United States. Not surprisingly, it isolates those groups with the highest RDAs, RDAs ranging from 1,200 to 1,300 milligrams per day, as the most prone to failing to meet their calcium quotas: boys and girls between the ages of nine and thirteen; girls between the ages of fourteen and eighteen; women between the ages of fifty-one and seventy, and both men and women older than seventy. Transfer this population of Americans that the NIH defines as wanting in calcium to the United Kingdom and many, if not the vast majority, of them would instantly be considered okay. In other words, whether you're meeting your calcium needs depends not on *how much* you're consuming but *where*. It depends not on the actual numbers but who is crunching them.

The lack of science behind the calcium RDAs is indicative of a more general problem with the Dietary Reference Intakes that Marion Nestle calls attention to in her interview of David Mark Hegsted. She prompts, "But the science isn't there to back them up." Hegsted agrees: "No. You know these are a best guess. Even at best." He should know, for he played a key role in writing the first Dietary Guidelines for Americans that were published in 1980. According to Hegsted, little had changed since 1980: "All these years later, they've been revised I don't know how many times and they're still pretty much the way we wrote them." Which is to say, unsubstantiated by "the science."

The 2010 Guidelines' recommendations for calcium and dairy illustrate Hegsted's point perfectly. Despite the growing consensus that calcium intakes above 800 milligrams per day are unnecessary and even unhealthy, especially when derived from animal sources, the USDA continues, as it has done for decades, to stand by calcium RDAs that range from 1,000 to 1,300 milligrams for everyone older than three. No amount of evidence seems capable of convincing the agency to turn down the volume on calcium.

Imagine for a minute if the USDA joined WHO in saying that, for populations with the greatest risk of hip fracture, 400 to 500 milligrams is sufficient to prevent osteoporosis. Such a recommendation would have a domino effect in North America. It would also require revising the three servings per day of dairy prescription that equates to about 900 milligrams of calcium that has long been the gold standard. If the USDA accepted that 500 milligrams of calcium is all we need, then the current dairy recommendations would lose their primary justification. Say the USDA also heeded the findings of the Swedish studies published in the *British Medical Journal* that more than 800 milligrams of calcium per day might increase the risk of bone fractures among women and, as discussed in chapter 4, that three or more glasses of milk per day may do the same. Then the recommendations would really be in trouble because when seen through the lens of studies such as these, and others with consistent findings, they are worse than unwarranted; they are hazardous to our health.

SPICING IT UP

Besides being potentially dangerous in their own right, the calcium and dairy recommendations have had the incidental but not insignificant effect of overshadowing the importance of other nutrients critical to bone and overall health, including vitamin D, magnesium, and vitamin K. I have already mentioned that dried basil compares favorably to milk on the calcium front: three tablespoons of dried basil contains 33 percent of the DV, which is slightly higher than the calcium in one cup of nonfat milk at a lower cost and less than half the calories. That's not all the lightweight herb is heavy in. Three tablespoons of dried basil spikes the food it's sprinkled on with 321 percent of the DV for the bone-building vitamin K compared to milk's zero percent; 75 percent of the DV for manganese, a nutrient that the USDA describes as critical for "normal development of bones and connective tissues," compared to milk's zero percent; 75 percent of the DV for iron compared to milk's effective negative percent; 24 percent of the DV for dietary fiber, in which the standard American diet is woefully lacking and which the 2010 Guidelines have identified as a nutrient "of concern," compared to milk's zero percent; 27 percent of the DV for magnesium, compared to 7 percent in a cup of nonfat milk; 12 percent of the DV for potassium, which isn't much more than milk's 11 percent but still worth noting, considering that potassium is another among the 2010 Guidelines' nutrients "of concern"; and 12 percent of the red-blood-cell–producing folate, compared to 3 percent in a cup of milk. Dried basil even contains a little protein, just over 3 grams in 3 tablespoons. Tallying up the numbers, milk is a weak contender with respect to bone, red blood cell, heart, and colon health.

I grew up in a got-milk culture. Ads, government pamphlets, friends' parents, elementary school lessons all told me that milk is essential. Even though I didn't fully believe it, I couldn't escape falling for it to some extent. Just as Maxine wondered "if not milk, then what?" to give her son Oscar, I too was insecure about how to keep strong without milk. I began taking calcium supplements at a young age and continued to do so religiously until I discovered how prevalent calcium is in my wide-ranging plant-based way of eating. Nobody told us growing up that foods high in calcium are not hard to find. I had no idea that the salmon and spinach salad sandwich that I frequently brought to school for lunch contained the same amount of calcium as a glass of milk. Even as a graduate student I didn't realize that my dinner routine of rice and beans topped with steamed greens, nuts and seeds, and tahini sauce was not only a powerhouse of protein but also calcium. I can't remember the last time I had a glass of milk or a piece of cheese, but every day I have chia, flax, sesame, sunflower, and pumpkin seeds; almonds and walnuts; carob powder that I shake over the seeds for a perfect snack of calcium, carbohydrates, protein, fat, and roasted earthy sweetness; lentils and amaranth seeds; and an array of vegetables. If I eat a wide variety of mostly whole, unprocessed foods, I now know I will naturally and easily meet my body's calcium needs.

Remember that even the National Dairy Council recognizes that the calcium in vegetables such as broccoli, bok choy, and kale is better absorbed than the calcium in milk. Its argument against substituting vegetables for milk is not based on the quality of calcium in plant-based foods but the quantity of greens you'd have to eat. How much exactly? A little more than two cups of broccoli provides the same amount of calcium as one glass of milk. The NDC doesn't think Americans will go that distance. I'm more optimistic. Try one cup of bok choy mixed with one and one-half cups of kale for a salad at lunch followed by two cups of broccoli with dinner and you will have consumed the calcium equivalent of three glasses of milk without the negative impact that animal protein has on calcium balance. If your palate is more like that of George H. W. Bush—who in 1990 publicly declared "I do not like broccoli" in response to questions about his ban of broccoli on Air Force One—than that of Michelle Obama, who has cultivated a peaceful edible setting by planting rows of the mini trees in the White House garden, don't worry. You don't have to live on broccoli to fill your calcium needs without dairy, calcium-fortified foods, or supplements. Here's a cheat sheet of other naturally excellent sources of the mineral: sesame seeds, whole or ground into butter; almonds; black beans; canned salmon and sardines with their bones; tofu; kale and turnip greens; quinoa, amaranth, and chia seeds; carob powder; and dried herbs, especially savory and basil.

Doctors David Ludwig and Walter Willett call on the government to change its approach to dairy. For starters, they suggest that the guidelines should "designate a broader acceptable range of intake, such as **zero** [emphasis added] to two or three cups per day, instead of a universal minimum requirement." This tweak would convey, in a diplomatic way, that dairy is not essential. The USDA has done the same for alcohol and empty calories respectively: for alcohol it has set an acceptable range of zero to one drink per day for women and zero to two drinks per day for men; for empty calories, it charts appropriate intake levels that vary according to age and gender, running from a low of zero to 120 calories for children between the ages of four and eight to a high of zero to 330 calories for males between the ages of nineteen and thirty. The doctors' proposal would put dairy in this category of frill rather than fundamental—where it has belonged all along.

I have a complementary, more sweeping proposition: replace the dairy group with dried herbs and spices, which ounce-for-ounce are more nutrient dense than their fresh counterparts. Dried basil is plentiful, relatively inexpensive, and delicious. It adds so much nutritious flavor with barely any sodium and none of milk's sugar or fat. For those who don't take to basil, there are plenty more dried herbs and spices—cinnamon, savory, dill, sage, rosemary, marjoram, and thyme, to name a few—to choose from with similar nutritional profiles. The color orange increases appetite. Substitute an orange circle for blue on MyPlate to represent this sensational food group, and Americans will benefit. Maintain the status quo, with dairy at the head of MyPlate, and we risk breaking down.

David Mark Hegsted conclusively established the state of the union of the Dietary Reference Intakes when he affirmed Marion Nestle's assertion that they are not backed by science. Since his passing in 2009, others have picked up the mantle. Doctors such as David Ludwig and Walter Willett understand that the current guidelines are subjecting North Americans to one giant experiment. We've been warned. We'd better jump off the hamster wheel before we make ourselves too weak to take the leap.

CHAPTER 10

A-Not-Okay: Mad Cow-Engineering to Make Milk for All and All for Milk

In November 2012 Barbara O'Brien, president of the Innovation Center for U.S. Dairy, declared at the joint annual meeting of the National Milk Producers Federation and Dairy Management Inc. that "fluid milk is in crisis." California's "Got Milk?" campaign briefly saved the days of the early to mid 1990s. In his commentary on the crisis that O'Brien identified, Tom Quaife, editor of *Dairy Herd Management*, a print and digital resource that provides business information to commercial dairy owners, noted that lifestyles and habits are changing. He gleaned a worrisome trend from the US Department of Health and Human Services' National Health and Nutrition Examination Surveys: 43 percent of teenagers, those between the ages of thirteen and seventeen, don't drink milk. Statistics forecasting dark clouds on milk's horizon are omnipresent. In a 2014 article "Competition Gulps Market of Cow's Milk," Fort Wayne Indiana's *Journal Gazette* reported a series of downward-trending numbers: per capita consumption of milk has dropped 25 percent from 1975 to 2012; the decline in consumption between 2011 and 2012 was the sharpest in more than a decade; and the number of preteens who drank milk three or more times per day fell from 31 to 18 percent between 1978 and 2008. A few weeks earlier a post to Eau Claire

Wisconsin's online news site, "Dairy Milk Consumption Down, Plant Milk Trending," expressed the slide in pounds rather than percentages: between 1987 and 2012, milk consumption in the United States fell from 237 pounds to 195 pounds. For Wisconsin, which produces more milk than every state except California, the downturn is as momentous as it is for dairy processors. Concern about dairy's fate is spilling from dairy farms to dairy states to dairy industry conference rooms such as the one in Orlando, Florida, where O'Brien was speaking. Hence O'Brien's ambitious mission to save fluid milk and Quaife's decision to pick up the ball.

In his editorial, Quaife identified milk's packaging as part of the reason for its plunge in popularity: too many gallon-sized jugs and not enough single-serve containers in retail refrigerators. He related his first-hand experience of what he presented as an inexcusable situation. On his way to the Orlando airport the week he heard O'Brien speak he had stopped at a convenience store for some low-fat chocolate milk only to discover, with frustration, that all they had was whole milk. He didn't have to explain where he was going with the anecdote, but he did anyway: "A good starting point would be to provide the kids with choices—cold milk in accessible places in convenient packaging in a variety of flavors." I take that to mean skim and 2 percent for the fat watchers; whole milk for the minority indulgers; flavored milk in various degrees of wholeness for those who can't stand plain; and perhaps other, as yet nonexisting choices that would push milk closer to the industry's objective of making milk everybody's favorite.

THE REALITY OF MILK ALLERGIES AND SENSITIVITIES

The intensity of the industry's longing to be most popular in the class of on-the-go beverages is evident in its refusal to give up on even the allergic and the intolerant. Start with the allergic. My sister is allergic to March. I don't know what it is about the onset of spring, but something blooms in the Northeast, where she has lived most of her life, that gives her an itchy throat, a runny nose, and headaches. She doesn't consider herself lucky. Most people who suffer from allergies don't. But at least she knows that with the passing of March, so goes her discomfort. Allergies are one of the few remaining conditions that have a straightforward treatment: avoid the allergen and avoid its miserable effects. As Ruslan Medzhitov, an immuno-biologist at Yale School of Medicine, reminds us, our response to allergies, in Kara's case coughing and sneezing in the presence of March, work to protect us: "The body's reaction serves as a signal to the sufferer: here's a bad place. Get out." Kara can't escape March, but she can endure until the April rains wash her troubles away.

While environmental allergies are often challenging to resolve because the trigger is difficult to isolate, food allergies can be easy to pin down and therefore manage. It doesn't take more than a few rounds of toast for break-fast followed by a bout of the runs to figure out that the bread is the likely cause of upset. The cure is also easier than having to leave home, which is really the only option for those who can't bear March. Allergic to glu-ten? Don't eat wheat toast for breakfast. Allergic to peanuts? No PB&J for lunch. Allergic to shellfish? Avoid the seafood paella on the dinner menu. Among the roughly 3 to 6 percent of humans allergic to milk? Don't drink milk. Sounds simple enough. But milk is different. We're encouraged not to get rid of it so fast.

If you're allergic to milk, contact with it, or more precisely, one of the proteins in it, will cause your immune system to produce antibodies that lead to a range of reactions, from a rash to anaphylaxis, which restricts breathing and can be fatal. The precise percentage of the population that is allergic to milk is hard to quantify. Some cases go unreported or undiag-nosed. There is also the question of how to classify those who have a sensi-tivity rather than an outright allergy. This sizable group exhibits many of the same symptoms as the allergic, the major difference being that contact with milk does not trigger detectable levels of antigens in the blood or a reaction to a skin allergy test.

Given the absence of a way to reliably test for food sensitivities, they are not often discussed in doctors' offices. Yet outside the thick walls of medical clinics, talk of food sensitivities is all around. Physicians may not be able to define or explain the phenomenon, but like much that defies description, you know it when you see, hear, or experience it. When I told Julie, the "junior stylist" who was giving me a bargain $35 haircut one sweltering August day, that I was writing a book on milk, she gushed about her boyfriend's remarkable recovery from a case of full-body eczema. He had tried every kind of medication. Nothing helped. Finally, he gave up on the doctors. After some experimenting, he healed himself. The miracle antidote: a milk-free diet. The eczema, which covered his back, cleared up almost instantly. Julie admitted that it hasn't been easy, since even dairy alternatives such as soy cheese contain casein, the milk protein responsible for many milk allergies and sensitivities. But he manages by reading labels carefully.

Yes, the story of Julie's boyfriend is a nonclinical tale of one man's tribulation, trial, and DIY solution. But that doesn't make his milk sensitivity any less real or recurrent. You don't have to take Julie's word for a cause-and-effect relationship between dairy and irritating skin conditions. Take to the streets, and episodes like the one Julie recounted can be heard in cafés, playgrounds, dog parks, and supermarkets. Almost everyone has a story of some sort of food sensitivity that they or friends have experienced.

In his book *Wheat Belly*, cardiologist Dr. William Davis writes about the 20 percent increase in severe acne that has been observed among milk-drinking teenagers. He chalks the relationship between milk and acne up to milk's "unique insulinotropic property." The studies he cites, which link the protein in bovine products to insulin production at levels disproportional to the natural sugar in milk, suggest that milk's protein rather than sugar content is the culprit. He notes that in populations where acne is uncommon, among the Inuit and African Bantus and Zulus, so is dairy.

The website learnstuff.com identifies milk as "the number one cause of food allergies among infants and children." Even governments that encourage milk drinking highlight milk as a common allergen that causes serious problems. That's why Canada has decided to require "common allergens" to be identified in "plain language" in the ingredients lists of food labels. The rule covers ten foods and one preservative: peanuts, tree nuts, **milk**, eggs, shellfish and crustaceans, fish, soy, wheat, sesame seeds, mustard, and finally sulphites.

THE ODDITY OF A COW CALLED DAISY

Despite milk's consistent inclusion on "common allergen" lists, boosting consumption of it continues to be a priority the world over. The tension between the push for and against milk built to a jarring crescendo when news of Daisy spread in October 2012 from her birthplace in New Zealand to India and CNN. Daisy is a calf that produces milk without detectable levels of beta-lactoglobulin (BLG), a protein that is not a common component of human breast milk and is a known allergen. Daisy was also born without a tail. That part of the tale was mostly lost in the brouhaha surrounding the details that led to her very existence. The researchers at New Zealand's AgResearch, a government-funded agriculture institute, had genetically engineered cow cells to suppress BLG production. They injected these cells into cow eggs, fertilized them, and then implanted the embryos into cows. After a failed first round, Daisy was born. Impatient to test the success of their cloning experiment, the researchers gave Daisy, a calf too young to produce milk, hormones to induce lactation. Corks must have been flying the day the results came back. The researchers had succeeded in creating a first: a cow that made milk without measurable levels of BLG. They also got more than they experimented for: milk with double the casein, another cow's-milk protein.

Leaving aside the fact that the aforementioned Cornell University nutritional biochemist T. Colin Campbell has found a correlation between casein consumption and the growth of cancer cells, casein is, like BLG, a known allergen. Yet Daisy's milk is being hailed as "hypoallergenic." Hope, my sister's dog, is hypoallergenic. That doesn't mean that while my sister's not allergic, her friends who are allergic to dogs break out in hives when they go near Hope; that means almost nobody is allergic to her. Even if BLG were a more common allergen than casein, which it isn't, milk that has none of one allergen and double the amount of another does not make it "hypoallergenic" according to any medically meaningful definition of the term.

To add to the madness of holding up Daisy's casein-concentrated milk as the fix for the milk allergic, some argue that BLG, a component of whey, is essential for digesting milk. The president of GE Free New Zealand, Claire Bleakley, estimates that of the 3 percent who are allergic to milk, only a 0.1 percent are allergic to BLG. Her organization argues that "breakdown products" rather than BLG trigger most allergic reactions. If I were a New Zealand taxpayer, I would be wondering why my government is funding a game of genetic roulette before settling key questions regarding potential health benefits. If it is true that BLG is a necessary and relatively minor component of milk, and if only 0.1 percent of people are allergic to it, Daisy is not as attractive as her name and her engineers make her out to be.

The AgResearch scientists aren't letting doubts about BLG's allergenicity slow them down. They look forward to breeding Daisy so they can assess the composition and quantity of milk she produces from, in their words, a "natural" lactation. "Natural" they say, presumably in contrast to Daisy's hormonally induced lactation. The Oxford dictionary defines "natural" as "established by nature." Daisy isn't natural. Her missing tail isn't natural. Her milk isn't natural. By nature unnatural, she can't have a "natural" lactation. Substituting "humans" for "nature" in the dictionary definition of "natural" produces the scientists' interpretation of the word. They beckon us to enter a brave new world where nature is no longer, so that the tiny percentage of people who are allergic to BLG can drink milk.

There is a more sensible alternative. If those who can't tolerate milk gave it up, they would send a signal to the scientists with big research budgets to do the same. As you must be able to see by now, milk is not essential for any body's good health. Cow's milk may not be nature's "perfect" food, as a century of propaganda has made it out to be, but the campaigning got something right: milk is *nature's* food. Best keep it that way for everyone's sake, including the cows that need their tails to swat the flies away. Given the dairy industry's consistent emphasis on "natural" in its ever-evolving promotion of milk, even it should agree. "Name the Ingredients" is one of many milk ads designed to keep the connection between milk and nature strong in the consumer mind. In this thirty-second mock game show, two contestants are asked to name the ten ingredients in "imitation milk." They fail and the clip ends with the slogan: "Real. Simple. Got Milk?" If the dairy industry means what it says, Daisy and her milk can't be part of the picture.

MILK TAKE 2

While scientists, government regulators, and consumer advocates debate and investigate whether Daisy is the first step toward a future in which everyone can drink milk, there is already milk on the Australian and UK markets earmarked for the allergic and sensitive. It's called a2 milk and it's sold by the a2 Milk Company. Founded in 2000 by the late scientist Corran McLachlan, PhD, an honorary Senior Research Fellow at the School of Biological Sciences in Auckland, and the late Howard Paterson, a wealthy New Zealand entrepreneur, the company's name is self-explanatory to those who are familiar with the minutiae of milk protein makeup. The milk contains only one of the two types of protein—individually known as A1 and A2—that make up the casein of most milk, including the majority of milk from the high-producing Holstein variety of cow common in North America. The theory, which is based in part on a study that pediatrician Dr. Bob Elliott conducted in 1997 showing a correlation between A1 protein and diabetes in mice, is that the A1 protein in milk is responsible for many of the ills that have been linked to milk, from allergies and sensitivities to autism, diabetes, and heart disease. In 2003 the a2 Company launched its milk with no A1 protein in New Zealand and Australia. The cows that produce milk for the a2 Milk Company have been selected for what has been described in the popular media as a "genetic quirk." Fittingly, former X-factor judge Dannii Minogue is lending her star power to promote the milk-with-a-missing-link. Minogue vows that even before debuting in this role in the fall of 2012, she swore by the product. After a lifetime of feeling "icky and nauseous" from drinking cow's milk or consuming anything made with it, she now enjoys custard made with a2 milk and gives a2 milk to her son.

Since going public, the a2 Milk Company has benefited from the 2007 book *Devil in the Milk,* which chronicles the one hundred plus studies that corroborate McLachlan's initial hypothesis that the A1 component of casein is messing with people's health. The company received another boost in 2014 when a small first-of-its-kind human trial conducted at the School of Public Health at Australia's Curtin University found notable differences between the subjects' tolerance of A1 and A2 milk. In short, the thirty-six participants reported more bloating and abdominal pain and looser stools when drinking milk with A1 protein versus milk without it. The results have caused everyone from the study's lead researchers to prominent nutritionists to call for larger, more detailed studies. However, the a2 Milk Company's indictment of A1 protein as the cause of digestive disorders such as those described by Minogue and experienced by the Curtin study's participants is also attracting criticism. Some health experts have dismissed a2 milk, which costs almost twice as much as regular milk, as a fad that unfairly demonizes run-of-the-mill milk that contains both A1 and A2 protein. They accuse the a2 brand of dealing another blow to an already diminishing market for regular milk. They believe that Minogue and the millions like her—some say one in five Brits share Minogue's beef with standard bovine milk—are misdirected, their complaints "unfounded," and their example detrimental. In one of the many articles covering Minogue's promotion of a2 milk, Catherine Collins, the principal dietitian at London's St. George's Hospital, voices the perspective of the skeptics: "Put simply, these types of products are fashionable—there is often nothing medically wrong with people who feel they are milk sensitive." To her all the fuss is made up: "bloating is a normal part of digestion . . . These people seem to obsess about their waistline increasing after eating and will seek out pseudo-scientific 'intolerance testing' which tends to confirm they are sensitive to various foods, normally the ones we eat most—dairy and wheat."

INSENSITIVITY

"These people" is disconcerting from one whose profession is supposedly built on the understanding that we are each born with unique constitutions, conditions, and predispositions. When my neighbor Kaya was sick in bed, she had a craving for lamb chops. I went to the local butcher and picked her out a couple, remarking to myself how fundamentally dissimilar we are. I can't digest lamb chops at the best of times, let alone if I felt, as Kaya looked, as if I were dying. Clearly our stomachs are not made of the same fabric. Mine knots with just one bite of red meat. Kaya's is more elastic. What goes for the gut goes for the nose. When I went to my sister's for a housewarming dinner, mine picked up the licorice flavor of fennel seed in the vinaigrette. Ina, another guest, only detected orange essence.

No two people respond identically to a glass, or two, or three of milk either. My sister suffered from chronic ear infections until my mum stopped giving her cow's milk altogether. I get gassy from one glass. Julie's boyfriend is overtaken by eczema. As you'll read in the next chapter, the two-year-old daughter of my friend Ghada turns colicky and irritable. Ro, the man of all trades who lives down the lane, can drink milk without immediate repercussions but chooses not to because he's vegan. Although Collins lumps all the milk sensitive together, we are not one "people" except in that not one of us avoids milk because of a waistline obsession.

In his July 7, 2012, Opinionator column for the *New York Times*, cookbook author and food journalist Mark Bittman distinguishes himself from the 90 percent of Asian Americans and 75 percent of African Americans, Mexican Americans, and Jews who are lactose intolerant, as well as the "estimated 1.3 million children" who have been diagnosed with a milk allergy. He counts himself among the dairy sensitive rather than allergic. Growing up with milk at every meal, he talks about living with a "chronic upset stomach." Over time his digestive distress moved up to heartburn. Not being a darling of the big and small screen, his complaints weren't dismissed as those of a dieter. Instead he was "treated as a neurotic."

Maybe you can relate: you don't respond well to the conventional advice for healthy eating. Milk, a part of many nations' recommended dietary guidelines, makes you bloated or causes acid reflux. You are sure of this but your doctor can't prove it with a test. Rather than listen and work with you, your doctor diagnoses you as a worrier and sends you away with some pills, maybe a proton pump inhibitor such as Prevacid for the acid reflux. You leave the doctor's office, the door closes, and the red neon exit sign directs you out to a place that is worse than the one you came from. Before: everyday an upset stomach. After: everyday an upset stomach *and* a drug dependence. The impasse you set out to overcome has grown more insurmountable.

Can you imagine where this conventional approach to problem solving might lead if you were facing life or death? I can. In 2002 my mum was diagnosed with Hodgkin's lymphoma. She underwent chemotherapy, which she found excruciating. A couple of years later her oncologist found an apparently unconnected non-Hodgkin's lymphoma on her leg. She underwent radiation therapy, which was easier. Then, in 2007, the same oncologist detected another, according to him, unrelated non-Hodgkin's lymphoma in her neck. He proposed another round of chemotherapy with decent odds for a long remission. She refused. For what, she wondered, so she could live a few more low-quality years? She was sixty-seven, slight, had never fully recovered from the first round of chemotherapy, and had had enough. On a house visit, her GP sat at the edge of her bed, where she lay weak but strong in her resignation. The growth on her neck had become so large it risked blocking her airway, which, she was warned, would not be a comfortable way to die. She was ready to begin palliative care sooner rather than later. She understood this meant taking morphine, which would relieve her discomfort. All she wanted was a gentle hand to help execute her plan. Instead, her GP hit her with a heavy dose of hostility. He looked at her hard—I was sitting next to him—and said aggressively: "So you're prepared to take drugs to kill you but not to keep you alive." It wasn't a question. I was too shocked to respond appropriately. This may sound like extreme insensitivity. However, having sat by the side of my mum, dad, and sister in many hospital rooms over the past decade, I regret to say the GP's apparent lack of compassion was not out of the ordinary.

Mark Bittman's ordeal seems to be finally over. It took him more than sixty years to discover that by forgoing milk and milk products, he could, as he writes, "devour linguine puttanesca (*with* anchovies) and go to bed an hour later" without any Tums, his favorite flavor wintergreen. In addition to his new-found freedom from a lifetime of heartburn, he no longer has to endure the distress that we all experience when doctors diagnose as crazy anything that their tests can't pick up.

In 2004 the Queensland Health Department slapped the a2 Milk Company with a $15,000 fine for false and misleading advertising about the health benefits of the company's product. Since then the chief executive of the Australian branch of Parmalat, the multinational corporation in the business of producing and distributing dairy products worldwide, has accused the a2 Milk Company of damaging the entire dairy industry by "denigrating normal milk" and confusing consumers. If the public, private, and health sector workers who denounce a2 milk as nothing more than a "designer" product are proven correct, they must assume some of the blame for a2 milk's growing market share. Had Minogue's health care provider reassured her from day one that dairy is not essential, that she could easily get all the calcium she needed from an assortment of other whole foods and that she could make all the milk she wanted from the almonds, cashews, and other nuts, beans and seeds that are so plentiful in the bulk bins of supermarkets, Minogue, who felt sick whenever she drank cow's milk, may have happily accepted going without. I'm guessing she never received the type of advice that would have made no milk a nonissue. She, like the rest of us, grew up surrounded by the missive, hammered in at school and spread on billboards and now the Internet, that milk is critical.

REINVENTING MILK

The two-pronged proposal that *Dairy Herd Management* editor Tom Quaife tabled in 2012 in response to the "fluid milk crisis"—diversify packaging so that milk is available everywhere for every occasion, and ensure that milk can be reliably and widely found in different flavors and fat levels— is tame in light of recent developments. Since the 2012 meeting between the National Milk Producers Federation and Dairy Management Inc. that Quaife was commenting on, DMI's CEO, Tom Gallagher, announced the more proactive plan to partner with Coca-Cola, Krogers, and five others to, as one October 2014 headline read, "ignite fluid milk innovation." Still others with more radical ideas, including milk made to smell like peaches and apples for a Japanese market that doesn't take well to the scent of milk, have stepped up to the plate. These movers and shakers, whether private corporations or publicly funded scientists, are out to redefine not only the game but also the players. While Quaife was stuck on packaging, they are playing with biology and big dollars to make everybody willing and able to drink milk.

Dr. Scott Spies, of the Matthews Children's Clinic, has some sound words for the milk allergic, sensitive, and averse. Maybe you've never heard of Dr. Spies or the Matthews Children's Clinic. I hadn't until my research led me to a small piece that aired on Charlotte, North Carolina's WBTV. The segment, summarized in words on the station's webpage, opens with a question frequently found on vegan websites but rarely posed elsewhere: "How Can You Lead a Healthy Life If You Can't Drink Milk?" Leave out the "how" for the question that Dr. Spies addresses: "If some children and adults don't like milk it's very possible to lead a very healthy lifestyle without milk." He has nothing against milk. He simply doesn't think it's necessary. This small recognition, expressed by a member of the community of physicians and dietitians who believe milk is generally a healthy food, is consequential. When milk proponents say milk is essential, which they directly and implicitly do repeatedly, they might as well say you can't lead a healthy life if you can't drink milk. Accept that the allergic can manage well without drinking milk, and the foundation upon which the dairy industry is built collapses, bringing down Daisy and a2 milk too. No wonder milk advocates tend to dodge the subject of those who can't drink it. When someone with Dr. Spies's credentials broaches the verboten topic, it understandably makes news. For a minute anyway, until coverage of local prom proposals and fishing forecasts overtake words that are too few and far between to be front page for long.

The health halo over milk protects public spending on it—whether in the form of price protections, resources to improve dairy production and processing procedures, or support for the introduction of new milk products—from reproach. However, if more physicians like Dr. Spies blow milk's cover, all the R&D going into making milk more widely available would be revealed for what it is: a looting of the public purse. If everyone swallowed the fact that milk, as Dr. Spies affirms, is not essential, then it would become just another product struggling to stay afloat in the dog-eat-dog food and beverage sector. It would drop from grace to become one among a bevy of products fighting for the consumer's limited, if expanding, stomach. In the age of enlightenment in which milk is perceived as dispensable, "Got Milk?" would lose its charm as a reminder from beneficent Big Brother not to forget one of life's necessities. The catchphrase would become just another siren song, no different than the ones that Coke composes to win the world over. When Coke says "it's the real thing," or when hip-hop artist G. Love sings, "I'd like to buy the world a Coke," we know Coke is trying to buy a share of our stomachs rather than improve the condition of humanity. Once we all acknowledge that the dairy industry's bottom line is the same as that of Coke and Pepsi, the industry will truly be in crisis. We're not there yet. But the number of bodies that are fighting back against milk's onslaught are forcing doctors such as Spies to come clean about milk. Each time this happens we move one step closer to saner ways than feeling we must, like it or not, drink three glasses of milk per day to keep fit and healthy.

CHAPTER 11

A History of Intolerance: Milk's Journey from Fermented Food to Unsavory Symbol of Power

My friend Ghada's two-year-old daughter Khloe was more irritable than usual. It wasn't hard to figure out why. One respiratory infection is enough to make a little girl cry, and Khloe's had become chronic. My erstwhile law school classmate and self-described "thorough" researcher, Ghada went to work. I learned of the outcome, to try eliminating milk from Khloe's diet, one day while we were talking on the phone. Our conversation had turned, as it so often does, to food. I didn't get very far into my description of my latest favorite concoction before she cut in: "I decided to stop giving Khloe milk so we don't buy any dairy anymore." She had one subject on her mind. The discussion took a quick right turn to the weighty subject of Khloe and her possible allergy to dairy. Although Ghada had cleansed her house of all things milk, she was still conflicted. She wasn't sure if Khloe was allergic but she wanted to see, but maybe Malik, her husband, was right. This time I interrupted her. "Right about what?" Malik, she explained, had made a point: there must be a really good reason to give kids milk since cultures everywhere have been doing it forever. I was surprised to hear Ghada repeat such a common misconception as if it had some merit. In the long story of humanity, milk drinking is an anomaly. It doesn't occupy a chapter or even a single letter. If Ghada hadn't read that bovine milk isn't and never has been a staple of most cultures, it had to be because this fact has not made it into the popular discourse about diet and nutrition. It's one of the best-kept secrets in North America. Strangely, everyone seems to know it, except you and everyone you know. This is when I realized that restoring balance to our relationship with milk would require debunking the myth that drinking cow's milk is and always has been ubiquitous.

Even if scientists succeed in breaking the allergy barrier to the universal consumption of milk, those who can't digest lactose, the naturally occurring sugar in milk, aren't going anywhere. They are many and their genes, which have been passed down through countless generations, are strong. A National Institutes of Health webpage about the genetics of lactose intolerance states: "Approximately 65 percent of the human population has a reduced ability to digest lactose after infancy." That's more than two out of every three humans in the world. A 2006 clinical report published in the journal *Pediatrics* arrives at the slightly higher statistic of 70 percent of the world's population, a statistic that the report's author, Dr. Melvin Heyman, teases out. He writes that the prevalence of lactose intolerance is: "50% to 80% in Hispanic people, 60% to 80% in black and Ashkenazi Jewish people, and almost 100% in Asian and American Indian people." In contrast, a majority of those of Northern European ancestry, a group that not coincidentally has strong dairy farming roots, is able to digest lactose into adulthood. Among some groups as few as 2 percent can't. However, these people make up a minority of the population, both globally and in America, a fact that Dr. Milton Mills, director of the Gilead Medical Group in Annandale, Virginia, wants policy makers to recognize once and for all. Taking the opportunity to comment on day two of the January 2014 meeting of the 2015 Dietary Guidelines Advisory Committee, which is tasked with advising government on writing the 2015 edition of the Dietary Guidelines for Americans, Dr. Mills emphasized that lactose intolerance is a major problem for populations of color. After citing statistics comparable to those of the *Pediatrics* journal article, he jumped straight to the point: "For the Committee to continue to encourage the consumption of foods that will necessarily make these people sick is a form of institutionalized government sponsored racism." As you will see, the assertion is not as radical as it may sound to the uninitiated in the history and current prevalence of lactose intolerance.

MUTATING REACTIONS TO MILK

Considering that the majority of humans today can't drink milk without reacting to the sugar in it, I arrive at a conclusion that is the opposite of Malik's: there must be a really good reason that most humans can't drink milk comfortably. History is on my side: drinking cow's milk is a new phenomenon. It only became common practice in the late nineteenth century, and even then mainly in Europe and the United States. However, the same can't be said for dairy, which has long played a role in civilizations spanning the globe. It all began 8,000 to 10,000 years ago when the aurochs, the wild ancestor of the cow, was domesticated in the Near East. In Northern Europe in the 1970s, archaeologist Peter Bogucki, PhD, dug up the next pieces of the puzzle of how dairy made its way into human diets: hole-studded clay shards about 5 centimeters wide dating to around 7000 BC and distributed across an area stretching from the Ukraine to France and from Hungary to not quite the Baltic Sea. Bogucki suspected that he had found the remains of vessels that were used to drain the whey from milk, the final step in cheese making. Current advances in chemical analysis support his hypothesis: residue detected in the clay is chemically consistent with cow's milk. When the research findings of Mark Thomas, PhD, an evolutionary geneticist at University College London, are added to the pot, Bogucki's theory gains more traction. According to Thomas's DNA research, the Neolithic Europeans who made the vessels didn't produce the enzyme, lactase, that is necessary to break down the sugar, lactose, in milk. In modern terminology, they were lactose intolerant. Drinking milk, as anyone without lactase knows, would have been no tea party for these ancient Britons.

The prevailing view of those who cannot digest lactose is embedded in the term that has been coined to describe them. If you are labeled "lactose intolerant," the implication is that you suffer from a deficiency, an illness to overcome. "Lactase impersistent" is the term that many scholars prefer to use. It is both impartial and more accurately describes the state of not being able to digest the lactose in milk. If you are "lactase impersistent," the enzyme lactase that is needed to break down lactose, a sugar that is found in both bovine and human milk, doesn't persist into adulthood. You don't lack the enzyme. You simply don't continue to produce it beyond babyhood, which was the only time we needed it before cows came along. That said, for expediency, here and elsewhere I sometimes resort to the value-laden yet familiar term "lactose intolerant."

Today, government, the dairy industry, and health experts, including the Academy of Nutrition and Dietetics, advise the lactose intolerant to persist. The USDA has written the blueprint for the strategy, which includes taking precautions such as drinking milk in small doses, and to slow digestion, trying whole milk or serving milk with solid foods. However, its tip to try chocolate milk is the most mindbending. Besides containing significant levels of oxalic acid, which binds with calcium to reduce the amount available to your body, cocoa beans and the powder and chocolate made from them also contain caffeine, which increases urinary and fecal calcium loss. More critically for the lactase impersistent, flavored milk has all the lactose of regular milk. Perhaps the backward thinking is that turning milk into the drink equivalent of ice cream will help the lactase impersistent tolerate the tsunami of side effects that every glass of milk threatens. The recommendation reminds me of another popular practice that perplexed me as a kid. Throughout my preteen years, visits to the doctor or dentist would inevitably end with the receptionist offering me a lollipop. I didn't understand the logic even then: give me something that's bad for me but tastes good because I don't feel good.

Now I recognize the Pavlovian logic. The vet gives Dixi a bone when he's finished with her because that way she'll associate the experience with the pleasure of the treat rather than the pain of the treatment and won't mind coming the next time. The USDA is counting on this theory working on your child when it advises in its 2013 newsletter "Milk for Kids with Lactose Intolerance": "Offer chocolate milk. It contains the same nutrients as white milk. But kids like chocolate milk and may be *more willing* [emphasis added] to drink it." The reasoning, if you can call it that, goes something like this: to ensure that your lactose-intolerant child will drink milk, give it to her chocolate flavored; she'll drink it and feel sick, but tomorrow, when it's time for the next dose, she'll drink it, remembering the appealing flavor rather than the aches and pains that bent her over. Congratulations. In the unlikely event that the stratagem works, you will have succeeded in making your child "more willing" to feel ill.

The farmers of yore could teach the USDA a lesson. They lived with scarcity as a routine part of their reality. Unlike most North Americans today, they really did need a good source of protein, fat, and minerals such as calcium. Yet rather than fight their DNA, Bogucki unearthed 7,000-year-old evidence that they listened to their stomach's cue. Instead of drinking in discomfort, they searched for and found a way to enjoy milk: cheese. Their discovery was ingenious. In the process of curdling milk into cheese, much of milk's sugar dissolves in the whey that is strained away. The result is a product that the hungry lactase-impersistent farmers could assimilate. The invention was as revolutionary as it was resourceful, helping the newly converted agrarians through slim times when crops failed and staples were in short supply.

"Offer cheese" is the fifth of six tips that the USDA doles out in its effort to persuade parents that "Even if your child is lactose intolerant, you can fit milk products in!" The preceding four relate to fluid milk. "Offer cheese," and "Try yogurt" appear as measures to be tried only after all fluid milk options fail. Seven thousand years ago Northern Europeans didn't have chocolate or processed sugar to make their milk taste better. They didn't have a human equivalent of a milk bone to trick their minds into believing that their stomachs were speaking nonsense. Even if they did have a spoonful of sugar to mix into their milk to make it go down, they would have known better. They couldn't afford to squander a precious resource by masking it only to throw it up later.

Although the Neolithic farmers didn't have chocolate or sugar, they did have whole milk, another of the USDA's proposed ways to get fluid milk into the lactose intolerant. Yet given the effort they expended to churn it into cheese, they must have had trouble digesting whole milk straight. The takeaways from the Stone Age: if you can't break down lactose, you will probably have a hard time breaking down milk, whole or not; and if milk makes you sick, either don't drink it or turn it into something that is acceptable to the whole body because camouflaging it, while seducing the senses, won't help the gut when it comes to digesting it.

There's an exception to the rule to avoid foods you can't digest: you're starving. When facing death or stomach upset, most of us would try the latter before succumbing to the former. This life-or-death scenario is the basis of a different theory of evolution than the one that Bogucki uncovered. Although the evolution of milk into cheese explains how dairy became a critical part of the diet of a lactose-intolerant group, it doesn't answer the more fundamental question of human evolution: how the descendants of a lactose-intolerant people developed the ability to drink a glass of milk without soon regretting it. Mark Thomas, the evolutionary geneticist whose DNA analysis pretty well sealed the thesis that Neolithic Europeans ate cheese, has some thoughts on the matter. Drawing on agricultural history, genetic analyses, and statistics, he has patched together an intriguing story for why roughly 30 to 35 percent of adults globally—mostly people of European, African, and Middle Eastern descent—are lactase persistent.

Although ancient history isn't usually the stuff of "best of" lists, Thomas's version of the artifacts made it onto NPR's the *Salt*'s catalog of the top twelve stories of 2012. Everyone, it seems, loves a mystery, especially when the much esteemed and maligned milk is the lead subject. The narrative begins 8,000 years ago in what is now Turkey. Then and there humans got the idea to milk other mammals. During the same time, mutations to the gene that produces lactase led to some adults being lactase persistent. Remember that most human babies produce lactase, the enzyme that enables them to digest the lactose sugar that the milk of their mother and other mammals contains. However most babies then as now stopped producing this enzyme after weaning, meaning lactase impersistence was the norm.

Thomas and his colleagues can't identify the first instance of lactase persistence. Some have postulated that the gene was first selected for in 5,500 BC. Ron Pinhasi, PhD, an archaeologist at University College Dublin, has an idea about when it first occurred in the Central European region known as the Great Hungarian Plain. He co-authored a study published in the journal *Nature Communications* in October 2014 that finds evidence of the mutation first appearing 3,300 years ago there. That's over 4,000 years after the people occupying the Great Hungarian Plain began milking cows. Whenever lactase persistence began to spread throughout Central Europe, all researchers on the subject can vouch for the mutation's far-reaching consequences. Most immediately, it provided a survival advantage for the early farmers of the region. When their crops foundered, milk from their cows was an obvious next best choice for nourishment. Thomas reckons that during times of scarcity, even those who couldn't digest milk would have tried to drink it out of desperation. However, for the lactase impersistent who were already malnourished, milk would have delivered the final blow. Starvation and diarrhea are not a match made for survival. Only the mutants with the gene that turned on the switch for making lactase for life would have thrived on milk and thus persisted to pass their aberration on. Not surprisingly, scientists have also found that the cow-herding cultures that acquired the mutation gave birth to more children; 10 percent more they say.

THE RISE OF A WORLDWIDE "WHITE REVOLUTION"

The geneticists' and archaeologists' facts, figures, and inferences tell the amazing tale of how one tiny tweak to the genome of a distant people shaped not only the destiny of certain individuals but also the courses of humanity: the deviation deserves much of the credit for introducing milk to breakfast, lunch, and dinner tables across North America, and increasingly the world. Thus, upon visiting the Guru Angad Dev Veterinary and Animal Sciences University in Ludhiana, India, one Friday in September 2014, Agriculture Minister Tota Singh promised to come down hard on the all-too-common practice in India of adulterating milk for economic gain. He didn't mince words in justifying his drive to stop the offenders: "It is important to sustain the white revolution." Even in China, where dairy farming is just beginning and lactase impersistence prevails, milk is touted as a necessity. Andrea Wiley, PhD, professor of anthropology and director of human biology at Indiana University, is interested in the diet-induced cultural transformation that is underway. She quotes Premier Wen Jiabao who, in standing up for milk in 2006, channeled the spirit of one of America's greatest visionaries: "*I have a dream* [emphasis added] to provide every Chinese, especially children, sufficient milk each day." Martin Luther King's speech that addressed the scourge of racism in America is more relevant to China's newfound devotion to milk than it might first seem.

In China, as in North America, role models from athletes to astronauts inspire milk drinking for strength building. Shanghai Bright Dairy and Food Corporation is one of China's largest dairy producers. Laying claim to ten pastures, 12,000 cows, and a 500,000-ton annual production capacity, it is invested in the notion that milk will make the people of China more robust. As a spokeswoman for Bright Dairy told *Wall Street Journal* reporter

Kathy Chen: "One cup of milk can strengthen a nation." The statement draws on, whether consciously or not, a history of Western discrimination against Asians for being smaller than Westerners. In Canada, for instance, the Nutrition Services division of the Department of Pensions and National Health approved a wartime advertisement entitled "Men without Milk." In his dissertation " 'Food Will Win the War': The Politics and Culture of Food and Nutrition during the Second World War", Ian Mosby, PhD, describes this piece of propaganda:

> *The ad showed a bow-legged Japanese soldier walking towards a ruined "oriental" city. "The short stature of the Japanese," the ad reads, "their bowed legs, their frequent poor eyesight are all blamed on inadequate diet—particularly lack of milk!"*

Note the exclamation mark. Subtlety is not the name of this federal department's game. The ad proceeds to contrast the diet of the victors with that of the vanquished. Whereas it depicts Japan as a country of barely ambulatory "men without milk," it boasts: "Canada drinks lots of milk. Canada likes the rich flavor and tempting taste which milk and its products give to our food." Canada and its allies, it might as well have said, won the war with milk.

"Men without Milk" was more than a relic of the conqueror's conceit. It reflected a deep-seated bias against the diets of cultures that did not place dairy front and center. Mosby points to a 1946 survey of children in British Columbia that illustrates the prejudice. The study identified a group of 157 Chinese students who had "poor" diets compared to the provincial average. It determined that the two major differences between the Chinese children and their schoolmates were scant milk and dairy in their diets and "thinness." Judging from this study, "Men without Milk," which ran around the same time that the study was conducted, reinforced an already widely held view that milklessness causes weakness.

The same anthem to drink milk for fitness that was playing across Canada was also blaring across the pond and south of the border. In 1943 Winston Churchill declared: "Milk in babies is the best investment." Back in the United States, a brochure published in 1942 by the Agricultural Marketing Administration branch of the USDA, "More Milk for More Children," explains the USDA's commitment to school milk programs. With the war underway and soldiers fighting overseas, civilians, it warned, were also under siege: "Millions of boys and girls are not drinking all the milk they need to build sound teeth and a strong framework for their growing bodies. A surprisingly large number are not drinking any milk—valuable as it is for growth, and as a weapon against one of the most dangerous enemies of democracy, malnutrition. Thus handicapped, children are not able to enjoy the full advantage of educational opportunities provided at community expense. They are not fully armed for citizenship." In heralding milk as building the backbones to protect democracy, the USDA made it the patriotic responsibility of every American to ensure that their children drank milk daily. A decision that was once private and domestic had risen in significance to military strategy.

The sweeping call to arms that rings throughout "More Milk for More Children" masks the utilitarian thinking behind the USDA's support of school milk programs. Following a brief outline of how the programs work, the USDA publication delivers a dollars-and-cents justification for their operation: "By broadening the market for fluid milk, chief source of the dairyman's income, the program provides farm incentive to produce enough milk to meet the urgent needs of the United Nations, whether military or civilian." Despite the USDA's stated concern that "a large number" of children weren't drinking milk, the school milk program was in reality designed to solve the pressing problem that farmers weren't producing enough milk to meet wartime production goals. While the war created a demand for large quantities of milk for processing into various wartime necessities such as cheese and dry and condensed milk, farmers couldn't afford to produce more milk unless they could sell a good deal of it as fluid milk, for which they received more money than for milk for processing. Enter the small but growing guts of the next generation. Bringing milk into the nation's classrooms would increase the demand for fluid milk so that farmers would ramp up milk production, which in turn would benefit the war effort. With its eye on this end, the publication observes: "Today, only a small part of that market is being tapped." However, this cold calculation reads as an anomaly amid the publication's otherwise highfalutin words about what's best for the nation's children and how milk will make them full citizens. If the USDA determined that the way to boost wartime milk production was through the mouths of children, it understood that the best way to frame its plan was gilded in words about making them strong. Fitting that "More Milk for More Children" was the creation of the Agricultural Marketing Administration. Rousing hearts and minds to solve an intractable problem of wartime economics is the work of skilled ad men.

TALL ORDERS

Although the war is over, the demand that it stimulated for fluid milk to process into cheese and powder is stronger than ever. "Men without milk" are no longer. So many countries are buying in that in 2000 the Food and Agriculture Organization launched World School Milk Day. FYI, it's the last Wednesday of every September. Since then more than seventy countries have participated in School Milk Day activities. The day is big enough to have been assigned an acronym, WSMD. A promotion of a promotion, a celebration of the celebration of milk that is the school milk program, it is also a bit much. If we were to set aside a separate day from Earth Day to celebrate the fact of Earth Day we would have the environmentalist's equivalent of WSMD. The method in the madness is to spread the word that school milk programs help "improve health, raise achievement, and improve social inclusion." Where the accent falls among the three aims depends on the country. Asian countries have tended to emphasize the health benefits of giving children milk in school. In China, milk, so say government and dairy industry moguls, makes children strong. From the perspective of Vietnam, that's not all milk has done for China. In 2013 Vietnam's deputy director of the Ministry of Labour, Invalids, and Social Affairs announced that he had submitted to the prime minister an initiative that would provide 2 million children in kindergartens and primary schools at least 200 milliliters of milk per day. Vietnamese boys and girls were falling short of the world standards for height. He was going to turn things around using China as his role model. Vietnamese officials had noted that a similar five-year program there had raised the average height of children by two centimeters.

Thailand also has a plan to make its citizens taller on milk. According to the public health minister, Thai youth tend to be short in stature because they don't drink nearly as much milk as the rest of the world. In June 2013, on World Milk Day, which is not the same as World School Milk Day, Thailand's deputy public health minister declared his government's intention to persuade Thais to drink at least one glass of milk per day. The bull's-eye: increase the average height of eighteen-year-old Thais by eight centimeters. There was a general recognition that hitting this target would be difficult given the number of deterrents: lactose intolerance is common among Thais; milk, the Thai word for which means "breast," is perceived as a drink for weaklings; and the nation's school milk program had developed a bad reputation for serving diluted and spoiled milk. However, these impediments didn't dampen the enthusiasm of officials such as Mauri Uotila, of the Bangkok office of the Food and Agriculture Organization. Speaking to the Associated Press, Uotila observed, "People here see tall European and American people drinking a lot of milk. I think, like all parents, they want taller children with stronger bones."

Comments such as these and the milk campaigns to which they are attached are troubling in more ways than one. First, they betray the readiness of governments to engage in national-scale experiments with the health of constitutions unconditioned to absorb the nutrients in bovine milk. Second, they reveal that the racial slurs inherent in publications such as "Men without Milk" have had a lasting impact on the subjects of discrimination.

One summer evening in 2014, I came across a telling exchange. A "Concerned Taiwanese," who had heard Wisconsin Public Radio's Dr. Zorba Paster tell a parent of an adopted Chinese child to feed the child more whole milk if the toddler wasn't gaining weight, wrote in to Paster's show with a rebuke that was posted on the Internet: "Well over ninety percent of Asians are lactose intolerant. Give them milk and they bloat up like a balloon. You are setting this family up for a miserable time. What is good for malnourished Europeans is not good for those with Asian ancestry. Please correct your awful advice." If, as the high incidence of lactase impersistence among Asians suggests is the case, the commentator is correct, the governments of China, Vietnam, and Thailand are leading their people down a path of destruction. Their milk frenzy promises a future tall on misery.

SCHOOL MILK PROGRAMS CAUSE MAYHEM

While the governments of countries in Asia hold forth the promise that school milk programs will elevate the collective stature, the governments of countries in the West have taken a slightly different angle. They emphasize the mental and social benefits of school milk programs. Thus MP Kevin Barron, while visiting a primary school in his constituency of Rother Valley in the United Kingdom in celebration of World School Milk Day, was quoted as saying, "Drinking milk is vitally important for children as not only does it help their general health but aids their concentration and performance at school." Meanwhile, on the same day at another primary school not far away, head teacher Wendy Stone underscored the important part "milk time" played in the school day: "As well as contributing to our healthy school ethos we use this time to develop our social skills."

Stone's words made me think of Lucas, the ten-year-old boy who used to live next door. I once brought over some cocoa powder I had bought in bulk for his mom to try. She hesitated to allow the bag past the front door for fear it might contain traces of milk protein. Lucas is allergic to milk. Contact with it, whether via the air, skin, or mouth could be fatal. Needless to say, she doesn't buy anything in bulk. The risk of cross-contamination is too great. Lucas is not unusual. Health Canada publishes safety fact sheets with titles like "Milk—One of the ten priority food allergens." And these just speak to the pervasiveness of milk allergies. They don't account for the millions more who are sensitive to milk, or lactase impersistent. In light of the huge number of children who don't get along with milk, it's hard to understand how the same administrators who recognize that milk is a real and present danger can promote it as social glue. If anything, it is the opposite, threatening more sickness, lowered achievement, and greater social isolation in classroom environments.

Consider the following hypothetical that builds from a photo I came across while reading about World School Milk Day. You're sitting at a table covered by a checkered plastic tablecloth. Your name is Nam. You're six years old. This is your first year at Blidworth Oaks Primary School in Nottinghamshire, England. Today is a special day. It's October 15, 2012, and Mark Spencer, MP for the Sherwood County constituency, is visiting. More precisely, he's here to honor, a little late, World School Milk Day, which fell on September 26. Blond Matthew and blue-eyed Naomi sit on either side of you. They eagerly await a photo shoot of the three of you drinking milk with the MP. You shy away. Milk doesn't do your body good. The last thing you want is to be photographed drinking it. You might grimace involuntarily. You don't say this. You already feel a bit different. The cameraman calls for "Pam" to move closer in so he can get you in the picture. You know he means you, but you move farther out of view because he hasn't *really* called on you.

Matthew and Naomi drink up dutifully and with glee. They receive praise from the MP and your teacher. You sit sidelined, your reluctance to embrace milk somehow a reflection of bad behavior, of your socially uncooperative nature. You're not imagining the silent rebukes. For months after WSMD, local papers in the United Kingdom run stories about the visits of various MPs to schools in their county constituencies. They report that milk is free for children in day-care or primary school and subsidized for school children aged five to eleven. The article covering the Sherwood MP's visit to Blidworth Oaks Primary School extols the many virtues of school milk: it "aids children's social development, including responsibility, independence and manners" and helps to ensure "improved concentration." The article concludes with a frequently cited quotation from John Sedgwick, the managing director of Cool Milk, a leading provider of free school milk in the United Kingdom: "Milk in schools continues to be incredibly popular and hugely successful in contributing to the healthy development of *all* [emphasis added] children."

Mr. Sedgwick is correct in identifying the popularity of milk in schools as a continuing trend. Similar school milk programs have spanned decades and continents. However, Sedgwick is mistaken that milk is healthy for "all" children. It's not good for Nam. It wasn't good for my sister and for most of our extended family. Count my sister among the roughly 75 percent of Jews who can't digest lactose. The ear infections that haunted her until my mum stopped giving her milk were the most severe of a list of symptoms that followed her every encounter with milk. It's not good for Suko either, the daughter of my sister's friend whose father is African American, another group of whom the majority are lactase impersistent.

Despite all the Sukos and Lucases out there, there are the Sedgwicks who continue to insist that in addition to its nutrients, milk "offers a variety of social opportunities." To school milk advocates, milk is a wonder food for children, working to encourage "social inclusion," develop "social skills," and provide "social opportunities." Social studies, however, turn up a different story. You don't have to dig deep to discover a social opportunity that school milk programs definitely provide: bullying. A 2010 survey of

350 parents of children with food allergies revealed that 35 percent of the children over five who were being studied had been bullied. Of those bullied, 86 percent had been tormented more than once. Although the perpetrators were mostly classmates, in some instances teachers and school staff had also participated. Over half the time the bullying was physical. Sometimes the allergen was thrown at the allergic child. Other times the child was forced to touch the allergen. Worst of all, some parents reported that their child's food had been spiked with the allergen, which is to say, deadly poison.

Such incidents should be a part of the discussion of any school milk program. But they're not. Instead, by spotlighting the most popular kids in the class, the programs' sponsors foster environments that make the milk-averse only more prone to harassment. When Alex Ohlendorf was a junior at Bonita Vista High School in California, he won the 2012 California Milk Processor Board's "Got Milk? Breakfast Billboard Photo Competition." The contest began with the CMPB soliciting high school teens from across the state to submit photos showing why milk is important to their health and academic performance. Alex's winning submission captures a few burly members of his varsity football team in an offensive line formation with open books under their hands and cartons of milk on their backs, ready to conquer the task at hand. The caption reads "Got Milk? Backing You Up." The CMPB found the entry witty. It awarded Alex $1,000, which he donated to his football team.

Alex took advantage of an opportunity to exercise his creativity. He should be commended for his generosity and for taking the job seriously. However, given the number of kids who break out in hives, just feel "icky," or experience an anaphylactic reaction when they drink milk, the contest warrants scrutiny. Chances are that there are more than a handful of kids in Alex's school whose bodies retaliate against them when they drink milk. Meet Leo. He's fictional but his story's not. Leo is in ninth grade. He's always avoided milk because his body fights back when he goes near it. But now he's in high school and the pressures are different. He sees Alex's photo blown up around town and the accolades that his milk-drinking schoolmates receive. He wonders what's wrong with him. From the looks of it, drinking milk is his pass to team excellence, both academic and athletic. Got milk, got the strong and successful behind you; got no milk, got no backup.

Leo's in a catch-22. If he drinks milk, he might vomit. If he doesn't, he risks being the butt end of intolerance, of going home with a black eye or two. Either way, the hospital is not far away. Maybe, you say, Leo can defend himself. Maybe he can. But what if my friend Ghada's son Mekhi, brother of Khloe, isn't so lucky. Now he gets a runny nose when he drinks milk. Once he graduates to high school he might get a bloody one if he doesn't. Making milk, one of the most common allergens, into a must creates a divisive, antagonistic school environment. There's no doubt about it, somebody is going to get hurt.

If Alex likes milk, by all means he should drink it. But Alex isn't everybody. At the same time that schools teach kids to respect that we come in all shapes and sizes, they have, in opening their doors to dairy industry campaigning, become the breeding ground for intolerance. Lucas will never have the same waistline as Alex. He doesn't have the genes to ever fit into Alex's big jeans. It doesn't make sense to expect his stomach to be the same as Alex's on the inside either. School milk programs, and the games that the dairy industry designs to enhance its visibility, do not create level playing fields. Not everyone at Bonita Vista High School looks like Alex. Not everyone dresses like him. Nor should everyone eat like him, as his winning photo exhorts his peers to do. Just as Alex is free to refuel with milk, so Lucas should have the liberty to hydrate with water without fear of exclusion, derision, or feeling downtrodden. No one food can be the vehicle to social inclusion.

Ghada's husband Malik is correct, there is a really good reason so many people all over the world give their children milk. But it has to do with economics more than nutrition. Read the headline of one story covering World School Milk Day: "Building foundations for future dairy *markets* [emphasis added]." Read beyond the headline to hear what the Food and Agriculture Organization's Michael Griffin has to say about the day that he helped to launch: "By creating demand, school milk programs can directly benefit dairy development. In Japan, for example, a school milk program helped increase its annual milk consumption from 5 liters per person at the start of [the] 1960s to 80 liters today. Imagine if the same result was achieved in China?" Griffin's question gives new meaning to Premier Wen Jiabao's dream. If it comes true, China's dairy economy will reach truly impressive heights.

Griffin concludes, "School milk is not an easy market, but from the industry as a whole it has to acknowledge that school children are tomorrow's consumers. One of the aims of WSMD and also World Milk Day which is held in June is to help develop the habit of milk consumption in children. If children do not grow up drinking milk or eating dairy products, they are not going to do so in later life when they are consumers." He thus leaks the underappreciated fact that the overriding purpose of school milk programs is, as it was during World War II, to build demand. Malik need not worry. Allergic, sensitive, lactase impersistent or not, Khloe will not suffer without milk, whether she goes without it for a day or for the rest of her life. Only the dairy industry has something to lose from the decisions of parents such as Ghada to stop giving their children milk: the stomachs to hold its future.

CHAPTER 12

The Big Mistake:
The Fitness of Lactase Impersistence

By invoking Martin Luther King in his 2006 speech about milk, Chinese premier Wen Jiabao insinuated that milk would restore equality to a relationship with the West that has been tainted by prejudice. Yet while the governments of Asian countries dream that milk will grow their citizens and economies, in America there is widespread recognition that power and prosperity depend on putting the brakes on growth rates. Enough Americans have expressed concern about the state of the next generation to push the USDA to issue, for the first time in thirty years, a new set of proposed standards for school snacks. The tabled rules, which were presented in February 2013, require snacks sold on school premises to be healthier and limited to 200 calories. Hailed by many as a long-overdue update of nutrition standards to reflect the current setting in which a third of children and teens are obese or overweight, they carry special weight for "Mission: Readiness." An umbrella of the nonprofit Council for a Strong America, Mission: Readiness is made up of retired admirals and generals. They aren't sugarcoating the problem. In September 2012 the organization released a report, "Still Too Fat to Fight," which details the degenerative state of the American military: one in four Americans is too heavy to join the forces and of those who are admitted, many carry weight that compromises their effectiveness in the field. Excess weight, the report states, leads to a greater risk of the largely preventable sprains and fractures that took more soldiers out of Iraq and Afghanistan than combat wounds.

THE EVOLUTIONARY ADVANTAGE OF THE LACTASE IMPERSISTENT

Growing bigger faster, it seems, is not a prescription for growing strong and mighty. Those who have been most vocal in contesting the healthfulness of cow's milk for humans, namely vegans and animal welfare advocates, have been saying the same for years. Foremost among the litany of reasons they have for avoiding cow's milk is one that derives from a simple observation: cow's milk is custom designed for calves, which double in size in forty-five days. Compared to human babies—we take quadruple the time, or 108 days to double in size—that's overdrive. The reverse is true when it comes to brainpower, which develops faster in humans than in the bovine body builders.

The differences in our growth patterns are reflected in the differences in the chemistry of human versus bovine milk. Human milk, on the one hand, is high in polyunsaturated fatty acids, such as linoleic acid, which are critical for brain development. Cow's milk, on the other hand, is lower in these fatty acids and higher in saturated fats and protein, both of which are good for rapid weight gain. Cow's milk, so the anti-milk enthusiasts argue, is formulated for cows, which grow to be seven times as heavy in body and three times as light in brains as humans. Humans need more and less. We need more of the brain-building essentials and less of the body-building baggage: more fatty acids and fewer of the saturated fats and bovine milk proteins that are killers for some humans. Advertise cow's milk for what it is, a weight-gain food, and it would quickly drop from the top of many grocery lists.

If the Chinese authorities want their citizens to grow fatter faster, ensuring that everyone drinks cow's milk every day is a good plan. However, if strength is what they're after, they might want to reconsider and listen to the American veterans who are saying America is not better for being bigger. Putting on the pounds is not the answer. Considering the chemistry of milk, maybe "Men without Milk" is. Although this caption once described men physically challenged in almost every way—sight, stature, and mobility—today "Men with Milk" could depict a similar picture: men immobilized by extra-large waists and blinded by obesity-induced type 2 diabetes. If cow's milk works the way it's supposed to and exponentially increases the size of its mammalian consumers, then "men without milk" will be the twenty-first-century picture of health in America.

In the New obesogenic World, the genetic predisposition toward lactase impersistence assumes new significance. During distant times and places, survival of the fittest meant survival of the lactase persistent. Not any longer, especially in North America, where there is a deathly overabundance rather than a dearth of food. US veterans aren't the only ones concerned. According to the Centers for Disease Control and Prevention, more than one-third of Americans are obese. If the surplus of diet books and products are any indication, still more are struggling to keep the weight off. That means that upward of 30 percent of Americans must cut back on calorie-dense foods in order to live long and productive lives. The USDA's "3-A-Day" recommendation for milk may be great advice for malnourished lactase-persistent farmers living 8,000 years ago. However, in modern-day North America, where calories are precious as a result rather than in spite of being cheap and ubiquitous, we have the luxury and the necessity, given the rise of obesity, of being choosy. The same qualities that made milk life preserving in ancient Turkey and a few other hand-to-mouth societies in Northern Europe, Africa, and the Middle East, make it deadly in a society where burning rather than storing calories is the key to survival.

Given that our food environment and needs have flipped 180 degrees since the time when humans first started drinking cow's milk, lactase impersistence could prove to be the new evolutionary advantage. Some simple math is revealing. Say every person older than nine who is lactase impersistent substituted water for the three glasses of low-fat milk that the USDA suggests everyone in this age range drink. Each person in this majority group—comprising roughly 90 percent of Asian Americans, 75 percent of African-American, Jewish, Mexican-American, and Native American adults, and roughly 2 percent of European-Americans—would drop 240 calories per day. Those calories translate into a lot of weight. Just ask Alice. In one of her "Go Ask Alice!" columns, which are brought to us by Columbia University, Alice says that if you eat 500 fewer calories every day, it will take about a week to skim off one pound. Following this formula, all else being equal, dropping 240 calories per day will make you twenty-five pounds lighter in a year.

Scaling up to the lactase-impersistent group as a whole, the number of pounds lost, or not gained if those calories were never drunk in the first place, is startling. Assuming, as the balance of estimates say, that about 60 percent of the total population of American adults—which was roughly 242,470,820 at the close of 2013 according to the US Census Bureau—are lactase impersistent, the group is approximately 145,482,492 strong. If each one of these 145 million-plus Americans lost twenty-six pounds per year, next year the United States would be about 3,782,544,792 pounds lighter. That's a lot of elephants in the room: over 250,000 to be exact. Although the number is too great for the average person to overlook, the USDA sees things differently. The USDA, along with the Academy of Nutrition and Dietetics and its graduates, and the dairy industry, continue their efforts to convert the lactase impersistent into milk drinkers. They do so by offering tips such as full-fat and chocolate milk, tricks which the USDA declares are not just for the kids: "For you, too! If you are lactose intolerant, these tips can help you too. Remember, your bones need calcium that milk provides to stay strong and healthy." In the tradition of the most artful politicians, the prompt is both true and false. True, your bones need calcium to stay strong and healthy. True, milk provides calcium. False, your bones need the calcium that milk provides to stay strong and healthy. There is only one sensible way forward for the lactase impersistent: to embrace their body's rejection of milk and opt for less calorie-laden sources of calcium.

A SAVORY IDEA

Although still treated as handicapped by the USDA and traditionally trained dietitians and physicians, the lactase impersistent and milk allergic are situated to be tomorrow's role models. They more than anyone have an incentive to look outside the dairy section for total nutrition. They don't have to search in the dark either. The supermarkets are well lit and full of choice. The members of the calcium-rich class of plants are as high in nutrients as they are low in calories. At lunch ramp up the flavor and nutrition of your salad or soup bowl by mixing in a quarter cup of dried savory and you will be adding more calcium to your dish than if you were to pour a glass of milk on top. At midday add a quarter cup of the dried ground leaves to boiling water for some savory tea. Just be sure to have a spoon on hand for the leaves that line the bottom of the cup. Every one counts. For dinner add a quarter cup of them to sautéed vegetables, or mix them into mustard and slather onto tofu or chicken. Do this, a quarter cup of savory three times a day, and you will exceed the 1,000-milligram DV for calcium by about 125 milligrams. At the end of the day, savory, which costs just under $19 per kilogram at my store and has twelve calories per tablespoon, rings in at ninety-four cents and 144 calories for 1,125 milligrams of calcium. The savings are huge. Consider that skim milk contains about 300 milligrams of calcium per eight-ounce glass. You would therefore have to drink almost four glasses of milk to reach the calcium equivalent of three-quarters of a cup of dried savory. Even at the deal price of $4 per gallon of milk and 80 calories per 8-ounce glass of skim milk, the cost of obtaining the same amount of calcium from milk works out to about $1 dollar and 332 calories.

In short, skim milk costs six cents and 188 calories more than dried savory for 1,125 milligrams of calcium.

If you're trying to bulk up, dried savory, which has less than half the calories per milligram of calcium as skim milk, may not be the ideal source of calcium for you. If, however, you are among the majority who are trying to cut corners, paying six cents less for half the calories is a good deal. There's a bonus. Three-quarters of a cup of dried savory not only exceeds the DV for calcium but also packs in a little more than 100 percent of the DV for iron, in which milk is deficient; 50 percent of the DV for vitamin A; 90 percent of the DV for dietary fiber, which is missing from the typical North American diet that counts ketchup as a vegetable and white bread as a staple; and 3.5 grams of protein, about the same amount of protein as in half a glass of milk.

Savory does fall short in some critical areas. Three quarters of a cup dried has zero sugar; zero cholesterol; less than 12 milligrams of sodium; and less than 3 grams of saturated fat. That's a heart-healthy profile, even compared to "nonfat" milk, which in the four glasses needed to equal the calcium in three-quarters of a cup of savory, also contains 50 grams of sugar; 20 milligrams of cholesterol; 412 milligrams of sodium; and one gram of saturated fat. A born-and-bred bargain hunter, I'd rather save in every way by paying for my calcium in savory. Why spend my money on the insipid watery fluid that is a USDA favorite for calcium when I can choose something that is cheaper, less calorie dense, more nutrient dense, lasts forever, and is full of flavor?

I don't mean to offer savory as the magic bullet to meeting your calcium needs. No food should be a one-stop shop for any nutrient. Not even the most ardent carnivores or committed cattle ranchers would shoot to obtain 100 percent of their protein from beef. Why should we accept, as the USDA urges us to do, that we should derive all of our calcium from milk? My mum used to say if she could put my sister and me together, she'd have the perfect child. The same can be said about food. Mixing and matching is the key to excellence. Just as no one person can excel at everything, so no single food can deliver all things to everyone. Turmeric is an excellent and necessary addition to curry. However, it is not sufficient. Without coriander, mustard seeds, cumin, fenugreek, paprika, cayenne, cardamom, nutmeg, cinnamon, cloves, ginger, and black pepper, you don't have curry. All you have is the yellowy orange root of the *Curcuma longa* plant that is bitter on its own. Everything in combination. The more variety in your diet, the merrier your mouth, mind, and body. The purpose of the milk-savory comparison is to emphasize that with a bit of rethink there are many easy and wholesome ways to incorporate calcium in your day-to-day without milk. You have nothing to lose except calories by experimenting with green sources of calcium.

The cost, calorie, and nutrition advantage that the lactase impersistent have to gain if they honor their genetic makeup is clear as day. Now for the flipside: the burden that the lactase persistent have to bear by following the USDA's dairy recommendations. The short answer is a diet that is seriously off-kilter. The long answer takes off from the 2,000-calorie-per-day foundation upon which the USDA's dietary guidelines are based. If you're nine or older and following the USDA's advice to drink three glasses of milk every day, you will be obtaining anywhere from 12 to 23 percent of your calories, depending on the milk's fat content, from one food. The percentages shoot up if you follow the USDA's dairy guidelines while on a calorie-restricted diet. In that case, milk may even approach one-quarter of your caloric intake for the day. You don't need a dietitian to tell you that diversity is critical to a healthy diet. Losing weight, one of the most common New Year's resolutions, on a well-balanced diet therefore paradoxically precludes following the USDA's nutrition guidelines. The USDA's 3-A-Day dairy recommendation is simply too heavy for a large proportion of the population to soundly carry.

WINNING WITHOUT MILK

In 1995, the *New Yorker* reported that according to the National Institutes of Health and McNeil Consumer Products, a distributor of pills that break down the lactose in milk so that the lactose intolerant can digest it, 30 to 50 million Americans were lactose intolerant. More recent statistics reveal that the number has skyrocketed, broaching the 150 million mark. Those who cannot digest milk are destined to become an even more formidable presence in North America as the continent becomes as diverse as the spectrum of plant-based, nutrient-dense foods that exist outside of the all-white dairy group. No wonder the dairy industry and government agriculture departments, neither of whom want to see the stream of dairy money that has flowed into the economy dry up, are pulling out all the stops to persuade the lactose intolerant not to give up. "Got milk?" carries a renewed sense of urgency.

If you're among the majority who are lactase impersistent, don't buy the propaganda. Those who carry the lactose-digesting enzyme, lactase, into adulthood are the freaks of nature. True, milk may make you bigger. But as former military leaders are telling us, bigger is not better. Unlike our Neolithic ancestors who needed calories wherever they could find them, most of us today could do with less fat and calories. Believe it or not, you who have been labeled with an affliction, you who have been marginalized as "lactose intolerant," hold the trump card. Should you recognize and play it, you will be the winners.

CHAPTER 13

Whole Truth:
The Facts About Cutting Milkfat

For as long as the USDA has been in the business of publishing Dietary Guidelines for Americans, it has been quietly admitting dairy's role in the big health menaces of our day. It doesn't say its "3-A-Day" dairy recommendation may contribute to obesity and heart disease. Twentieth-century technology that enables dairy processors to easily extract the fat from milk has given the USDA a way out of radically reforming its take on dairy. Rather than reevaluate the role of the Dairy Food Group as a whole, it emphasizes the benefits of substituting low-fat and fat-free dairy for full-fat milk products, as if stripping the fat from dairy is sufficient. A confluence of reason, observed and hard facts, and recent research, however, suggests that it isn't.

WHOLE HYPOCRISY

Whole milk is not healthy. That's what the USDA and FDA say, albeit indirectly. Hence the USDA's aforementioned "Key Consumer Message" about dairy found at ChooseMyPlate.gov: "Switch to fat-free or low-fat (one percent) milk." Not even two percent makes the cut. The USDA isn't the only branch of government that refuses to talk about whole milk and health in the same breath. According to FDA regulations, any product that contains 4 grams of saturated fat per "reference amount customarily consumed" (RACC), which is an 8-ounce cup in the case of fluid milk, is disqualified from making a health claim. Whole milk, which contains 4.5 grams of saturated fat per RACC, exceeds this 4-gram threshold and therefore cannot carry a label that "expressly or by implication" characterizes it as having a relationship to a "disease or health-related condition." All the advertising about milk being high in calcium and essential to bone building is, according to these FDA rules, off-limits for whole-milk products. Only nonfat and low-fat milk products, most of which are flavored and filled with sugar to make them drinkable, have the privilege of making health claims on their labels.

Whole-milk products are forbidden from expressing or implying not only that they ward off diseases such as osteoporosis but also that they are "healthy," period. The FDA has specific requirements for using the word and variations on it such as "health," "healthful," "healthfully," "healthfulness," "healthier," "healthiest," "healthily," and "healthiness." No product is permitted to even mention the word or any of its derivations on its label unless it meets the FDA's definition of being low in total fat—3 grams or less of fat per RACC—and saturated fat—1 gram or less of saturated fat per RACC and not more than 15 percent of calories from saturated fat. Whole milk, which contains almost 8 grams of total fat and over 4 grams of saturated fat per RACC, doesn't come close to qualifying. "Low-fat" 1 percent milk and "reduced fat" 2 percent milk, both of which contain just over 1 gram of saturated fat per 8-ounce serving, almost but don't quite make the grade. Only "nonfat" milk passes muster.

The rules, which apply to milk products, have absurd consequences. For instance, they disqualify plain yogurt made with whole milk from making claims about being a probiotic. Strawberry-cheesecake–flavored yogurt made with nonfat milk and a generous amount of added sugars, however, gets the go ahead. Maybe that's why it's so hard to find single-serving containers of plain whole-milk yogurt in supermarket refrigerators. They can't compete with their low-fat high-sugar neighbors that can boast about being good for your gut even though they're not. I sought confirmation from the FDA that I was interpreting the regulations correctly and wasn't overlooking any exceptions, but received no reply.

The FDA's regulations are not academic. Their teeth are piercing the profits of massively lucrative products. CytoSport, with its line of Muscle Milk protein drinks and bars, is one company that has fallen into the claws of the law. Muscle Milk, a leading sports nutrition brand in the United States, generates over $300 million in annual sales and claims almost a quarter of the share of the sports nutrition category. Just as CytoSport was gearing up to storm the UK market, it received a warning letter from the FDA. Muscle Milk products, the FDA stated, were misbranded. The letter was followed by a complaint from a California plaintiff that CytoSport had been misleading consumers with claims that Muscle Milk drinks and bars provide "Healthy, Sustained Energy" and "Healthy Fats." Muscle Milk protein shakes contain more than 3 grams of fat per serving. As such they do not meet the FDA's definition of "low fat" and so cannot sport the word "healthy" on their label. The same goes for Muscle Milk protein bars, which contain more than 3 grams of total fat and 1 gram of saturated fat per serving.

In the fall of 2013 a judge in California provisionally approved a $5.3 million settlement between the plaintiff and CytoSport. The terms of the agreement were twofold. CytoSport would stop baiting customers with the promise of "Healthy, Sustained Energy" and donate $85,000 to the American Heart Association. The judgment sends the message that the buyer does not bear full responsibility for being aware of the fat that is everywhere. Seller beware, "health" and "high fat" cannot be uttered together. More importantly, it signals that according to the FDA, none of what you read about the importance of dairy in maintaining a healthy diet applies to low-fat, reduced-fat, or whole-milk products. Curiouser and curiouser. On the one hand, the USDA has singled out milk from all the many nutrient-dense whole foods on this planet to make into a food group. On the other hand, the FDA has ruled that the group's truest member, its originator, cannot wear the health badge of honor. The two positions are as irreconcilable as the words "high fat" and "healthy" are to the FDA.

The fact that the USDA's definition of and recommendations for dairy are consistent with the FDA's health claim regulations only reinforces the incongruity at the core of the Dairy Food Group. In delineating the food group, the USDA states: "All fluid milk products and many foods made from milk are considered part of this food group." So while all fluid milk counts, not all foods made from it do. High fat ones that are low in calcium, such as cream cheese, cream, and butter are excluded. Whole milk makes it into the group, but just barely. Slapped with the USDA's caveat that "Most Dairy Group choices should be fat-free or low-fat," it is treated as a second-class dairy citizen. FDA and USDA aversion toward whole milk begs the question: how can dairy deserve to fill prime stomach real estate three times a day, 365 days of the year, when the same agencies behind the 3-A-Day dairy recommendation have declared the family's founder distasteful?

WHAT HAPPENED TO WHOLE MILK?

In the days when milk was delivered door-to-door, the message about milk from dairy producers, retailers, and public officials was unequivocal: milk is nature's perfect food. The focus was on how to keep it from becoming contaminated rather than on anything inherently bad about it. The debate that played out in local jurisdictions across the country was whether to pasteurize or to certify milk to ensure its safety. Physicians pushed for on-farm inspection programs, arguing that pasteurization destroyed much of milk's nutrition. But the cost of such programs proved too prohibitive. One by one, cities and states caved to the efficiency of technology that removed high-billing experts from the economics of protecting milk's purity. Pasteurization became the norm and whole milk the form. My dad in Toronto and my mum in Brooklyn only knew whole milk growing up in the early 1940s.

Gone are the days that my dad spoke of when he and his brothers fought over the cream that rose to the top of the glass jars of silky dense fluid that the milkman delivered. However, even when the milkman disappeared, whole milk didn't. All my friends were drinking whole milk well into the 1970s. My memory is consistent with the statistics. Sales of low-fat and skim milk combined didn't surpass sales of whole milk until 1988. The massive overhaul of the milk supply that has relegated whole milk to a special occasion, to use sparingly for rich dishes, desserts, and perhaps an extravagant cup of coffee, happened in a heartbeat relative to the number of years North Americans enjoyed it. In 1980, just as my friend Amy was learning how to master the art of Kraft Macaroni & Cheese, which required enough literacy to read directions, a little whole milk and a dollop of butter, the USDA had other plans for whole milk and butter, and they didn't involve dinner. Together with the Department of Health and Human Services, it issued the first Dietary Guidelines for Americans. The USDA's website describes the Guidelines, which are updated every five years, as the "cornerstone of Federal nutrition policy and nutrition education activities."

Page one of the 1980 Guidelines reveals that reducing saturated fat has always been a target of the government's ongoing experiment in creating an effective national nutrition strategy. Laid out are seven recommendations that are numbered in super-sized and varying fonts on what appears to be a page of schoolbook graph paper. The bubbly delivery makes even number three on the list, which is bold and colored in cautionary red, non-threatening: "Avoid too much fat, saturated fat, and cholesterol." Page twelve acknowledges that while there is controversy about what's appropriate for healthy Americans, for the population as a whole, reducing fat is "sensible." Accordingly, chapter 3 counsels Americans to limit their butter and cream intake.

Further along, the initial red light against fat turns to yellow: "The recommendations are not meant to prohibit the use of any specific food item or to prevent you from eating a variety of foods. . . . If you prefer whole milk to skim milk, you can reduce your intake of fats from foods other than milk." This concession to whole-milk devotees indicates that in 1980 there were enough of them to warrant recognition. Evidently in 1980 whole milk was still okay with the USDA, as long as we cut fat elsewhere. Lose the butter in the mac & cheese, maybe. In 1980 most parents still considered whole milk a healthy food to keep around at all times. Yes, everyone knew not to do as my grandfather did. "Have a little toast with your butter" we'd be tempted to say when he joined us every so often for brunch on Sunday. Yes, Amy and I followed the unspoken rule that we could have a scoop or two, but never a container of ice cream after dinner. However, setting limits on how much whole milk a person could have was not part of the zeitgeist of the late seventies and early eighties. Amy's mom would have been thrilled if Amy and her brothers poured themselves a glass of whole milk for breakfast, lunch, and dinner. She'd prompt them when they didn't.

I didn't know about the Dietary Guidelines for Americans in 1980, but I knew the convenience store down the street, Becker's, inside out. All the kids in the neighborhood went there for popsicles in the summer and candy year-round. I watched as the open refrigerator at the back of Becker's underwent a dairy makeover during the course of a few short years. Already by the early 1980s whole milk was no longer the one and only, the symbol of all things pure and healthy. It was fighting for shelf space with skim and 2 percent milk, which were taking over. I don't remember a fourth option, fat-free, but it was just around the corner. My parents avoided the store altogether. They still only got whole milk, in both senses of the word "got": they only *bought* whole milk, when possible straight from the farm, because they didn't *understand* milk that was packaged in large quantities in varying degrees of fat. But my parents were outliers. Becker's, a chain of stores that had over 90 franchises throughout Ontario, represented middle Canada. Its offerings reflected what the majority were buying: advice from Health Canada and the USDA to avoid saturated fat and cholesterol. These had become enemy combatants number one and two in the fight against cardiovascular disease and hypertension that was disturbing the peace of post–World War II North America.

The renovation to Becker's dairy section kept pace with the evolution of the Dietary Guidelines for Americans. Side by side, the 1985 Guidelines seem light-years, not merely five years, away from the 1980 edition. Although the seven recommendations that introduced the 1980 Guidelines remained much the same, the presentation is markedly different. Three-dimensional hexagons, each drawn in a different color of the rainbow, replace the numbers that previously preceded the recommendations. These hexagons are linked vertically on page one, and then spherically, like honeycomb structures, in the following pages. Having a geometric figure front the seven recommendations matches the Guidelines' ambition for precision. Whereas the 1980 Guidelines were prepared to discuss and negotiate, the 1985 Guidelines assume a firmer, more unforgiving tone. They read more like the words from a stern schoolmaster than a kindly kindergarten teacher. There is no consoling the Amys of America who preferred their milk whole. Instead, top among the 1985 Guidelines' multiple suggestions for how to "avoid too much fat, saturated fat, and cholesterol" is the instruction: "Use skim or low-fat milk and milk products." Here began the end of whole milk, in abundance at Becker's, in a tall glass beside a short stack of Oreos, on cornflakes, or with dinner.

The Dietary Guidelines for Americans have become more militant in their opposition to saturated fat and cholesterol with each five-year cycle of renewal. The 1985 edition dropped the part about whole milk being okay. In 1990, the Guidelines stopped speaking in the abstract about saturated fat. They provide a concrete allowance: "An amount that provides less than ten percent of calories (less than twenty-two grams at two thousand calories per day) is suggested." Finally, in 2000, whole milk is lumped together with villainous foods such as butter, cream, and ice cream that are fronted by the admonition: "Keep your intake of these foods low."

At the same time that the Dietary Guidelines for Americans were getting stricter about cutting down on whole milk and its products, they were growing in stature. The four-by-nine-inch "brochure" that contains the first generation of Guidelines expanded in the second millennium to the full-sized eight-and-a-half-by-eleven-inch "booklet" that has become the layout for the twenty-first century editions. This scaling-up coincided with the Guidelines' rise from relative obscurity to recognition by the president of the United States. On May 27, 2000, President Bill Clinton dedicated his Memorial Day Weekend radio address to the release of the most recent Guidelines. Although he acknowledged that the weekend was about honoring those who fought for freedom, he chose to concentrate on the food that Americans would be eating at the picnics and backyard barbeques where they were gathering in celebration. While recognizing that nutrition-labeling laws were helping Americans eat better, he called attention to an "alarming trend": more and more Americans were overweight or obese. The population's rising largesse was so concerning because, he said, "Obesity and bad eating habits contribute to four of the leading causes of death: heart disease, stroke, cancer, and diabetes." Despite the gloomy news, he optimistically declared, "Today I am releasing the federal government's new Dietary Guidelines 2000." The Guidelines, he went on to say, "serve as the gold standard of nutritional information. They determine, among other things, the nutritional content of the lunches served to twenty-six million of our children every day in school." They sure do, in ways that promote both sickness and health.

SPILLED MILK

There is no doubt that the Dietary Guidelines for Americans are improving school meals. I don't have fond memories of the canned creamed corn and the flat, square, greenish hamburger patties that my school served up for lunch. Crowned by yellow Jell-O, or, if we were lucky, chocolate pudding mixed from a package, these meals were nothing more than stomach filler. The idea behind the arranged marriage between the Dietary Guidelines for Americans and school meal programs is to turn meals once made to get children through the school day into sustenance for now and the future. The lunch lady who picks up a copy of the Guidelines will read about the importance of variety in "Building Healthy Eating Patterns," the title of chapter 6 of the 2010 Guidelines. The word "variety" appears over forty times throughout the 2010 Guidelines' six chapters: "Eat a *variety* [emphasis added] of vegetables"; "Choose a *variety* [emphasis added] of protein foods"; "Increase the amount and *variety* [emphasis added] of seafood"; "Choose from a *variety* [emphasis added] of strategies to increase physical activity"; "The USDA Food Patterns recommend selecting a *variety* [emphasis added] of foods within each food group"; "Spices, herbs, and lemon juice can be used as alternatives to salt to season foods with a *variety* [emphasis added] of flavors." And the kicker: "Americans should select a *variety* [emphasis added] of food sources of potassium to meet recommended intake rather than relying on supplements." Good idea, if only it were applied consistently. The government's evident appreciation of the value that variety brings to the table conflicts with its attempts to push Americans to select one single food, milk in its multiple iterations, to meet the recommended intake of calcium. The USDA would do well to take a leaf out of its own book. Variety is the life of food. It adds color and intrigue to our most fundamental daily activity. Variety is to food what quilts are to covering, elevating the functional into the soulful.

Unfortunately, the Guidelines' unspoken premise that food must be interesting to be enriching is undermined by its priority to lead Americans away from the temptation of whole dairy. The Healthy, Hunger-Free Kids Act (HHFKA), which was passed in 2010, illuminates how the whole-milk prohibition that the 2010 Guidelines encodes is negatively influencing the nutritional content of school meals. Section 202 of the HHFKA, "Nutrition Requirements for Fluid Milk," amends the section of the National

School Lunch Act (NSLA) that requires schools to serve milk with vary-ing levels of fat. Full-fat milk was part of the deal until section 202 of the HHFKA declared no. It states that schools "shall offer a variety of fluid milk," and that "Such milk shall be consistent with the most recent Dietary Guidelines for Americans." The final rule passed in January 2012, "Nutrition Standards in the National School Lunch and School Breakfast Programs," explains what section 202 means for school cafeterias. Twenty-five pages into the rule, which is eighty-one pages in full, there's a table titled "Summary of the Final Rule Meal Requirements." It contains the amount of fruits, vegetables, grains, meats/meat alternatives, and fluid milk that school breakfast and lunch programs must provide to comply with the HHFKA. The footnote to "Fluid Milk" clarifies: "Fluid milk must be low-fat (one percent milk fat or less, unflavored) or fat-free (unflavored or flavored)." The small font discloses big change: for the first time in its long history of feeding school children, the government will no longer condone giving children full-fat milk in school. Two percent milk is also forbidden. It's official. Any milk with more than trace levels of fat has been blacklisted.

If the government were more observant, it might have thought better of amending the NSLA so as to ban whole milk from school quarters. All it had to do was look at the statistics that its own USDA had already gath-ered. In 1997 the USDA's Economic Research Service (ERS) published a report, "Estimating and Addressing America's Food Losses," that found that milk accounted for much of the food loss in America. Of the 54,474 mil-lion pounds of fluid milk available for human consumption in 1995, 17,431 million pounds were lost. The statistic isn't surprising. I've heard more than one parent grumble about how their kids drown their cereal in milk only to abandon their bowl with the last spoonful of snap, crackle, and pop. The frustrated cleaner-uppers bemoan all the milk and money they pour down the drain each morning. Although the morning routine now, it wasn't always so. When I slept over at Amy's, cereal and milk in the morning was a given. So was finishing every last drop of the sweet cereal milk that was left after the cereal was all gone. It was the best part. We weren't particularly waste conscious. It was the whole milk difference. I don't blame kids these days for running away before their full bowl of milk is found out. The plain, nonfat milk they pour is nasty. We can only skimp so much before the customer catches on and refuses to accept a product that has been reduced to a handful of nutrients suspended in a watery, semi-translucent solution.

Milk isn't only a waste product of breakfast. Insiders have told me that after lunch, the school cafeteria is a mess of garbage bins spilling cartons of untouched, sometimes even unopened, milk. I don't have to go inside to believe it; the wreckage overflows onto the path in front of the high school I walk by every day. Single-serve cartons of milk are scattered about, forming puddles on the concrete and asphalt. I have looked but have never found whole milk among the cartons of casualties. If the ERS report is correct, 32 percent of fluid milk available for drinking never reaches America's big mouth. That gives milk the distinction of having the second-highest loss rate of all the foods that the report measures. Gallons upon gallons of perfectly good but bad-tasting milk are feeding our landfills. I wonder if less milk was lost when Amy and America still had the USDA's approval to drink the whole thing.

THE ICK FACTOR OF FAT-FREE MILK

In her December 2013 editorial, Samantha Perry, editor of West Virginia's *Bluefield Daily Telegraph*, nails what many Americans think of fat-free milk. Reacting to the torrent of "How to Eat Healthy" columns that inundate the papers during the holiday season, she plays the devil's advocate for full-fat milk: "When I was younger, living at home with the folks, my mom once poured me a glass of one of those milk impostors. I took one drink, spit it out, and quickly termed it 'devil's juice.' After I was married, I refused to allow any of these 'healthy' milk products in my house. For twenty-one years I am proud to say our 'fridge has housed only whole milk.

Bad action, perhaps. But it's a quirk that cements my role as the poster child for unhealthy eating habits." Perry's confession explains why children and teens aren't drinking their milk, even when it's freely handed out to them. The waste inside and outside the trash bins speaks for itself: fat-free milk is foul tasting to more people than Perry. Yet Perry is the one who feels deviant for allowing only whole milk into her home. She, like the rest of Americans, has been indoctrinated by USDA Food Pyramids, Plates, and the complementary materials they generate into believing that her whole milk habit makes her an ad for errant eating.

Perry isn't exaggerating the degree to which whole milk is looked down upon from on high in Washington today. As the Dietary Guidelines for Americans have become more detailed, as they have expanded from eleven pages in 1980 to ninety-five pages and sixteen appendices in 2010, as they seek to reach beyond healthy Americans aged two and older to those who are also "at increased risk of chronic disease," their intolerance of whole milk and whole-milk products has become visible. Figure 5-2, titled "Examples of the calories in food choices that are not in nutrient dense forms and the calories in nutrient dense forms of these foods," of the 2010 Guidelines selects six foods to make the point that not all forms of food are created equal. The chosen ones are: beef, chicken, cornflakes, potatoes, applesauce, and milk. Using a bar graph, the figure pairs the calories in the "nutrient dense" form of the food alongside the calories in the same food that is "not in nutrient dense" form. Moving from top to bottom, the graph thus compares an extra-lean ground-beef patty to a regular ground-beef patty; baked chicken breast to breaded fried chicken strips; cornflakes to frosted cornflakes; baked potato to French fries; applesauce to sweetened applesauce; and lastly, fat-free milk to whole milk. If whole milk is to fat-free milk as French fries are to a baked potato, the graph leaves no doubt about the USDA's current take on whole milk: it's unhealthy. Whole milk, the 2010 Guidelines communicate pictorially, is fat-free milk's evil twin.

But what if Perry is correct? What if any cow's milk but whole cow's milk is "devil's juice"? The HHFKA, which forces milk with virtually all of its fat removed on children, doesn't sit well with the objective to train the next generation to prefer foods that will sustain them beyond their youth. As teaching aids, low-fat and fat-free milk are lacking in more ways than fat. To be as blunt as these tools are for carving out models of healthy eating, milk stripped of its fat is plain and worse than simple. Disagreeable to eye, mouth, mind, and stomach, it is totally unacceptable. Without added color, flavor, and sugar, fat-free milk looks and tastes no better than the effluent from some faraway processing plant. Teaching children to build healthy eating patterns by skimming off the cream of the crop and giving them the leftovers is as futile as teaching them to read with the letters X, Y, and Z. Our vocabulary would be severely limited if we didn't learn A, B, and C and every other letter in between. Whole foods are the ABCs of meaningful and vibrant living. Exposure to them is critical to fluency in healthy eating.

The government's incorporation of the Dietary Guidelines for America into school meal planning is motivated by good intentions and high expectations. The Guidelines' horizon is long. As the introduction explains: "The ultimate goal of the Dietary Guidelines for Americans is to improve the health of our Nation's current and future generations by facilitating and promoting healthy eating and physical activity choices so that these behaviors become the norm among all individuals." Six-year-olds don't set the kindergarten curriculum. If they did, they might watch cartoons all day. Similarly, juvenile palates should not dictate what's for school lunch. When they do, hamburgers, French fries, fried chicken, pizza, and soda dominate the menu. Although not even the experts have solved the mystery of how to eat to attain maximum health and well-being, everybody knows that the daily diet of fried foods, ketchup, cookies, and cola that most children would choose is not one on which they will reach their potential. The joint work of government legislators and agencies to clean school premises of the sticky sweet carbonated beverages that are implicated in diseases ranging from obesity and diabetes to cancer and chronic inflammation is therefore not hugely controversial. However, their embrace of milk as an essential part of school meal programs and their prohibition against schools providing it in its whole form is not only perplexing but also vexing.

You've read the statistics. You've seen the garbage. No one with any senses, not even the young who lean toward foods on the tasteless end of the spectrum, wants the equivalent of chalk water to wash down their sandwich. Expunging whole milk from school meal programs, as the HHFKA has done, has left children with no good choice but milk with a sugar profile much the same as the soft drinks that schools are racing to remove from their vending machines. Just over 70 percent of the milk served in schools is flavored, which means sweetened, too, usually with sugar or high-fructose corn syrup. Low-fat chocolate milk contains 25 grams of sugar per 8-ounce glass, or roughly 4 teaspoons of sugar, compared to the 12.5 grams in the same amount of plain milk. Eight ounces of Coca-Cola contains 26 grams of sugar. By encouraging schools to serve students flavored milk, the government is merely substituting sugar for sugar: it is taking it out in cans of soda and introducing it back in cartons of flavored milk.

THE SUGAR-SWEET COVER-UP

Dr. Walter Willett, who has been called the "world's most-cited nutritionist," isn't impressed. He is critical of the type of fat-free approach to dietary reform on display in the government's rules regarding school milk: "Often sugar is substituting for fat, and many times the new low-fat product is worse than the original full-fat version." For those who drink milk, he suggests that full fat is best, in part because, as he notes, "unfortunately, in many low fat dairy products the fat is replaced by sugar, and these will almost certainly induce more weight gain than the full fat versions." That's exactly what's happening in the case of flavored low-fat milk. Fat has been swapped for sugar. And as Dr. Willett points out, "if you're removing mostly good fat and replacing it with refined starch or sugar, that's not going to be good on balance for our long-term well-being." There's more weight to gain than lose from trading high-fat dairy for high-fructose corn syrup.

The 1980 Dietary Guidelines for Americans kicked into high gear the campaign against saturated fat that was gaining momentum in the 1960s. Their demonization of my grandfather's favorite nutrient was accompanied by an equally simplistic assessment of what to do instead. The notification to "avoid saturated fat" is followed by exactly the type of advice that Willett decries: "If you limit your fat intake, you should increase your calories from carbohydrates to supply your body's energy needs." By endorsing milk that has had its fat removed and carbohydrates added back, the USDA is repeating the mistake that it made thirty-five years ago: encouraging us to substitute carbohydrates, which in North America have become synonymous with refined sugar and grains, for fat. The agency's steadfast adherence to a directive that the current research is proving deeply flawed serves as a reminder that the USDA, and the Dietary Guidelines for Americans that it underwrites, are and always have been prone to error. But that's to be expected given what Dr. Willett is not shy to admit: the dairy picture is "very complex"; and the "relation between diet and health is unusually complicated to study, and that's probably why we don't have all the final answers even yet." Against such uncertainty it would be foolish to rely on anyone, including the USDA, for the final word on anything as specific as a 3-A-Day prescription for fat-free milk.

The dairy industry recognizes what the government, which is stuck in the 1980s, hasn't: delivering products that substitute simple carbohydrates for fat is not the formula for a strong and healthy future. Aware that their young clientele aren't drinking the plain milk options that meet the government's standards for fat, and attuned to the calls from parents and health experts to remove excess sugar from children's diets, dairy processors have submitted a proposal to the FDA. In March 2009 the International Dairy Foods Association (IDFA) and the National Milk Producers Federation (NMPF) petitioned the FDA to allow dairy processors to artificially sweeten milk without having to declare the fact on the front label. More precisely, they want the FDA to amend the standard of identity for milk "to allow optional characterizing flavoring ingredients used in milk (e.g., chocolate flavoring added to milk) to be sweetened with any safe and suitable sweetener—including non-nutritive sweeteners such as aspartame." Practically speaking, they want to call milk sweetened with aspartame, the same sweetener found in diet soft drinks, "milk." Currently, they can't. If they sweeten flavored milk with a non-nutritive sweetener they must include a nutrient content claim, such as "reduced calorie," on the label. In defense of the petition, the IDFA and NMPF state that "lower-calorie flavored milk would particularly benefit school children who . . . are more inclined to drink flavored milk than unflavored milk at school." They accept having to list the non-nutritive sweetener as an ingredient on the back. But they vehemently oppose calling attention to their product's low-calorie formulation by having to make a nutrient content claim on the front. They argue that children won't choose milk that is marketed as "reduced calorie."

The dairy industry has a strong incentive to keep low-fat and fat-free milk at the top of the government's dairy agenda. It isn't all about keeping the kids happy and fit. If the USDA and health experts who advise it have gotten it wrong all these years, if whole milk turns out to be better than fat-free, the 3-A-Day dairy recommendation is bound to break down because three servings per day of whole milk translates into about 450 calories, which is too many for an already overstuffed nation to handle healthfully. Reducing or eliminating the 3-A-Day recommendation is clearly not in the dairy industry's interest. No surprise then that it has come up with a compromise that may be its best hope for keeping the dairy group alive and kicking.

The government's solution to increasing the amount of milk children drink without increasing the fat around their stomachs is counter to everything we're learning about the causes of obesity. Pushing copious amounts of saturated-fat–reduced, sugar-saturated milk on school children is a bad idea for more reasons than what we are discovering about how readily dietary sugar converts to body fat. The government's sponsorship of milk with more sugar and less fat doesn't mesh with what doctors such as Walter Willett are saying about the dietary fat/body fat connection: "many studies have not supported the idea that fat in the diet is specifically related to greater fat in our bodies." But the dairy industry's fix isn't any better. The situation it is creating in school cafeterias couldn't be more convoluted. First it delivered up vast quantities of whole milk. Then it took out the fat. Then it added sugar and flavor. Now it wants to take out the sugar and add a non-nutritive sweetener. The solution is especially disagreeable in light of the news that broke in September 2014 about an Israeli study published in the journal *Nature* that found that artificial sweeteners change the microorganisms in our gut in ways that may lead to glucose intolerance; increase the numbers of bacteria in the gut that are linked to gut inflammation; and, like sugar, lead to spikes in blood-sugar levels. The report concludes that artificial sweeteners "may have directly contributed to enhancing the exact epidemic they themselves were intended to fight." Experts are calling for more research into the observed effects of artificial sweeteners on gut health and glucose tolerance. Yet the dairy industry wants to substitute aspartame, one of the artificial sweeteners studied, for sugar and is asking to hide the fact from consumers because it says children won't choose milk that sounds like a diet food. All these mind and body games are being played in the name of nudging children to drink three glasses a day. There is some truth to the claim that whole milk is nature's perfect food. It is perfect for calves. However, the mocked-up milk that has been reconstituted to suit North Americans' waists and tastes isn't fit for anyone. It isn't nature's food, let alone perfect for any mammal, bovine or human.

A decade ago whole foods didn't mean much more to the average consumer than a chain of high-end supermarkets that sell some whole foods and a whole lot more packaged, purportedly healthier versions of highly processed favorites such as soft drinks, chips, and Hot Pockets. Today whole foods is reclaiming its original meaning as a description of food rather than where to buy it. Michael Pollan's book *In Defense of Food*, which reached number one on the *New York Times* non-fiction bestseller list when it was released in 2008, deserves some of the credit. The yellow band encircling the head of lettuce on the book's cover states the "Eater's Manifesto," giving away the between the covers: "Eat Food. Not too Much. Mostly Plants."

The answer to the billion-dollar question of what humans should eat to be healthy that the book sets out to discover is slightly but not much longer than three sentences. First, Pollan explains what he means by "eat food": "you're better off eating whole fresh foods rather than processed food products." In one stroke, Pollan thus pens the whole-foods diet. Not to be confused with the Whole Foods diet of chic urbanites with fat paychecks, Pollan's lower-case "w," lower-case "f" diet means eating outside of our obesogenic environment. It means passing by the fast, fattening, and tantalizing foods that are within a stone's throw of anywhere you stand. The whole-foods diet, which is as diverse in content as it is in the numbers who follow it, is shaped by a few principles: eat outside of the box; stock up on the fresh foods that line the perimeter of supermarkets; and substitute plants cooked in your kitchen for the products of food-processing plants.

Michael Pollan isn't the only one talking about the nourishment that comes from digging down rather than driving around. On this point the Dietary Guidelines for Americans are in agreement. The core of the 2010 edition contains recommendations for "Foods and Food Components to Reduce" and "Foods and Nutrients to Increase." Highly processed foods, specifically refined grains, fall within the former category. Hence, one of the Guidelines' "Key Recommendations": "Limit the consumption of foods that contain refined grains, especially refined grain foods that contain solid fats, added sugars, and sodium." Later the 2010 Guidelines add color to their negative opinion of processed foods: "Consume more fresh foods and fewer processed foods that are high in sodium." The first three bullet points in the summary of "Foods and Nutrients to Increase" are all about whole foods: "Increase vegetable and fruit intake; Eat a variety of vegetables, especially dark-green and red and orange vegetables and beans and peas; Consume at least half of all grains as whole grains. Increase whole-grain intake by replacing refined grains with whole grains." And yet another iteration of the Guidelines' refrain, which is repeated throughout the ninety-five pages, to increase intake of whole fresh foods and reduce consumption of refined foods: "Americans should emphasize naturally occurring carbohydrates, such as those found in whole grains, beans, peas, vegetables, and fruits, especially those high in dietary fiber, while limiting refined grains and intake of foods with added sugars."

At the same time that the 2010 Guidelines rally Americans to incorporate more whole foods into their diet, they describe the downsides of the refining process: it "results in the loss of vitamins, minerals, and dietary fiber." The practice of enriching, it explains, is only a partial remedy, returning "some, but not all, of the vitamins and minerals that were removed during the refining process." Refined grains that are enriched with vitamins such as iron, thiamin, riboflavin, and niacin, for example, remain lacking in fiber and other nutrients that their whole counterparts retain. What goes for whole grains goes for whole milk. You can refine it and enrich it and load it with sugar but what you're left with is less than the original. Children deserve more.

CHAPTER 14

Making It Without Milk: Colorful Recipes That Leave Dairy Out of the Picture

"Because 73 percent of the calcium available in the food supply is provided by milk and milk products . . . it is difficult to get recommended levels of calcium by consuming non-dairy sources." Even if this statement by the American Dairy Association and National Dairy Council were true, even if milk and milk products accounted for a large majority of the calcium available in the food supply, spotlighting the fact is hardly a ringing endorsement for milk. If most of the calcium in the food supply comes from dairy, then when you consider how plentiful and accessible dairy is alongside the fact that the 2010 Dietary Guidelines for Americans have identified calcium as a "nutrient of concern," the dairy industry has some explaining to do.

The way the calcium and dairy recommendations have been set, the Guidelines' finding that Americans aren't meeting the former means they aren't meeting the latter either. And if they're not meeting the latter, it's not because there's a shortage of milk products. As Joe Satran discovered during his weeklong engagement with MyPlate, meeting his calcium RDAs with dairy, which is the intended consequence of following the USDA's MyPlate dairy guidelines, created what he called the "The Dairy Problem." The "problem" in short was that he was consuming more milk and milk products than he would have liked. The fact that, as a population, Americans aren't meeting their calcium RDAs means Satran is not the only one who finds three servings of dairy per day unappetizing. If Americans are calcium deficient, it's because advising Americans to obtain all their calcium from dairy isn't working.

My plate is different. It's loaded with calcium-rich foods that don't include cow's milk and everything that goes with it, including the sugar that most can't digest and the casein that so many can't breathe in, let alone swallow.

MY BIG BEAUTIFUL PLATE

June is Dairy Month. June 1 is World Milk Day. The last Wednesday of September is World School Milk Day. It's about time we have a month in which we hear none of it. I hereby proclaim May "Milkless Monday Month." In celebration, I urge you to take the Milkless Monday Challenge. There's only one rule: every Monday try to meet your calcium RDAs without any milk products, calcium-fortified foods, or supplements. Even if you don't want to eliminate dairy from your diet entirely, you will benefit by participating. Why? Because if you fill your calcium RDAs without dairy, calcium-fortified foods, or supplements, you will find yourself eating very healthfully. You may even lose weight. I've made the challenge easy by providing four menus, as well as tips, snack suggestions, and desserts that will help you succeed. My hope is that when you become more aware of the non-dairy calcium-dense foods that surround you, your Twitter feed will nourish your friends and your friends' friends so that eventually people will stop being surprised when I tell them that dried basil is, gram for gram, a higher source of calcium and other essential nutrients than most foods, including milk and milk products.

Before you dig in, a few fundamentals. First, forget what they say about reducing the size of your plate. The idea behind the diet advice is that you will eat less if less fits on your plate. Whoever says that to lose weight you need to cut down portion sizes is wrong. A great way to lose weight or simply stay healthy is to eat plenty of bulky, fibrous veggies. The menus that follow are plant- and, specifically, vegetable-heavy. The Big Kale Salad (see Menu Four), for instance, won't fit into your typical single-serve salad bowl. Since plant foods tend to take up a lot of space, you will need at least one big plate and a serving-sized bowl to eat from, a couple more if you don't like having to wash the same dish over and over. In addition to a spacious serving dish or two, the following will be helpful: a hand blender, a regular upright blender, a coffee grinder, a food processor, a box grater, and a zester. The hand blender is a must for quickly turning a chunky soup into a creamy one and chia and flaxseeds into pudding. The regular blender is great for making nut milk. The coffee grinder turns seeds into flour. The food processor is good for making pesto and hearty sauces. The box grater shreds vegetables in an instant. And the zester, mine is eight inches long and one inch wide, works for nutmeg as well as citrus. Of course, you will also need the basics, including a pot, a pan, a stovetop, and a toaster oven if not a full-size oven.

I will continue to provide tips along the way, but I want to get something off of my chest right away. Carob. It's not a hippie thing. It is sweet, earthy, slightly nutty, and high in calcium and fiber, another on the 2010 Dietary Guidelines for Americans' list of "nutrients of concern." Carob has been maligned as chocolate's healthy substitute. It's not. It's its own bean. The trick to carob is not to expect chocolate. At the risk of sounding like a flower child—I'm not, I came of age during the era of big hair and Boy George rather than beaded bracelets and the Beatles—I encourage everyone to give carob and all the other plant foods highlighted in these menus a chance.

About the recipes more generally, they contain no wheat or added sugars and feature ingredients with low glycemic loads. They are designed to be convenient for singles and families to make, and to be nutrient- but not calorie-dense. An estimate of the number of calories and milligrams of calcium, magnesium—a mineral that studies show North Americans are low in and that is equally as important as calcium in building strong bones—and grams of protein accompanies each recipe. The numbers should be read with the understanding that they are best estimates and have not been lab-tested. The totals are based on online nutrition data sites and food package labels. For example, my 300-gram bag of black, organic chia seeds says each 2-tablespoon serving contains 77 calories; 15 percent of the Daily Value (DV) for calcium, which equals 150 milligrams; and 24 percent of the DV for magnesium, which equals 96 milligrams. These are the numbers I rely on in totaling the nutrients in recipes that contain chia seeds. Because your bag of chia seeds may say something different, it's not an exact science. However, there is a constant. As you consider the numbers, remember that the DV is 1,000 milligrams for calcium and 400 milligrams for magnesium.

The recipes are also amenable to substitutes. For instance, dried figs contain about three times the amount of calcium as raisins and dried dates by weight. One half cup contains 12 percent of the DV for calcium, or 120 milligrams. If you want to maximize calcium intake, I therefore encourage you to try using figs wherever the more familiar and traditional raisins and dates are called for in these recipes. Slice or chop them into raisin-sized bits when replacing raisins. When using them instead of dates, soak them as you would the dates.

Finally, the recipes riff off each other to maximize efficiency and minimize waste. Thus the eggshells that are the by-product of a frittata become the ingredient for an eggshell powder that is added to a breakfast cookie for a calcium kick. And the sweet-potato skins that are left over from making salmon burgers morph into a side dish for chili. While this chapter contains menus for four milkless Mondays, you can enjoy the recipes any and all days of the week. You'll see, it's easy to make it without milk.

Onward, green soldiers.

HOMEMADE ALMOND MILK

Almonds are a good source of calcium, as is the milk made from them. While you can buy almond milk, much of it has unwanted additives such as carrageenan, a derivative of seaweed that has been linked to an increased rate of malignant tumor growth in laboratory animals and chronic gastrointestinal inflammation in humans. Due to widespread concerns, one big seller of almond milk, WhiteWaveFoods, maker of Silk almond milk, has announced that it will stop using carrageenan in its products. However, it's starting the phase-out with Silk soy and coconut milk, so it may be a while before its almond milk is carrageenan-free.

Most store-bought almond milk is also not made from raw almonds. That's because a USDA rule that took effect in 2007 makes the pasteurization of almonds grown in California, including those certified "organic," mandatory. The FDA has approved propylene oxide treatment, steam treatment, oil roasting, dry roasting, and blanching as acceptable methods of pasteurization for the purposes of the rule. The FDA also permits pasteurized almonds to be labeled "raw." Since no rules prohibit the sale in the United States of unpasteurized almonds from other countries, if you want to be sure your almonds are truly raw, look for the organic "raw" ones from Spain. Smaller, flatter, and slightly darker in color than the common California variety, they also tend to be less expensive. Try them in this recipe.

MAKES THREE CUPS OF ALMOND MILK AND ONE CUP OF ALMOND MEAL.

1 cup raw almonds*

3 cups water plus 2 cups water for soaking the almonds**

You can substitute your favorite nuts or seeds for the almonds. Cashews, hazelnuts, hemp seeds, and sunflower seeds are all good alternatives, although not as high in calcium as almonds.

**Use filtered water for all recipes if possible*

STEPS

1. Soak the raw, unpeeled almonds in 2 cups of water overnight or for at least 4 hours. After soaking, drain the almonds and rinse under cold water.

2. Transfer the soaked almonds to an upright blender. Add 3 cups of water and blend until smooth.

3. If you're using a hand blender, transfer the soaked and rinsed almonds to a wide-mouth jar that can hold up to 4 cups of liquid. Add 1 cup of water and blend on high speed until smooth. Remove the hand blender, add the remaining 2 cups of water, and continue to blend. Adding the water in stages will prevent splashing.

4. Line a strainer with a piece of cheesecloth and place the strainer over a large bowl. Pour the almond mixture into the lined strainer. Pick up the sides of the cheesecloth, forming a bag, and squeeze the "milk" out of the almond meal into a bowl.

Store the almond milk in a glass jar in the fridge. It should keep for up to a week. Reserve the almond meal for menu items including smoothies, carob banana muffins, and salmon burgers.

NUTRITION

Each one-cup serving contains:
Calories: 92
Calcium: 84 mg
Magnesium: 84 mg
Protein: 7 g

Check out how much more protein you, compared to the commercial processors, can wring out of almonds: 7 versus the 1 gram that is typical of store-bought almond milk. That said, commercial milk, which tends to be fortified with ingredients such as calcium cabonate, can contain up to three times as much calcium. If you do decide to go the carton route, be sure to always choose unsweetened. Anything else is calcium-fortified sugar water.

MENU ONE

BREAKFAST
Pudding of Champions

LUNCH
Aztec Tabbouleh in a Nest of Lettuce Leaves with White Bean
   Hummus and Root Vegetable Sticks

DINNER
Herbed Salmon Amaranth Burgers with Coleslaw

MENU TWO

BREAKFAST
Carob Banana Muffins

LUNCH
Three Sisters Chili

DINNER
Spinach–Wild Mushroom Frittata with Broccoli and Romesco Sauce

MENU THREE

BREAKFAST
Cookie Monster

LUNCH
Big Kale Salad with Tahini Lemon Dressing and Roasted Beets

DINNER
Miso Ginger Tofu Stir-fry with Gomasio

MENU FOUR

BREAKFAST
Carob Almond Smoothie

LUNCH
Mustard Greens and Black Bean Tortillas with Mole Sauce and Fresh Salsa

DINNER
Collard White Bean Soup with Crispy Sage Leaves and Garlic Baked Potato with
  Nettle Pesto

BREAKFAST

PUDDING OF CHAMPIONS

Chia seeds are a favorite of endurance athletes. Lore has it that the ancient warriors of Central America and Mexico mixed chia seeds with water to provide them with stamina. I eat this pudding every day. The flavorful combination of seeds and spices never fails to uplift the spirits. Like the Energizer Bunny, it's the breakfast that keeps you going and going and going.

MAKES 1 SERVING

2 tablespoons flaxseed
2 tablespoons chia seeds
1 heaping teaspoon cinnamon
¼ teaspoon ground dried stevia leaf*
2 whole cloves
¼ teaspoon grated nutmeg
¼ teaspoon anise seeds
1 cardamom pod
½ teaspoon orange zest
¼ inch piece of fresh ginger, cut into slivers or grated, or 1 teaspoon dried ground ginger
1 cup room-temperature, hot, or boiling water, or homemade almond milk
⅓ cup water**
sliced fruit of choice (suggestions follow)

*Look for green stevia powder that is made simply from dried, ground stevia leaves.
**Or make some of your favorite herbal tea, ginger would pair well, and use in place of all or
  part of the water.

STEPS

1. Using scissors, cut the cloves and cardamom pod into a four-cup-deep bowl. Be careful not to cut your fingers.

2. Add the remaining ingredients except for the liquid and combine with a spoon.

3. Add the one cup of hot or boiling water or almond milk. Mix with a spoon and let sit on the counter for at least 20 minutes to thicken.

4. After 20 minutes, use a hand blender on low speed to mix the contents of the bowl, adding as you do so the remaining 1/3 cup of water until you reach your desired consistency. I like the pudding on the thinner side so I add the full 1/3 cup of liquid, sometimes a little more, which I make sure is hot or boiling if it's cold out.

5. Remove the hand blender and mix in desired fruit. Try a few slices of apple for some sweet and sour crunch, a few segments of orange cut into bite-size pieces for some tangy juiciness, a few slices of banana, and a handful of fresh (or frozen and defrosted) cranberries, strawberries, and raspberries.

NUTRITION

Each serving of pudding made with one cup of homemade almond milk contains:
Calories: 285
Calcium: 314 mg
Magnesium: 266 mg
Protein: 15 g

Each serving of pudding made entirely with water contains:
Calories: 193
Calcium: 230 mg
Magnesium: 182 mg
Protein: 8 g

AZTEC TABBOULEH

The Aztecs didn't eat tabbouleh. They couldn't since they didn't have one of the dish's signature ingredients, lemon. But I bet they would have if they could have. They probably ate something close to it.

MAKES 4 SERVINGS

½ cup quinoa, rinsed

½ cup dried lentils, rinsed

2 cups water

1 cup fresh tomatoes, diced if large or halved if cherry-size

¼ cup chia seeds

½ cup chopped green onions

1 cup fresh parsley, chopped

1 tablespoon dried mint

1 garlic clove or shallot, finely chopped

½ cup fresh lemon juice

2 teaspoons grated lemon zest

2 tablespoons extra virgin olive oil

¼ teaspoon plus one pinch of sea salt

½ teaspoon freshly ground black pepper

8 to 12 whole romaine lettuce leaves, washed and dried

1 avocado, peeled and quartered

1 lemon, quartered

STEPS

1. Combine the quinoa, lentils, and water in a medium-size pot over high heat. Add the pinch of salt and bring to a boil. Reduce the heat to medium-low and simmer, covered, for 15 minutes. Turn off the heat and let sit covered for another 5 minutes, or until all the water is absorbed. Uncover, stir, and set aside to cool.

2. In a large bowl combine the lentil-quinoa mixture, tomatoes, and chia seeds.

3. In a small bowl combine the green onions, herbs, garlic, lemon juice and zest, olive oil, salt, and pepper into a dressing.

4. Pour the dressing over the lentil-quinoa-chia-seed mix and season to taste with salt and pepper.

Divide the lettuce leaves among four plates. Spoon the tabbouleh on top. Garnish with a quarter of an avocado, sliced, a lemon wedge, and a drizzle of extra virgin olive oil. Serve with White Bean Hummus (p. 191) and Root Vegetable Sticks (p. 193).

NUTRITION

Each serving of tabbouleh contains:

Calories: 235

Calcium: 147 mg

Magnesium: 122 mg

Protein: 11 g

A quarter of a Hass avocado adds to each serving:

Calories: 81

Calcium: 6 mg

Magnesium: 15 mg

Protein: 1 g

WHITE BEAN HUMMUS

Everybody knows that beans and grains make a perfect protein. Fewer know that beans and seeds do, too. Hence the nutritional sensibility of the tahini-bean combination that makes hummus hummus.

Besides being sensible, hummus is wonderfully versatile. Add a couple of tablespoons of cider vinegar or lemon juice to a couple of tablespoons of hummus and you have a dressing for a salad or steamed vegetables.

MAKES 2½ CUPS

2 cloves garlic, peeled and minced

2½ tablespoons olive oil

½ teaspoon ground cumin

3 tablespoons lemon juice

2 cups canned white beans, drained and rinsed

3 tablespoons tahini (sesame paste)

¼ teaspoon sea salt

1 tablespoon water

STEPS

1. In a food processor, blend together garlic, olive oil, cumin, and lemon juice.

2. Add white beans, tahini, salt, and water and continue to blend until smooth. For a thinner consistency, add an extra teaspoon or two of water.

Spoon onto Big Kale Salad (p. 212). Or for a snack scoop into a bowl, then sprinkle with paprika and either Za'atar (p. 192) or toasted sesame seeds, drizzle with olive oil, and serve with raw vegetables.

NUTRITION

Each 2-tablespoon serving contains:

Calories: 78

Calcium: 29 mg

Magnesium: 27 mg

Protein: 3 g

One tablespoon of toasted sesame seeds per serving adds:

Calories: 52

Calcium: 88 mg

Magnesium: 32 mg

Protein: 2 g

ZA'ATAR

Brings the taste of the Middle East to something as basic and all-American as a baked potato.

MAKES ⅓ CUP

4 tablespoons dried ground thyme
2 teaspoons dried ground sumac
1 teaspoon dried ground oregano
1 tablespoon toasted sesame seeds
¼ teaspoon sea salt

STEPS
In a small bowl combine all the ingredients.

Store in an airtight container un-refrigerated for up to one month.

NUTRITION
Each tablespoon contains:
Calories: 22
Calcium: 96 mg
Magnesium: 15 mg
Protein: 1 g

ROOT VEGETABLE STICKS

There's more to root vegetables than carrots and potatoes. It's hard not to fall for the crisp texture and flavor of kohlrabi, which is reminiscent of jicama only less waxy and fruity, or a fiery radish, or a perfectly balanced sweet and mildly spicy turnip. If you're lucky enough to find any among this group of roots with their heads of greens intact, don't throw them out. Cut them off, bag them, and store them in the fridge for a stir-fry or soup or for making a dinner fundamental, a bed of steamed greens. If you haven't tried carrot tops you're in for a pleasant surprise. They're very fragrant, even more "carroty" than their lower bodies.

MAKES 1 SERVING OF HUMMUS DIPSTICKS

4 large radishes (about 1½ ounces), washed and cut into one- to two-inch long sticks
1 small turnip (about 2 ounces) scrubbed and cut into two-inch long sticks
½ medium kohlrabi (3½ ounces), peeled, or not—I don't bother—stems trimmed (reserve for making soup stock) and cut into 2-inch-long sticks
1 medium carrot (about 2 ounces), scrubbed and cut into 2-inch-long sticks

NUTRITION

Four large radishes contain:
Calories: 4
Calcium: 9 mg
Magnesium: 4 mg
Protein: 0.4 g

3½ ounces of kohlrabi contains:
Calories: 27
Calcium: 24 mg
Magnesium: 19 mg
Protein: 2 g

One small turnip contains:
Calories: 17
Calcium: 18 mg
Magnesium: 7 mg
Protein: 0.5 g

One medium carrot contains:
Calories: 25
Calcium: 20 mg
Magnesium: 7 mg
Protein: 1 g

HERBED SALMON AMARANTH BURGERS

Unless salmon is really fresh, like the salmon that my grandfather and Uncle Ian used to bring back with them from their fly-fishing trips to the Bonaventure River in the Gaspé Peninsula, canned salmon is a good bet. First, it's almost always wild, in part because farmed salmon is too fatty to can easily. Second, it tastes better than most "fresh" wild salmon, which usually isn't. Third, unlike "fresh" wild salmon, it's affordable. Fourth, you can eat the bones, which are a great source of calcium. I like the crunch, but if you don't, you can mash them up so you don't notice them.

This recipe is inspired by a dinner that Helena, my parents' Swedish friend, improvised one evening when she was teen-sitting me. Comfort food.

MAKES 8 BURGERS

2 15-ounce cans of salmon

2 large eggs

1 medium sweet potato, baked, peeled, and mashed*

½ cup ground almonds (or half a cup of the almond meal left over from making the almond milk)

3 tablespoons fresh parsley, chopped fine

2 teaspoons dried dill

2 tablespoons onion, finely chopped

2 teaspoons fresh lemon juice

½ teaspoon sea salt

1 teaspoon ground cumin

1 teaspoon ground paprika

1 teaspoon ground black pepper

½ cup cooked amaranth**

2 tablespoons of olive oil for sautéing

STEPS

1. Drain the canned salmon and discard the liquid. (Or give it to a furry friend. I mix the liquid into my dog, Dixi's, dinner. She loves it.) If you don't like the texture of the bones, break them down using a fork or your hands. Use your hands to squeeze any remaining liquid out of the salmon and transfer the salmon to a large bowl.

2. Crack the eggs into the bowl with the salmon. Add all remaining ingredients, except for the oil. Stir well with your hands or a wooden spoon.

3. Line a plate with parchment or waxed paper. Form the mixture into 8 burgers. Place them on the plate and refrigerate for at least 30 minutes and up to 8 hours.

4. Remove the plate from the fridge and pat the burgers dry with a paper towel.

5. Heat the oil in a large skillet over medium-high heat until hot but not smoking. Working in two batches, carefully add burgers to the pan and cook until golden brown and cooked through, about 3 minutes per side.

6. Transfer burgers to a paper-towel–lined plate and serve immediately or keep warm in an oven set at 250°F.

*To bake the sweet potato, preheat oven or toaster oven to 425°F. While your oven is already on, why not roast some beets for a lunch salad, too. Scrub the potato and a couple of average-size beets (about 7 ounces) under running water. Trim away any sprouts or green spots on the potato and any dark spots on the beets. Slit the top of the potato with a shallow stroke of the knife and rub the beets with a little olive oil. Place everything on a baking sheet and bake until the potato and the beets are soft when pierced with a knife and some of the sweet potato's sugars begin to caramelize onto the tray, 50 to 60 minutes. Don't worry about overcooking. The longer the potato and beets cook, the more their natural sugars will caramelize. When done, remove the potato and the beets from the oven and allow to cool. When cool, scrape out the insides of the potato for the salmon burgers and store the potato skins and the beets separately—if stored together, the beets will stain the sweet potato skins red—in the refrigerator. (Toast the skins on a tray in a toaster oven until dark and crunchy, about 5 minutes, for a snack or as a side to go with Menu Two's Three Sisters Chili.)

**To cook the amaranth, pour a cup of water into a small pot. Add 1/3 cup of amaranth seeds and a pinch of salt and bring to a boil. Reduce the heat to medium-low and simmer, covered, for 15 minutes. Turn off the heat and let sit covered for another 5 minutes, or until all the water is absorbed. Uncover, stir, and set aside to cool. Makes 1/2 to 2/3 cup of cooked amaranth. If there's extra, freeze for another occasion or refrigerate to eat with soup, chili, stir-fry, or mixed into breakfast pudding or into a smoothie as a protein-rich thickener.

Serve salmon burgers with coleslaw (p. 197) and condiments: Dijon or seed mustard; nettle pesto (p. 231); or extra tofu mayo (p. 198). All go nicely.

Once the burgers have cooled, you can freeze any uneaten ones in a ziplock freezer bag. When you want a quick meal, remove from freezer, let defrost in the fridge in a glass container for a few hours, then reheat in a 250°F oven.

NUTRITION

Each salmon burger contains:

Calories: 250

Calcium: 300 mg

Magnesium: 70 mg

Protein: 26 g

COLESLAW

No reason not to have seconds of this twist on the side dish that asks you to exercise portion control when made the usual way.

MAKES 2 ONE-CUP SERVINGS

1 cup thinly sliced red cabbage*
½ cup grated carrot
1 green onion, thinly sliced
2 tablespoons fresh parsley, roughly chopped
1 tablespoon fresh dill, finely chopped
3 tablespoons tofu mayo (p. 198)
1 teaspoon lemon juice
¼ teaspoon sea salt

Green cabbage will work, too.

STEPS

Combine all ingredients in a medium-size bowl and toss until evenly coated. The longer it sits the softer and more flavorful it will become.

Serve with salmon burgers (p. 194).

NUTRITION

Each 1-cup serving contains:
Calories: 63
Calcium: 34 mg
Magnesium: 19.2 mg
Protein: 1.6 g

TOFU MAYO

Take mayonnaise, subtract the cholesterol and saturated fat, keep the delicate flavor and creamy texture, add protein, and you have yourself this take on a traditional condiment. Once you try it, you're going to want to be sure you always have some on hand.

MAKES ½ CUP OF MAYO

3½ ounces silken tofu*
½ teaspoon apple cider vinegar
½ teaspoon Dijon mustard
1 tablespoon olive oil
¼ teaspoon sea salt

Ming Yu, the farmer at my market who makes tofu from scratch says that if you want to eat tofu the way it was originally made in China, it should be prepared with nigari, which is essentially magnesium chloride, a derivative of sea salt that acts as a coagulant. Packaged tofu made this way, with nigari or magnesium chloride, is not hard to find. Read the label and look for either one of these ingredients.

STEPS
Place all ingredients in a 2-cup wide-mouth jar. Using a hand blender, blend on low until creamy. Alternatively, combine all ingredients in a large bowl and whisk quickly until smooth.

NUTRITION
Each 2-tablespoon serving contains:
Calories: 50
Calcium: 8 mg
Magnesium: 7 mg
Protein: 2 g

BREAKFAST

CAROB BANANA MUFFINS

My mum used to talk about how she ate cake for breakfast as proof of her unhealthy beginnings. Maybe you fantasize about having cake for breakfast and eating it guilt-free, too. These muffins, which are like crumbly cake in a different shape, are your and every child's dream come true.

MAKES 12 MUFFINS

¼ cup coconut oil

¼ cup carob powder

¼ cup chia seeds

¼ cup plus two tablespoons water

¾ cup ground almonds (or almond meal from the almond milk)

¼ cup sesame seeds

1 tablespoon cinnamon

¼ cup unsweetened dried coconut, ground

½ teaspoon baking powder

2 small ripe bananas, peeled (about 3½ ounces each after peeling)

1 tablespoon vanilla extract

¼ cup olive oil

½ teaspoon salt

¼ cup walnut pieces

STEPS

Preheat oven to 350°F.

1. Grease a 12-cup muffin pan.

2. If the coconut oil is hard, place the jar in a bowl of hot water until it liquefies.

3. In a mixing bowl combine the coconut oil and carob powder until smooth.

4. Spread the mixture onto a piece of parchment paper and freeze until set, about fifteen minutes.

5. In a small bowl mix the chia seeds with the water and let sit for ten minutes, until goopy.

6. Remove the hardened carob–coconut oil mixture from the freezer and break into quarter-inch chunks with your hands.

7. In a medium-size bowl mix the almond meal, sesame seeds, cinnamon, ground coconut, and baking powder.

8. In a larger bowl, mash the bananas with the vanilla, chia-seed mixture, olive oil, and salt. Add the almond-meal mixture and stir until combined. Fold in the walnuts and carob–coconut-oil chunks.

9. Divide the batter evenly among the 12 muffin cups and bake the muffins for 16 to 18 minutes, until they are golden brown and a toothpick inserted into their centers comes out clean.

Allow to cool for 10 minutes before removing from muffin tin. Serve with a cup of homemade almond milk.

Store in the fridge for up to a week or in a ziplock freezer bag in the freezer.

NUTRITION

Each muffin contains:	One cup of homemade almond milk complements the muffin with:
Calories: 124	Calories: 92
Calcium: 88 mg	Calcium: 84 mg
Magnesium: 51 mg	Magnesium: 84 mg
Protein: 3 g	Protein: 7 g

THREE SISTERS CHILI

In the good old days when McDonalds didn't rule the Americas, the three sisters—corn, beans, and squash—did. This chili honors the wisdom of the sisterhood that has been buried by the bullshit of factory farming.

MAKES 6 SERVINGS

2 cups dried black beans

8 cups water plus 5 cups water for soaking the dried beans

2 tablespoons olive oil

1 medium onion, finely chopped

3 cloves garlic, peeled and minced

1½ tablespoons chili powder

1 teaspoon ground cumin

1 tablespoon dried ground oregano

½ teaspoon chili flakes

1 cup butternut squash (five ounces), scrubbed and cubed*

1 cup green peppers, washed, seeded, and chopped

1 teaspoon sea salt

1 18-ounce (or 16-ounce if that's all you can find) can of tomatoes**

1 cup frozen corn kernels

2 tablespoons apple cider vinegar, divided

¼ cup chopped scallions or cilantro

desired amount of tangy tofu cream

toasted pumpkin seeds for garnish

*Leave the skin on. It's thin and contains many nutrients.

**I follow my mum's advice and always choose the cans of "whole" tomatoes. They retain more of their flavor. You can either break them up with your hands as you add them to the chili or with a spoon as you stir. However, if you prefer a more uniform consistency, buy the tomatoes "chopped" or "crushed."

STEPS

1. Rinse beans and place in a pot with 5 cups of water. Cover and soak overnight un-refrigerated.

2. When ready to make the soup, drain beans and rinse again. Set aside.

3. In a large saucepan, or Dutch oven, heat oil over medium high heat. Add onion and garlic and cook, stirring occasionally, until onion is translucent, 3 to 5 minutes.

4. Add chili powder, cumin, oregano, and chili flakes. Cook, stirring often, until spices begin to brown, 2 to 3 minutes.

5. Add the beans, squash, and green peppers. Stir to coat with the spices. Add the water and salt and bring to a boil. Reduce to a simmer and cook covered until the beans are tender, about 50 minutes.

6. Add the tomatoes with their juice, the corn, and half the vinegar. Bring to a boil, reduce to a rapid simmer, and cook uncovered until chili is thick, about 10 minutes, stirring every few minutes to makes sure chili isn't sticking to the bottom of the pot. Just before turning off the heat mix in the remaining tablespoon of vinegar.

Ladle into four bowls and top with tangy tofu cream (p. 203), chopped scallions or cilantro, and toasted pumpkin seeds. If you have sweet-potato skins in the fridge, now's the time to use them. Toast in a toaster oven for about 5 minutes until crisp and eat with the chili.

The flavor of the chili will improve with time. Store in the refrigerator for a few days. You can also freeze it in a large glass container or in a few smaller single-serve containers. To defrost, leave the container overnight in the refrigerator on a plate to hold the water that the container will sweat. For a quicker defrost, remove the container from the freezer and place in a sink partially filled with cold water. When the contents are soft enough to cut into, take out the amount you want, place in a pot, and reheat on low on your stovetop. I refreeze what I don't reheat, but it's probably best to refrigerate the remainders and eat within a few days.

NUTRITION
A sixth of the chili, about 2 cups, without toppings, contains:
Calories: 295
Calcium: 125 mg
Magnesium: 135 mg
Protein: 17 g

TANGY TOFU CREAM

Limes are miraculous. Case in point. They turn silken tofu into a perfect substitute for sour cream.

MAKES ½ CUP

3½ ounces silken tofu
1 teaspoon lime juice
½ teaspoon lime zest
1 tablespoon olive oil
¼ teaspoon sea salt
½ teaspoon paprika, optional

STEPS

Combine all ingredients in a 2-cup bowl. Using a hand blender, blend until smooth. Add ½ teaspoon paprika if desired.

NUTRITION

Each 2-tablespoon serving contains:
Calories: 50
Calcium: 8 mg
Magnesium: 6 mg
Protein: 2 g

SPINACH–WILD MUSHROOM FRITTATA

Before I grew old enough to make my own breakfast and lunch and cook for others, my mum, an excellent cook, took care of the meals. Except when it came to eggs. Then my dad was in charge. His years spent in Paris taught him a lot, including how best to cook eggs. I learned from him that omelets are best eaten *baveuse*, or slightly runny, and that frittatas should be left to cook on their own. This one's for you, Dad.

MAKES 6 SERVINGS

1 cup dried wild mushrooms

1 cup boiling water

12 large eggs

1 tablespoon olive oil

½ cup diced onion

4 cups raw spinach, washed

½ cup flat-leaf parsley, chopped

4 basil leaves, chopped

¼ teaspoon salt

1 teaspoon cracked black pepper

STEPS

1. In a small glass bowl, cover the dried mushrooms with one cup of boiling water and soak for 20 minutes until mushrooms are soft and rehydrated.

2. When rehydrated, remove the mushrooms and keep the soaking water. Wring any extra moisture out of the mushrooms, and cut into ¼-inch slices. Strain the mushroom water to remove grit.

3. Crack the eggs into a large bowl and set aside.

4. (Optional) Wash eggshells with hot water and store in a container in the fridge for making eggshell calcium powder.

5. Heat the oil in a heavy ovenproof skillet over medium heat.

6. Add onion and sauté until translucent, 3 to 4 minutes.

7. Add the mushrooms, spinach, and herbs, and continue sautéing until the spinach wilts, another 3 to 5 minutes. Turn off the heat.

8. Turn on the oven broiler.

9. Whisk the eggs with ½ cup of the mushroom water and the salt and pepper.

10. Return the skillet with the spinach, mushrooms, and onions to medium-low heat.

11. Pour the eggs into the skillet over the cooked vegetables. Cook until the edges of the eggs have set, about 3 minutes. The eggs should still be a bit wet.

12. Remove the skillet from the stove and place under the broiler until the top is golden brown.

13. Remove from the broiler and allow to cool for 15 minutes before slicing.

Serve warm with steamed broccoli (p. 208) and Romesco sauce (p. 206). Refrigerate any frittata leftovers for a quick and easy cold meal.

NUTRITION

Each 1/6 portion of the frittata contains:
Calories: 213
Calcium: 35 mg
Magnesium: 19 mg
Protein: 6 g

ROMESCO SAUCE

Fisher folk are a resourceful lot. They have a lot of good ideas, especially when it comes to baiting picky eaters. Smother a big plate of steamed vegetables with this sauce from the shores of northeastern Spain and you'll be on your way to converting the most pigheaded vegetable denier—we all know at least one or two—into an evangelist in short order.

MAKES 6 SERVINGS

2 large red bell peppers
2 plum tomatoes, cut in half lengthwise
4 cloves garlic, unpeeled
¼ cup olive oil, divided
½ cup almonds plus ten for garnish
1 tablespoon apple cider vinegar
1½ teaspoons paprika
¼ teaspoon salt
3 tablespoons flat-leaf parsley, chopped

STEPS
Preheat oven to 375°F.

1. Line a baking sheet with parchment paper.

2. Place the whole peppers, unpeeled garlic cloves, and the tomatoes, cut-side down, on the baking sheet and rub everything with one tablespoon of olive oil. Cook for one hour on a middle rack, turning peppers every 20 minutes to make sure all sides cook evenly.

3. While the peppers, tomatoes, and garlic are cooking, spread the almonds in a single layer on a separate baking sheet. Place in the oven on the top rack above the one with the vegetables and toast for 8 to 10 minutes, until slightly darkened. Remove from the oven and let cool.

4. After one hour the peppers should be soft and have black patches on their skins. Turn the oven off, remove the peppers, tomatoes, and garlic, and transfer them to a large bowl. Cover with a plate for 20 to 30 minutes. The steam will help release the pepper skins.

5. Remove the plate and, using your hands, remove the tomato and pepper skins. Discard the skins or reserve for soup stock.

6. One by one, open the peppers over a plate or sink, and remove and discard the seeds. The peppers will have hot liquid inside, so be careful. Return the peppers to the bowl with the tomatoes and garlic.

7. Remove the garlic cloves from the bowl one at a time and squeeze their contents into a food processor. Discard the peels. Add the remaining oil, the ½ cup of almonds, the tablespoon of vinegar, the paprika, and the salt to the garlic and blend until smooth.

8. Add the roasted peppers and tomatoes with their juices to the food processor and blend again until smooth.

Serve warm or at room temperature over steamed broccoli (p. 208). Garnish with the toasted almonds and the chopped flat-leaf parsley.

NUTRITION
Each ½-cup serving contains:
Calories: 220
Calcium: 45 mg
Magnesium: 47mg
Protein: 5 g

STEAMED BROCCOLI

I love broccoli. Cooked just right it turns from a dull to a robust bright green. Even little ones find the trees cooked just so irresistible. I've had the pleasure of witnessing the budding love affair between plant and young animal on more than one occasion.

MAKES 4 SERVINGS

4 pounds broccoli (3 big bunches)*
½ cup water

A pound per person may sound like a lot, but if it's your only vegetable for dinner and it's next to a bowl of Romesco sauce, pesto, or tahini lemon dressing, you'll wonder where the broccoli disappeared to so fast.

STEPS

1. Wash the broccoli and peel the bottoms of the stems if tough.

2. Cut the stems into one-inch rounds.

3. Slice the broccoli tops in half.

4. Place the water, then the broccoli stems, then the broccoli tops in a large pot, cover, and bring to a boil.

5. Once the water boils and you see steam escaping from the pot, turn the heat off. Let the pot sit on the stove covered for 2½ minutes.

6. Remove the lid and pierce the broccoli stems and tops with a knife. The broccoli should be deep green and firm yet easily pierced. Using tongs, remove all done pieces onto a plate. Return the lid and allow any undercooked pieces to rest in the pot until done. The broccoli will continue to cook in the hot water without additional heat.

7. Once all the broccoli is done, pour any liquid that's left in the pot into a mug and drink immediately for a nutritious pre-dinner tonic.

NUTRITION
Each serving contains:
Calories: 153
Calcium: 212 mg

Magnesium: 96 mg
Protein: 13 g

BREAKFAST

COOKIE MONSTER

If you're alone in the kitchen when you begin baking, you might not be when the cookie's ready to come out of the oven. I never need help cleaning up the crumbs of this monster.

MAKES ABOUT 2½ POUNDS OF COOKIE, OR GRANOLA DEPENDING ON HOW YOU BREAK AND EAT IT

½ cup raisins*

1 cup raw almonds

½ cup hazelnuts or filberts

3 cups rolled oats

1 cup raw sunflower seeds

1 cup raw pumpkin seeds

¼ cup sesame seeds

¼ cup chia seeds

2 tablespoons ground flaxseeds

2 tablespoons cinnamon

½ teaspoon ground or grated nutmeg

½ teaspoon allspice

¼ teaspoon sea salt

1 tablespoon eggshell powder (optional, p. 211)

½ teaspoon vanilla extract

1 cup apple cider

Depending on how sweet your tooth is, leave the raisins out or add a whole cup rather than ½ cup.

STEPS

Preheat oven to 375°F.

1. Soak raisins in ½ cup of boiling water for 15 minutes.

2. Chop almonds and hazelnuts.

3. Combine all the dry ingredients in a large mixing bowl.

4. Add the vanilla, apple cider, and the raisins with their soaking water to the dry ingredients and mix with a wooden spoon until combined. If there are any dry spots, add enough water so that the entire mixture is wet.

5. Dump the contents of the bowl onto a 15-by-21-inch greased baking sheet, or the largest baking sheet you have.

6. Using a fork, flatten the mixture onto the baking sheet so that it covers the entire sheet. Use two sheets, or bake in two batches if you don't have one large one. Dip the fork in a bowl of ice-cold water every so often to prevent the cookie from sticking to the fork.

7. Bake for 50 to 60 minutes or until golden brown.

8. Remove the baking sheet from the oven and, using a metal spatula, transfer the cookie to a large cooling rack. You can try to keep it as one giant cookie. I *have* succeeded, but don't be discouraged if it breaks into pieces as you transfer.

Once cool, transfer to a cookie jar or freeze in a ziplock freezer bag. The cookie/granola is even good straight from the freezer.

Eat on the go or smashed in a bowl with homemade almond milk.

NUTRITION

Each 3½-ounce serving with eggshell powder contains:

Calories: 405

Calcium: 324 mg

Magnesium: 165 mg

Protein: 14 g

Each 3½-ounce serving without eggshell powder contains:

Calories: 405

Calcium: 124 mg

Magnesium: 159 mg

Protein: 14 g

Bonus: the cookie recipe can also be used as topping for apple crisp (p. 211).

EASY APPLE CRISP

Core and slice four apples with their nutrient-packed skins into a baking dish. Add a handful of cranberries, fresh or frozen, ¼ cup of apple cider, one tablespoon of lemon juice, and one teaspoon of cinnamon. Combine with your hands and cover with 1 to 2 cups of uncooked cookie mixture. Bake in a 375°F oven for 50 minutes, or until top is golden brown and fruit is bubbling.

EGGSHELL CALCIUM POWDER

Don't just save your eggshells for the garden. They're good for you, too.

12 eggshells   1 cookie sheet

1 pot of water   1 coffee grinder

STEPS

Preheat oven to 200°F.

1. Wash the eggshells.

2. Bring the pot of water to a boil. Carefully submerge the shells in the boiling water and allow to cook for 10 minutes to sterilize the eggshells.

3. Using a slotted spoon, transfer the shells from the pot to a cookie sheet and dry in the 200°F oven for 10 minutes.

4. Once the shells are dry, turn off the oven, remove the sheet from the oven, and crush the shells into small pieces with your hands.

5. Transfer the pieces, in batches, to the coffee grinder. Grind the shells into a powder and store in an airtight container away from heat and light.

NUTRITION

One teaspoon of eggshell powder contains:

Calcium: 800 mg

Magnesium: 2 mg

BIG KALE SALAD

One bone-building bowl of salad coming up.

MAKES 1 SERVING

1 medium-size roasted beet (3½ ounces raw), cut into wedges*

3 cups raw chopped kale

¼ teaspoon sea salt

1 tablespoon dried ground basil

1 teaspoon dried ground oregano

1 small carrot (2 ounces), washed, scrubbed, and grated on the large holes of a box grater

½ small zucchini (2 ounces), washed and grated on the large holes of a box grater

¼ cup fresh parsley, dill, or a mixture of the two

1 cup chopped fresh tomato

2 tablespoons chia seeds

2 tablespoons raw or roasted pumpkin seeds (optional)

2 tablespoons tahini lemon dressing (p. 214) or herb vinaigrette (p. 215)

See salmon burger recipe for roasting directions. If you don't have roasted beets on hand, substitute ½ cup of grated raw beets.

STEPS

1. Wash the kale; cut off the stems and set them aside.

2. Cut the raw kale leaves into ½-inch strips and transfer to a medium-to-large serving bowl.

3. Add the sea salt, dried basil, and oregano, and rub into the kale until the kale begins to break down. It will turn from pale green to darker green and begin to release some of its water.

4. Cut the kale stems into thin slices and add to the serving bowl. Add all the remaining ingredients except the chia seeds and toss.

5. Sprinkle the chia seeds on top.

Serve with dressing of choice (see recipes for tahini lemon dressing and herb vinaigrette that follow), a handful of raw or toasted pumpkin seeds, and a scoop of white bean hummus.

NUTRITION

Each undressed salad with roasted beets contains:

Calories: 306

Calcium: 675 mg

Magnesium: 298 mg

Protein: 20 g

TAHINI LEMON DRESSING

Tahini, lemon, and garlic: a great way to dress any vegetable, roasted or raw.

MAKES 1½ CUPS PLUS 3 TABLESPOONS (27 TABLESPOONS TOTAL)

1 clove garlic, peeled and finely chopped
¾ cup water
¾ cup tahini
2 tablespoons lemon juice
scant ½ teaspoon sea salt
1 tablespoon toasted sesame seeds

STEPS
Combine all ingredients in a large bowl. Using a hand blender, blend on a low setting until smooth. Alternatively, place all ingredients in a food processor and blend until smooth.

NUTRITION
Each 2-tablespoon serving contains:
Calories: 69
Calcium: 53 mg
Magnesium: 6 mg
Protein: 2 g

HERB VINAIGRETTE

My mum spent years trying to convince my dad to give up his conviction that he acquired while living in Paris that 3:1 is the proper oil to acid ratio for a vinaigrette. My mum perferred closer to 1:1. So do I, as reflected in this recipe. Whether or not you choose to emphasize the "vinaigre" in vinaigrette, the vinaigrette is a perfect medium for dried herbs, many of which, such as the ones featured in this recipe, contain more calcium by weight than cow's milk.

MAKES 2½ CUPS

¼ cup apple cider vinegar

½ cup plus 1 tablespoon lemon juice

scant ½ teaspoon sea salt

¼ teaspoon cracked black pepper

¾ cup plus 2 tablespoons extra virgin olive oil

1 tablespoon fennel seeds, toasted in a dry skillet until fragrant

1 tablespoon mustard seeds, toasted with the fennel seeds

¼ cup fresh parsley, finely chopped

¼ cup fresh mint, finely chopped

1 small scallion (3 inches long), including tops and bulbs, roughly chopped

1 tablespoon dried ground basil

1 tablespoon dried ground thyme

1 tablespoon dried ground sage

1 teaspoon dried ground oregano

1 teaspoon lemon zest

1 teaspoon orange zest

STEPS

In a 3-cup bowl combine vinegar, lemon juice, salt, and pepper. Add remaining ingredients and whisk with a small spoon.

NUTRITION

Each 2-tablespoon serving contains:

Calories: 85

Calcium: 19 mg

Magnesium: 6 mg

For a calcium- and protein-packed quick snack, mash a couple of tablespoons of this dressing with a few canned sardines—look for water-packed sardines that are not smoked—and sandwich between 2 lettuce leaves.

MISO GINGER TOFU STIR-FRY

Miso, a fermented bean- and grain-based paste, brings this dish, and your gut, alive.

MAKES 4 SERVINGS

½ cup dried shiitake or morel mushrooms

½ cup boiling water

4 generous teaspoons brown rice miso

1 cup cilantro, chopped

2 limes, zested and juiced

2 tablespoons apple cider vinegar

3 tablespoons olive oil, divided

1 14-ounce package extra-firm tofu,
    drained, cut into half-inch slices, and
    patted dry with paper towels*

1 small onion, sliced into thin crescents

1 clove garlic, peeled and squeezed through
    a garlic press if you have one, or sliced if
    you don't

2 inches fresh ginger, peeled and minced

4 fresh shiitake mushrooms, sliced thin

1 head broccoli, cut into 1- to 2-inch pieces

16 leaves (stalks intact) bok choy (also
    known as pak choi), washed, stacked,
    and sliced horizontally into ¼-inch strips

1 small red pepper, seeds and stem
    removed, quartered, then thinly sliced
    lengthwise

1 cup frozen green peas

¼ teaspoon toasted sesame oil, optional

4 cups raw dandelion greens and stems
    (7½ ounces), washed and shredded
    (you can substitute mustard greens or
    spinach)**

For a chewier, meatier texture, freeze the tofu slices and thaw before cooking.

**Dandelion greens were originally brought to North America for eating rather than weeding.*

STEPS

1. In a small bowl, cover the dried mushrooms with the half cup of boiling water and soak for 20 minutes, until mushrooms are soft and rehydrated. Keeping the soaking water, remove the mushrooms, wring any extra moisture out of them, and cut into quarter inch slices.

2. In a small bowl combine the miso paste, mushroom water (strained if gritty), cilantro, lime juice and zest, and vinegar.

3. Heat 2 tablespoons olive oil in a heavy, preferably cast-iron, skillet (it should have a lid, which you will need later) over medium-high heat until hot but not smoking. Sauté tofu slices for 2 minutes per side and transfer to a paper-towel–lined plate.

4. Return skillet to medium heat. Add the remaining tablespoon of olive oil and sauté onion, garlic, and ginger for 2 minutes.

5. Add the mushrooms, broccoli, bok choy, red pepper, and green peas. Cover and cook for 3 to 5 minutes, until broccoli is tender.

6. Turn off the heat and add the miso sauce and tofu. Toss until the tofu is warmed through.*

7. Stir in ¼ teaspoon toasted sesame oil if desired.

*Miso is a fermented food and therefore, for optimal nutrition, should not be cooked. Be sure the heat is turned off before adding the sauce.

Divide the dandelion greens among four plates. Top each plate with a quarter of the stir-fry. Garnish with Gomasio (p. 218) or toasted sesame seeds.

NUTRITION
Each plate, including one cup of shredded dandelion greens, contains:
Calories: 197
Calcium: 343 mg
Magnesium: 82 mg
Protein: 13 g

One tablespoon of Gomasio per serving adds:
Calories: 52
Calcium: 88 mg
Magnesium: 32 mg
Protein: 2 g

GOMASIO

Gomasio adds a burst of umami to anything you choose to sprinkle it on, whether a bowl of quinoa , a stir-fry, or some hot, freshly popped corn.

2 cups raw unhulled sesame seeds
1 teaspoon sea salt
1 strip kombu seaweed, 6 inches by 1 inch

STEPS

1. Heat a cast-iron skillet to medium-high heat and lightly toast the salt and kombu until the salt turns a light gray color.

2. Remove the kombu, let cool and then break into pieces and return to the pan.

3. Add the sesame seeds and toast for another 6 to 8 minutes, stirring constantly until the seeds are golden brown.

4. Remove from heat, transfer to a bowl, and allow to cool.

5. Once the sesame seeds and kombu are cool, place them in a coffee grinder and grind to the consistency of cornmeal.

Store in an airtight container unrefrigerated for up to one month.

NUTRITION

Each tablespoon contains:

Calories: 52   Magnesium: 32 mg
Calcium: 88 mg   Protein: 2 g

For an easy snack, sprinkle Gomasio on steamed edamame. Buy the edamame frozen and follow directions for cooking. One cup of frozen edamame without Gomasio contains:

Calories: 130   Magnesium: 72 mg
Calcium: 71 mg   Protein: 12 g

BREAKFAST

CAROB ALMOND SMOOTHIE

They call it "silken" for a reason.

MAKES 2 SERVINGS

1 small banana, frozen*

1 tablespoon carob powder

1 cup homemade almond milk

3 tablespoons silken tofu

½ teaspoon vanilla extract

1 tablespoon almond butter

1 tablespoon chia seeds

2 tablespoons frozen blueberries or other berries (optional)

To freeze bananas, peel and cut into half-inch rounds. Transfer to a ziplock freezer bag and freeze. The pieces will stick together but are easy to separate with a knife. Straight from the freezer they're like bites of ice cream, a perfect after-dinner sweet.

STEPS

In a 4-cup jar, combine all ingredients and blend on medium high with a hand blender until smooth. You can also make this smoothie in a standard upright blender.

NUTRITION

Each 1-cup serving without berries contains:

Calories: 160

Calcium: 185 mg

Magnesium: 84 mg

Protein: 4 g

MUSTARD GREENS AND
BLACK BEAN TORTILLAS

I would never be so foolhardy as to imagine I could recreate Oaxaca street food in my kitchen. I lack the proper ingredients, heat sources, and, most of all, the innate know-how. If you're ever in Oaxaca City, take a trip to the market, where you'll find stalls serving up handmade corn tortillas with zucchini flowers. You'll have to suspend your disbelief in the magic of simplicity to believe the experience will change you forever. It's hard to imagine anyone being angry after tasting such a delicacy.

Cue the dreams of bright colors, hot and dusty streets, and the evanescent taste of plants in full splendor.

MAKES 1 SERVING

1 teaspoon olive oil

¼ small onion, thinly sliced

2 cups mustard greens, washed and shredded

1 pinch of salt

½ cup canned black beans, drained and rinsed

3 tablespoons mole sauce (p. 222)

2 6-inch lime-treated corn tortillas*

2 tablespoons cilantro, finely chopped

¼ avocado, sliced

Lime-treated tortillas have more calcium.

STEPS

1. In a medium-size skillet heat the olive oil over low heat and add the onion. Stirring occasionally, cook until translucent, about ten minutes.

2. Turn the heat to medium high and add the mustard greens and pinch of salt to the skillet. Stir occasionally until the greens are wilted. Remove the onions and greens from the skillet and set aside.

3. Add the beans and mole sauce to the skillet. Turn the heat to low and heat until warm.

4. While beans are warming, place a small skillet on medium-high heat. Add the tortillas to the dry hot skillet for thirty to forty-five seconds per side, until softened and warm.

5. Remove tortillas and arrange on a plate. Divide the beans and greens between the two tortillas and garnish with fresh cilantro and sliced avocado.

Serve with fresh salsa (p. 224) and tangy tofu cream (p. 203).

NUTRITION

Each 2-tortilla serving with a quarter of an avocado contains:

Calories: 418

Calcium: 276 mg

Magnesium: 134 mg

Protein: 18 g

MOLE SAUCE

Cacao deserves to be made into so much more than sweet chocolate.

MAKES 1 CUP

1 tablespoon olive oil

5 tablespoons (1/3 cup) finely chopped onion

1 tablespoon chopped garlic

1 teaspoon dried ground oregano

½ teaspoon ground cumin

1 pinch ground cinnamon

1 tablespoon chili powder

1 tablespoon ground almonds

1½ cups water

1 teaspoon raw cocoa powder*

1 teaspoon raisins soaked in one tablespoon warm water

¼ teaspoon sea salt

Most cocoa powder that is not raw has been Dutch-processed, which means an alkalizing agent such as potassium bromate or potassium carbonate is used to reduce the bitterness and darken the color. The process also reduces the nutritional content, specifically the levels of phytonutrients that make cacao the wonder food that it is. I have found that alkalizing agents aren't always listed as an ingredient, so unless you buy raw, or unless the label specifically states that the powder has not been Dutch-processed, it's hard to know.

Remember that cacao contains oxalic acid, which inhibits your body's uptake of calcium, so best not to make a habit of using large amounts of cacao in combination with calcium-rich foods. However, no need to worry here. This recipe, which only contains one teaspoon of cocoa powder per cup of sauce, won't seriously set you back.

STEPS

1. In a small saucepan, heat the oil over low heat. Add the onion, garlic, oregano, cumin, and cinnamon. Cook, stirring often, until onions are translucent, about ten minutes.

2. Add chili powder and almonds and cook for another three minutes.

3. Slowly stir in water and bring to a boil, then reduce to a simmer.

4. Stirring occasionally, cook uncovered until the sauce is reduced by half, about thirty minutes.

5. Remove saucepan from heat and stir in the cocoa powder.

6. Add the raisins with their soaking water and salt and, using a hand blender, blend until smooth.

NUTRITION

Each 2-tablespoon serving contains:

Calories: 28

Calcium: 15 mg

Magnesium: 6 mg

Protein: 3 g

FRESH SALSA

Mild or spicy, blended or chunky, this salsa is a must on top of or on the side of the black bean tortillas.

MAKES 1¾ CUP

1¼ cups fresh tomatoes, roughly chopped

½ medium onion, finely chopped

1 tablespoon lime juice

½ teaspoon ground cumin

¼ teaspoon chili flakes (if you like a bit of a kick)

1 clove garlic, peeled and finely chopped

¼ teaspoon sea salt

¼ cup cilantro leaves, washed and roughly chopped

STEPS

1. Combine all of the ingredients in a sturdy bowl with a high edge.

2. Optional: for a uniform consistency, use a hand blender on a low setting to blend the salsa until you reach your desired consistency.

NUTRITION

Each ¼ cup contains:

Calories: 12

Calcium: 9 mg

Magnesium: 5.5 mg

Protein: 0.5 g

COLLARD WHITE BEAN SOUP

One of the most discerning palates I know mistook the collards and lemon in this soup for sorrel. If you're a fan of sorrel, but have a hard time locating the elusive and zesty plant, try this recipe for a passable imitation.

MAKES 6 SERVINGS

1 cup dried white beans

6 cups water, divided, plus two cups of water for soaking the dried beans

1 small leek

1 bunch collard greens (12 ounces or 4 cups chopped)

1 tablespoon olive oil

1 small onion, finely chopped

1 teaspoon sea salt

¼ teaspoon cracked pepper

1 medium head cauliflower, cut into bite-size pieces (4 cups)

5 tablespoons lemon juice (or juice of one large lemon)

1 teaspoon lemon zest

1 cup chopped fresh parsley, divided

STEPS

1. Rinse beans and place in a pot with 2 cups of water. Cover and soak overnight outside of the refrigerator.

2. When ready to make the soup, drain beans and rinse again. Set aside.

3. Slice the leek lengthwise and cut the halves into ½-inch semicircles.

4. Immerse the half-moon pieces of leek in water, wash well, and drain.

5. Wash collard greens and cut out the stems. Trim ends off the stems and chop into ¼-inch pieces. Stack collard leaves in a pile and slice into one-inch ribbons, and then turn the pile 90 degrees and cut the collard ribbons into one-inch squares.

6. In a large heavy pot or Dutch oven heat oil over medium heat. Add onion. Stirring occasionally, cook until onion is translucent, about 3 to 5 minutes. Add leeks and cook until soft, about another 5 minutes.

7. Add beans, 5 cups of water, salt and pepper and bring to a boil. Reduce to a simmer and cook covered until the beans are tender, about fifty minutes.

8. Add the remaining one cup of water and the cauliflower and bring to a boil, then add the collards, parsley (reserve a handful for garnish), and lemon juice and zest. Reduce to a simmer and cook uncovered, stirring occasionally, until the cauliflower is soft, about 12 to 15 minutes.

9. Let soup cool for 5 minutes and then, using a hand blender, blend in pot until smooth on a low to medium setting to avoid splashing.

Ladle into bowls and top with crispy sage leaves (p. 227), cracked pepper, chopped parsley, and a drizzle of olive oil.

NUTRITION
A sixth of the soup, about 1½ cups, contains:
Calories: 211
Calcium: 272 mg
Magnesium: 109 mg
Protein: 13 g

CRISPY SAGE LEAVES

My Auntie Susan, who incidentally *did* come of age during the era of "beaded bracelets and the Beatles," says sage makes you wise.

MAKES 10 CRISPY SAGE LEAVES

10 fresh sage leaves
2 tablespoons olive oil
1 pinch of sea salt

STEPS

1. Line a plate with a paper towel.

2. Wash sage leaves and dry them completely. Any water will cause the oil to splash out of the pan.

3. In a small skillet, heat oil over medium-high heat until hot but not smoking.

4. Carefully add the sage leaves to the oil, 5 at a time, and cook for 1 to 2 seconds until they change color from pale green to dark green.

5. Using tongs, remove the leaves from the skillet and transfer to the paper-towel–lined plate. Sprinkle with salt.

Serve immediately or store in a paper-towel–lined airtight container at room temperature for up to three days.

NUTRITION
Each crispy sage leaf contains about:
Calories: 12
Calcium: 10 mg
Magnesium: 3 mg

GARLIC BAKED POTATO

There's no better way to showcase a potato than by sticking it in the oven and letting it bake until crisp on the outside and fluffy on the inside. Don't forget to eat the skin, the most nutritious part. The skin is the perfect vehicle for any of the sauces or toppings contained in these menus.

MAKES 1 BAKED POTATO

1 medium russet potato (7½ ounces)
1 teaspoon olive oil
3–6 unpeeled garlic cloves (depending on how garlicky you like your potato)
1 tablespoon dried ground basil
1 teaspoon dried ground oregano
1 teaspoon dried dulse flakes
½ cup frozen green peas, optional

STEPS
Preheat oven to 425°F.

1. Scrub the potato under running water and pat dry. Trim away any sprouts or green spots.

2. Pour the olive oil into your hands and rub over the garlic cloves. Set the cloves aside for adding to the oven later.

3. Place the potato on a baking sheet.

4. Slit the top of the potato with a shallow stroke of a knife or prick it in a few places with a fork to allow the steam to escape as it bakes.

5. Place the potato in the oven and bake for 30 minutes.

6. After 30 minutes remove the baking sheet and add the garlic cloves.

7. Return the sheet to the oven and bake for another 20 minutes.

8. After 20 minutes remove the tray and check everything for doneness. The garlic cloves should be soft to the touch and the potato should be soft when squeezed or pierced with a knife. If you encounter any hard spots in the potato, return it to the oven for another 10 minutes.

9. While the potato is baking, follow the instructions for cooking the frozen peas.

10. Once the potato is done, remove it from the oven. Place the potato on a plate with the garlic cloves. Squeeze the potato open with your hands. Sprinkle the basil, oregano, and dulse flakes inside. Slice the tops off the garlic cloves and squeeze the insides on top. Store any uneaten cloves in the refrigerator. They're good cold on a salad.

11. Garnish with cooked peas if desired.

Serve with nettle pesto (p. 231); or tangy tofu cream (p. 203) and chopped scallions; or herb vinaigrette (p. 215); or Za'atar (p. 192); or spoon some of the collard white bean soup (p. 225) on top; or simply top with more herbs, salt and pepper, and a drizzle of olive oil.

NUTRITION

One medium baked potato without garnish contains:
Calories: 168
Calcium: 28 mg
Magnesium: 49 mg
Protein: 5 g

Three garlic cloves add:
Calories: 26
Calcium: 16 mg
Magnesium: 2 mg
Protein: 1 g

One tablespoon of dried ground basil adds:
Calories: 12
Calcium: 112 mg

Magnesium: 36 mg

Protein: 1 g

One teaspoon of dried ground oregano adds:

Calories: 5

Calcium: 32 mg

Magnesium: 5 mg

One teaspoon of dried dulse flakes adds:

Calories: 3

Calcium: 3 mg

Magnesium: 3 mg

Iodine: 165 mcg (110 percent of the DV for iodine)

Half a cup of peas adds:

Calories: 52

Calcium: 15 mg

Magnesium: 17 mg

Protein: 3.5 g

NETTLE PESTO

Pesto is one of the best ways to capture the fleeting flavors of the passing months. My mum made one and only one kind of pesto: basil. In the summer, when the herb was plentiful, she'd take out her ratty Cuisinart—aka "food processor," back then they were one and the same—yellowed and cracked like the pages of a well-fingered book, and begin making batches that she'd freeze in ice cube trays. Once the pesto had frozen, she'd pop the cubes from the ice cube trays into a ziplock freezer bag, storing away summer for cold winter nights when she'd take a cube out to add to a ratatouille, or a fish soup she was making for dinner.

These days I think pesto, and I think my sister. She always has some homemade in her refrigerator. The leading green changes with the season: ramps in spring; sage, basil, or garlic scapes in summer; and green peppers in the fall and winter months. Pesto makes everything taste better.

Nettles are April.

MAKES 2 CUPS

1 large pot of water
10 cups of young nettles (if unavailable, substitute dandelion greens, spinach or, for a lemony twist, sorrel)
1 bowl of ice water
5 cloves garlic, peeled
½ cup almonds, ground*
1 tablespoon lemon juice
¼ cup fresh lovage, or 2 tablespoons dried
½ teaspoon sea salt
½ teaspoon ground fresh pepper
½ cup olive oil, divided

You can buy the almonds ground, use the almond meal left from making almond milk, or grind the almonds yourself in small batches in a coffee grinder.

STEPS

1. Bring the pot of water to a boil.

2. Plunge the fresh nettles into the boiling water for 30 seconds. Using tongs, remove the nettles from the water and immediately transfer to the bowl of ice water to stop the cooking. Once the nettles are cool, remove and use your hands to squeeze the excess water out of them.

3. In a food processor, combine the garlic, ground almonds, lemon juice, lovage, sea salt, pepper, and half of the olive oil. Pulse until the ingredients are well mixed.

4. Add the nettles and the remainder of the olive oil. Blend until smooth.

NUTRITION

Each 2-tablespoon serving of nettle pesto contains:
Calories: 77
Calcium: 38 mg
Magnesium: 12 mg
Protein: 1 g

Sweet!

Treats can be healthy, too. The proof is in these puddings.

CHOCOLATE PUDDING

This dessert has been described as "heaven mixed with Betty Crocker icing."

MAKES 4 SERVINGS

1 medium-size ripe avocado

7 medjool dates, pits removed

3 tablespoons raw cocoa powder

½ cup homemade almond milk

¼ teaspoon salt

½ teaspoon vanilla extract

4 tablespoons chia seeds (garnish)

STEPS

Combine all ingredients except the chia seeds in a food processor and blend until smooth. If you prefer to use a hand blender, add ingredients to a 4-cup jar or bowl and blend on medium speed.

Divide among four bowls and top each bowl with one tablespoon of chia seeds.

NUTRITION

Each 1/2-cup serving without chia seeds contains:

Calories: 200

Calcium: 83 mg

Magnesium: 54 mg

Protein: 2.5 g

Each serving topped with one tablespoon of chia seeds adds:

Calories: 38.5

Calcium: 75 mg

Magnesium: 48 mg

Protein: 2 g

VANILLA PUDDING

Vanilla has gotten a bad rap. Guilty as charged. When I was a kid, I assumed anyone who, given a choice of flavors, picked vanilla, must be boring. Now I know better.

This recipe makes the vanilla bean pod optional since the pods are pricey and not always easy to find. However, if you know of a source, I encourage you to make the investment. You won't be disappointed. The beans and paste contained in the pod add a deep, rich, smoky flavor that vanilla extract cannot match. There's another option: ground vanilla beans. You can buy it in bags. At $18 for 100 grams of ground organic vanilla beans, it costs more than extract up front. But those 100 grams go a long way. One bag lasts me over six months, and I use it every day. I transfer the powder to a saltshaker. A few shakes is all you need to turn an unflavored smoothie into a vanilla shake, or vanilla pudding into *vanilla* pudding. Use it in place of vanilla extract in any of the recipes in this chapter.

MAKES 2 SERVINGS

4 cooking dates or 2 medjool dates, pits removed

1 inch-long piece of vanilla bean pod (or ½ teaspoon vanilla extract, or ¼ teaspoon ground vanilla beans)

¼ teaspoon orange zest

3 tablespoons chia seeds

½ teaspoon cinnamon

¼ teaspoon nutmeg

¼ teaspoon sea salt

1 cup homemade almond milk, divided

STEPS

1. If using cooking dates (medjool dates are soft enough as is), place them in a small bowl and pour just enough boiling water over them to cover. Soak until soft, about 15 minutes. Remove from the liquid, which you can use for sweetening tea or hot cocoa, and place on small plate.

2. If using the piece of vanilla pod, cut it in half lengthwise. Use a teaspoon to scrape out the vanilla beans and the paste lining the pod. Set the teaspoon on the plate with the dates. Add the empty pod to your vanilla extract bottle for extra flavor. Or cut a few small pieces of the pod into boiling water for vanilla scented water. There are myriad ways to use the fragrant bark that don't involve the garbage.

3. In a deep bowl or a 2- to 4-cup jar, combine dates, orange zest, chia seeds, vanilla seeds and paste (or extract, or powder), cinnamon, nutmeg, salt, and half the almond milk. Using a hand blender on low setting, gently blend pudding, pulsing with the hand blender to avoid splashing, until all ingredients are fully combined. Add the remainder of the almond milk and blend for 5 more seconds.

4. Let rest in the refrigerator until thickened, at least 30 minutes.

Serve cold or at room temperature.

NUTRITION

Each ¾-cup serving contains:

Calories: 165

Calcium: 238 mg

Magnesium: 90 mg

Protein: 4 g

SOME NUTTY IDEAS TO SNACK ON

One of my favorite snacks is frozen almond butter, or any nut or seed butter for that matter. Frozen sunflower and cashew butter are also delicious. I even like frozen sesame butter (tahini), but some may find it too bitter on its own. If you've never tried freezing your nut and seed butters, you're in for a delightful surprise. Simply place whatever jar you have in the freezer. If the jar hasn't been opened, open first and stir. Or don't. If you want a few "free" tablespoons of nut oil, freeze without opening and stirring. After the jar has frozen—I've never timed it but to be sure leave the jar overnight—a layer of frozen oil will form on the top that you can easily scrape off and use for cooking or baking.

After you've skimmed off the hardened oil, let the jar sit on the counter for about five minutes, long enough so you can chip away at the meat with a small knife. You won't need much of the creamy, rich, melt-in-your-mouth nut or seed butter to satisfy you. I keep all of my nut and seed butters in the freezer. They don't take long to soften on the counter if you want them to be spreadable and you can always return them to the freezer after softening.

For a sweet variation, peel a banana and slice in half lengthwise. Spread each half with softened nut butter, sprinkle with a little salt, sandwich together, cut into one-inch rounds, and freeze in a ziplock freezer bag. After-school snack or after-dinner dessert—you choose.

For a more mobile snack, and one that's fun for the kids to make and eat, cut an apple into quarters or eighths. Glue the apple back together with your nut or seed butter of choice.

Of course, there's always peanut butter on celery with a dash of salt. Almond butter on celery is good, too. Eat immediately or bag the boats for taking to school or work.

1. Reduce your consumption of sugar by using ground stevia leaves, carob powder, ground licorice root, or cinnamon in place of added sugars in recipes.

2. In place of salt, which depletes calcium stores, add apple cider vinegar, lemon juice, dulse flakes, mustard seeds, and/or dried herbs to your meals.

3. For the thick and creamy mouth feel of fat without the fat, use Dijon mustard for savory dishes. Use cinnamon, which imparts more of a gooey than a creamy texture, for sweet ones.

4. To reduce the fat and increase the protein and nutrient density of meals, use nut or seed butters, when the flavor combinations permit, instead of oil for sautéing. Try in stir-fries, for instance. I learned this trick when I stayed with a family in the rural outskirts of Harare, Zimbabwe. Oil was scarce, and freshly ground peanut butter was plentiful. After tasting sautéed greens with peanut butter I realized I, not the family with whom I was staying, was missing something.

5. For creamy oatmeal without the cream, mix 5 parts water to 1 part rolled oats in a pot and cook covered on the lowest heat on your stove top until the mixture begins to bubble, about 40 minutes on my electric stove. Be careful to catch the oatmeal before it bubbles over, because it will eventually, even on the lowest of low temperatures. Turn the heat off and let rest for a couple of minutes. When you lift the cover, don't stir. The top is all cream. Slip in a spoonful of nut or seed butter for extra richness. For a savory lunch or dinner, instead of the nut butter, crack an egg on top of the oatmeal immediately after turning off

the heat and lifting the cover. Return the cover and let sit until the whites of the egg turn from translucent to white, about 5 minutes. Or instead of the egg, add 2 tablespoons of dried lentils per serving of oatmeal and a few uncooked cubes of your favorite variety of squash—mine is kabocha—to the oats and water at the start. The lentils and squash will be done by the time the oatmeal begins to bubble. At the bubbling point you can also add ¼ cup of frozen peas per serving of oatmeal to the pot before turning off the heat. The peas will cook in the oatmeal on their own. Sprinkle the lentil-studded oatmeal with herbs and garnish with sliced avocado, a splash of cider vinegar, a dash of dulse flakes, and salt and pepper. Note: millet also turns creamy when slow-cooked this way, 5 parts water to 1 part millet.

6. To make popcorn in your toaster oven, place 3 tablespoons of dried popcorn kernels into the rimmed baking tray that comes with your toaster oven. For this magic trick, you don't need any oil. Cover the tray with another tray of the same size. Place in the oven, turn the temperature to 425°F and bake until the kernels stop popping, exactly 10 minutes in my toaster oven. Be careful not to leave the kernels in too long as the popped corn will turn from perfectly done, to toasted, to burned in no time. If you don't hear a pop for 5 seconds after the last pop, turn the heat off, quickly remove the sandwiched trays from the oven and remove the top tray to prevent further cooking. You will need oven mitts as the trays will be very hot.

Voilà.

Unholy Holstein Cow: Caution Killer Yields

You've probably heard about the dairy sector's role in global warming. A 2013 publication by the Food and Agriculture Organization, "Milk and Dairy Products in Human Nutrition," cites a report holding the sector accountable for about 4 percent of the greenhouse gas emissions caused by humans in 2007. Methane emissions from "enteric fermentation," the process by which cows digest food, are especially concerning. They are so high that they have caught the attention of the Obama administration. If you scan the Climate Action Plan that the President released in the spring of 2014 you will see that a "key step" is the development of a government partnership with the dairy industry to "reduce U.S. dairy sector greenhouse gas emissions by 25 percent by 2020."

Or maybe you've read that America's livestock are some of the heaviest consumers of GMO crops grown in America. You don't need me to tell you the extent to which dairy farming is shaping environments near and far. Or maybe you do.

GARBAGE IN, GARBAGE OUT

Did you know that dairy cows are fed sodium bicarbonate to counter the acidic effects of feeds high in fermentable carbohydrates such as corn?

Grain-based diets aren't the only cause of the digestive disorders plaguing dairy cows. As Elliot Block, PhD, explains in an article in *Dairy Herd Management,* "Overcrowded facilities force cows to gorge rather than eat small meals, which contributes to rumen acidosis." Block, not coincidentally a research fellow at Arm & Hammer Animal Nutrition, therefore recommends that dairies add at least half a pound of buffer per day to the ration of a cow consuming 60 pounds of dry matter. That's just the beginning of what high-producing dairy cows are given to keep them eating, lactating, and insect-free. In Canada, farmers are permitted to buy over-the-counter antibiotics to promote the growth of their cows without a veterinarian's prescription. They can and they do. And in the United States dairy farmers are allowed to give their dairy cows the synthetic recombinant bovine growth hormone rBGH, alternatively known as rBST (recombinant bovine somatotrophin), to boost milk yields. They can and they do.

A 2014 University of Kentucky publication details another protocol that some dairy farmers follow: adding insect-growth regulators such as methoprene and organophosphates to the mix. Everybody knows what happens when cows ingest poison: their milk turns to poison. They were on to this fact as far back as the days of Abraham Lincoln, when thousands of people reportedly died from drinking the milk of cows that had eaten white snakeroot, a plant that contains the toxin tremetol that can be fatal to humans. Abraham Lincoln's mother was, so the story goes, among those who suffered from what was then called "milk sickness."

The insecticides that are the subject of the University of Kentucky report transform cow manure from a breeding ground for fly maggots into a lethal substrate that kills the maggots before they mature into milking-parlor pests. The chemicals are also doing their part to convert a natural fertilizer into hazardous waste. It's a role shared by farm consolidation, which is making the waste visible and inescapable.

Dairies with 1,000 or more cows produce over 50 percent of US milk. The trend toward bigger isn't slowing down either. In her May 2014 *Yale e360* article "As Dairy Farms Grow Bigger, New Concerns About Pollution," journalist Elizabeth Grossman notes that the dairy operations that are growing the fastest are the ones with 2,000 or more cows. They're called "operations" for a reason. These are not farms like Old McDonald's, with barns and fences enclosing vast swaths of grass for grazing. They are controlled steely environments in which each cow is given just enough room to breathe. Needless to say, these confined feeding lots don't accept any old cow into their quarters. She has to be a high-milk-yielding breed to be worth the dairy operator's time and money. The Holstein breed of cow has become a favorite among dairies. The problem is that Holsteins are as prolific in making manure as they are in producing milk. Milking cows in general generate more manure than beef cattle and Holsteins take the cake, churning out twice the manure of the all-around less productive Jersey breed of dairy cow. A single cow produces about 120 pounds of manure daily. Multiply that by a thousand or two and you have an idea of the mountains of manure that accumulate each day on the large dairy operations that are spreading across North America. The Holsteins' impressive dumps are placing states such as Wisconsin, which proudly proclaims itself "America's Dairyland," in a bad predicament. When you consider, as the USDA has, that every 200 milking cows produce as much nitrogen as the sewage of a small community, Clean Wisconsin staff attorney Elizabeth Wheeler's assertion that Wisconsin has a nitrate problem is an understatement. There's simply too much manure seeping into the surroundings. One way of dealing with it is to store it in lagoons. However, if not watched closely, this diversion method risks collapsing into a delivery system of nitrate to groundwater.

The U.S. Environmental Protection Agency (EPA) is addressing the issue. It has identified poorly managed animal-feeding operations as an agricultural activity that causes nonpoint source pollution (NPS). As such, they are, an EPA website says, a "leading source of water quality impacts" on lakes and rivers as well as "a major contributor to contamination of surveyed estuaries and ground water." Too many milking cows manufacturing too much manure to be used gainfully creates enough of a public health and safety hazard without the added fact that the mounds that can't be made to disappear are laced with pharmaceuticals and pesticides.

OUTSIDE IN

Dairy Month, or June, muddies the waters more. Don't be fooled, the national holi-month did not originate with the promotion of your health in mind. It all started in 1937 under a different name, National Milk Month. National Milk Month, which was christened June Dairy Month two years later, became a way to boost demand for milk during the surplus stimulated by happy cows let out to pasture after a long winter. Back then, cows' internal clocks were synchronized with the seasons, programmed to spring their host to life along with the dandelions and long, leisurely days chewing the cud in the sun. Today Dairy Month is an anachronism. June is no longer peak milk month. The majority of milking cows in North America are pumped all days of the year under lock and key. They don't know June from January. They don't know the sweet smell of early summer grass after a good soaking or the feel of a gentle breeze tickling the tips of their ears.

Maybe you can't compare apples to oranges, but as Florida orange grower Jim Brewer does, you *can* compare modern methods of growing orange trees to twenty-first-century factory cow farming:

> like anything else in farming. . . . the faster we produce something the more money comes back the quicker and the quicker . . . so we burn them out so to speak. A tree that used to last to be eighty, ninety, a hundred years old or even older couldn't make it today because we give them such good fertilizer . . . Like a cow, like growing cattle, there are only so many calves you're going to produce with a cow. If you have

her having the calf every year, every year, every year, she won't last as
long as that cow that has one every 1.5 years or something like that . . .
So she's just going to die quicker.

Brewer chooses cattle breeding for his analogy because it epitomizes the crash-and-burn approach toward food production that dominates North American agriculture. Cows are literally bred and milked to death.

I could go on but others such as Elizabeth Grossman have done the job well. You get the idea; you know how ugly the picture is of the inhumane and polluting ways of industrial dairy agriculture. If we are what we eat, then cows are walking drugstores fueled by the same corn that is turned into ethanol to gas larger vehicles.

SCHOOL WATER

The picture on the other end of the milking operations that support the Dairy Food Group isn't any prettier. Kids vomiting. That's what Betti Wiggins, executive director of the Office of School Nutrition for Detroit Public Schools witnesses when the schools under her jurisdiction give children milk for breakfast before sending them out to play. "Milk is too heavy" she says, addressing a workshop I attended in the spring of 2014 about what experts in the field of school nutrition are discovering that schoolchildren need more than anything: access to more and cleaner water. Now that whole milk has been nixed from school breakfast and lunch programs, children, Wiggins says, are choosing water at the beverage stations in her school cafeterias. She can't even convince the kids to put milk on their cereal unless it's strawberry flavored. Wiggins doesn't blame them. She says the low-fat and nonfat milks that are a required offering "taste like wallpaper." Yet while the government provides Wiggins with funds for purchasing milk, it doesn't do the same for water. She's left with having to figure out how to supply her children with what they want, when and where they want it: bottomless glasses of drinkable water.

I learned from another presenter, who asked that I not use her name, that the runoff from dairies is one of the major obstacles to supplying Californian children and their families with round-the-clock access to potable water. If Wisconsin is "America's Dairyland," California is America's Dairy Heartland. It produces the most milk of any state in the nation. Being the largest milk supplier, it is also a heavy polluter. Dairy and other high input agriculture is uniquely impacting the ground water in the Central Valley of California, which is heavily contaminated with nitrates. If you saw the photos the presenter showed of the taps in schools and homes in the San Joaquin Valley, you would believe that in some places a bottle of Coke is a safer if not healthy alternative to tap water. This clean water advocate isn't asking for flavored milk in schools, which she doesn't see as a solution to improving nutrition and preventing obesity. She's fighting for a true life essential: clean water. All the while, nonpoint effluent from dairy agriculture is running amok over- and underground, thwarting her efforts from all directions. As the water workshop wrapped up, I was reminded of the Harvard School of Public Health's Healthy Eating Plate. On its plate blue doesn't stand for dairy but water, an essential nutrient that the true blue dairy group is ironically making scarce in counties across America. Water is critical. Milk is not and worse, the kick to get us to drink more of it is degrading what is.

THE UNHEALTHY LEGACY OF THE MAKE-BELIEVE THAT MILK IS ESSENTIAL

The cows aren't all right. The kids aren't all right. And yet the dairy industry continues to prop up the myth that milk is essential. Making the rounds during 2014's Dairy Month, the St. Louis District Dairy Council joined Missouri's News Channel 5 to answer, among other questions, "Why are milk and milk products important?" Topping the Dairy Council's list of reasons is: "Dairy is irreplaceable in the diet as a source of essential nutrients." You could say the same about any food that is a source of essential nutrients. You could say broccoli is "irreplaceable" in the diet as a source of essential nutrients. Its profile of essential nutrients is different than that of any other food and hence "irreplaceable." However, that doesn't make it an essential source of those essential nutrients. "Irreplaceable" and "essential" sound, but are not, synonymous. The Dairy Council's statement is good or bad wordsmithing depending on your perspective. It's just plain bad when you consider the consequences.

The effects of government and dairy industry efforts to convince Americans that dairy is essential are documented in a table in the 2010 Dietary Guidelines for Americans. Breaking down the table, which charts the nation's food preferences, provides some insight into the belly of America. It doesn't look healthy. The table, divided according to age group, lists the top twenty-five sources of calories for Americans, as gleaned from data collected by the National Cancer Institute for 2005–2006. When you add it all up, you see that despite the government's best efforts to nudge Americans to consume dairy mostly of the low-fat and nonfat variety, it is failing spectacularly. Who, seeing that "milk-based desserts" and "hard," "soft," and "processed cheese" are members of the Dairy Food Group, is going to choose plain fat-free or low-fat milk to meet their 3-A-Day MyPlate dairy requirement? Not very many, say the data that the National Cancer Institute has collected. Of the 265 dairy calories that the young group is consuming, only eighty-six of them come from reduced-fat milk.

The proportion is even lower for adult Americans. Of the 148 dairy calories that adult Americans consume each day, just under a quarter are in the form of reduced-fat milk. Clearly, American adults are not drinking glasses of milk, whole or fat-reduced. Nor, however, are they avoiding dairy fat altogether. While the 1980s Guidelines advised Americans to stick with whole milk if they liked it and trim saturated fat intake elsewhere, the table reveals that these days Americans are doing the reverse. They're cutting out whole milk altogether in exchange for other higher-fat and/or sugary dairy products such as ice cream and cheese. A June 2014 report authored by attorney Michele Simon entitled "Whitewashed: How Industry and Government Promote Dairy Junk Foods" finds the same. In it, Simon teases out the details, from government partnerships with the likes of Domino's Pizza to encourage greater cheese consumption in America, to the astonishing statistic that 11 percent of all sugar is used in the production of dairy products. The examples are telling. In Simon's words: "The assumption that eating dairy is essential has created a blind spot when it comes to criticizing unhealthy forms of dairy."

Herein lies a major part of the problem in pushing dairy on America. Dairy takes many forms, and the ones Americans like most contain unhealthy levels of sugar, fat, and salt. As a result, the Dairy Food Group has become a back door to bad habits. Haven't had your glass of milk today? Go ahead, the Dairy Food Group says, help yourself to the cheese plate laid out in the office meeting room. Still short a couple of servings of dairy? rocky road ice cream sounds nice, especially on a warm Dairy Month night. Make that rocky road frozen yogurt, that way you'll feel better about having seconds. But don't worry if you don't like frozen yogurt—I double-checked—ice cream is part of the Dairy Food Group, too. There's more good news for the ice-cream lover: you have to eat half as much more ice cream—one and one-half cups versus one cup for frozen yogurt—to make a dairy serving. If you ever wanted a reason to order two scoops instead of one, MyPlate gives you one. Actually, it gives you permission to go all out: add another scoop for a total of three and now you have a serving of dairy. Children cannot buy whole milk at school, but they and you can meet the USDA's 3-A-Day dairy recommendation with fattier and sugary products all hours of the day outside the school cafeteria.

Americans are assimilating government and dairy-industry messaging that dairy is "irreplaceable" by eating hunks of cheese and helpings of ice cream. These processed dairy products *are* irreplaceable sources of essential nutrients, the very ones we are saturated in, namely carbohydrates, fat, and salt. So as long as there are enough buckets of ice cream and wheels of cheese to go around, the Dairy Food Group will continue to be a menace to society, an excuse to fill up three times a day on three of North America's most ruthless and indiscriminate killers: sugar, solid fat, and salt.

. . . .

"I haven't given Oscar milk. He's two now. What do I do?"

While there are many difficult, unanswered, and perhaps unanswerable questions about milk, this is not one of them. The answer, dear Maxine, is simple: forget about it. Parents, as long as your kids continue to eat their veggies, you have nothing to worry about. If they don't love broccoli as much as Oscar clearly showed he did while visiting me in 2012, turn to the recipe chapter in this book for a wide array of calcium- and nutrient-dense foods to choose from that you and your growing family will thrive on.

Eat to Love

Leave it to my sister, the sometime jeweler, to find a gem: a clip of an interview between Terry Gross, host of National Public Radio's *Fresh Air*, and Maurice Sendak. Terry asked Sendak for a favorite reader comment. His response was priceless:

> *Oh there's so many. Can I give you just one that I really like? It was from a little boy. He sent me a charming card with a little drawing. I loved it. I answer all my children's letters—sometimes very hastily— but this one I lingered over. I sent him a postcard and I drew a picture of a Wild Thing on it. I wrote, "Dear Jim, I loved your card." Then I got a letter back from his mother and she said, "Jim loved your card so much he ate it." That to me was one of the highest compliments I've ever received. He didn't care that it was an original drawing or anything. He saw it, he loved it, he ate it.*

It takes a Sendak to draw out the most precious lesson from little Jim's instinctive (or to another, less tender man, destructive) act: eating is fundamentally an expression of love. As we grow out of the age of innocence, we tend to lose touch with such basics. Eating becomes less wonder full. Our fast-paced world pushes us toward the hyphenated and homogenized foods that have been redacted and repurposed into packages of quick and easy energy that have been stripped of love and integrity.

The massive dairies that provide most of North America with its milk deliver nothing that Sendak's pen pal would want to put in his mouth. Little Jim is hungry for love, not for the milk of sick, suffering, and barely living cows. He has a hankering for beautiful hand renderings, not the mechanized, drug-dependent output of crowded, miserable beings. Provide him with a plateful of trees and watch his imagination run wild. Maybe he'll want to climb the biggest. The next he'll gobble up. The last he'll set aside to admire.

The Dairy Food Group leads to so many deadening ends, from strings of pizza dinners, to late-night raids of super-sized ice cream cartons, to poisoned water. Open your kitchen to the magical kingdom of plants, however, and you can't go wrong. All ways point to love and prosperity. If you're not feeling creative, conjure Jim for inspiration.

ACKNOWLEDGMENTS

My mum and dad always come first because they were downright awesome parents. My dearly missed dad believed I was capable of doing anything, including beating the number-one-ranked under-sixteen tennis player in Canada when I came up against her at junior nationals. I didn't win more than a few games, which in tennis speak means I "got wiped." I continue to strive to be as great as he thought I was and could be.

I have nothing but admiration for my late and loving mum. Not mom: mum. It wasn't some oddball Canadian thing like Thanksgiving in October. She was born and grew up in Brooklyn. She never bothered to explain her preference. She didn't have to; mum was softer, more elegant. She was always a little different than other moms. That went for her approach to milk, too. Milk in our house was like "mom." We didn't use it as other families did. Although we pretty much always had milk in the house, my mum didn't consider it medicine. She didn't encourage us to take it by the glass as a nutritional supplement with each meal. Nor did we.

I am forever grateful for being born to Peter and Linda Hamilton and their fiercely supportive, nonconforming, quality ways. This book is an expression of my appreciation and my best effort to pay it forward.

There are so many living animals, my dog Dixi included, who deserve way more words than I have room for here. Start with my sister Kara, who makes multiple appearances throughout the book. Thanks to you I know I am not an island onto myself. I take much joy and comfort in sharing literally all of me with you.

When my aunt and uncle, the first farmers I ever knew, introduced me to the sweetness of their honey, they instilled in me a deep respect for the bees everywhere who are busy producing food to feed the world. Thank you Sue and Hugh for opening my eyes to the invaluable work of farmers of all stripes.

I owe my life to Ted Thorpe, Debbie Wiecha, Ben and Jesse Sosnicki, Elizabeth Stocking, Amanda VanHart, and all the other fruit and vegetable growers whose names I may not know but who have sustained me over the decades. Their greens, reds, yellows, and purples are to die for. I am constantly in awe of their adaptive and experimenting minds that benefit and improve all of humankind. I wish for a shop like Pots's 4 Life Natural Foods around everybody's corner where you can count on picking up farm-fresh bounty when there's no time to make it to market.

Thank you Maxine and Tina for visiting me with inspiration for this book and for the gift you both gave me that was years in the making: some of my best memories.

My dear Ghada, thank you for allowing me to use you as an example of the trouble that even the smartest and most meticulous among us have in navigating the world of dairy pronouncements and products. I hold you up as a model mother.

I'm indebted to you, Patty, longtime friend and long-ago college roommate of my mum, for reminding me what women of a certain age are forcefully and falsely told about their daily dairy needs. Really that's but a peep of what my heart says to you and Bob, my surrogate parents during and after college.

Daniel, the file folder I keep of your "finds" keeps growing. I'm convinced that you carry around an extra pair of eyes or two with you. You never stop seeing. I credit you for directing me to some important historical publications that highlight the government's long and active role in promoting milk consumption.

If I were reading aloud I'd stop here and clear my throat so I could shout out a thank-you to my literary agent, Rick Broadhead, for finding me but more importantly for your sincerity and rare dedication to getting every detail right. This book wouldn't exist without you.

Thank you, Brad Wilson, for your patience and sense of humor throughout. Your relaxed yet clear-sighted approach gave me both space to develop my ideas and the boundaries I needed to finish sooner rather than later. Every writer should be so lucky as to have such a thoughtful and thought full editor.

Paige Hazzan, although it is not part of your job description as editor, I have to say you are one great mediator. Of course, you are also a super vacuum cleaner. You helped me clear the manuscript of many distracting cobwebs and details. Your respect for my delivery means I must take the blame for the final product.

Thank you, Rob, for assigning yourself to this project. Besides being the resourceful and fast-on-your-feet publicist that you are, you understand where I'm coming from, from the quirky little lane that I live on to my notorious love of pumpkin seeds and kabocha squash. I could never have imagined I'd have the opportunity to work with the co-author of a book called *The Everyday Squash Cook*. Keep the thought-provoking questions coming.

I extend a more general thank-you to all the editors and great people at HarperCollins Canada and the United States who helped whip the manuscript into shape and push it through to publication and beyond, including Matt Harper, who seamlessly took over from Paige when she left to fulfill her dream of being a children's book editor; publicist Andy Dodds, who must have a magic wand up his sleeve; and the ever-so-supporting leader of the pack, Lisa Sharkey.

Big thank-you to Katie Mathieu for helping to bring the menus in this book to fruition. You stuck with me until we perfected each and every recipe, whether that meant adding some lovage here, or toning down the toughness of raw kale there. You were always full of bright ideas that you skillfully executed, including turning tofu mayo into sour cream with the right amount of lime, creating a Romesco sauce without bread, and featuring nettles in an early spring pesto. Due to your gentle touch, we can all enjoy the wild, prickly plant as a beacon of so much summer goodness to come.

Finally, but in no way lastly, huge thanks to the people and peoples who inspired the recipes for good eating contained herein. To each and to all: Atii niriliqta; Xitlacua cualli; Bon profit; Smaklig måltid; Nooshe jan; Es gezunterheyt; Buon appetito; Sihk faahn; Pamusoroyi; Kalí óreksi; Bil hana wish shifa'; Bom apetite; Hyvää ruokahalua; Prijatnovo appetita; Kripyā bhojan kā ānnaṅd lijîya; Guten appetit; Labu apetîti; Verði ér að góðu; Buen provecho; Ith do shàth; Kŏr hâi jà-rern aa-hăan; Douzo meshiagare; Eet smakelijk.

Bon Appétit.

REFERENCES

INTRODUCTION

"When milk prices soared in November 2014 in New Zealand . . . milk is considered a 'basic necessity'"

"Concern milk moving from a staple to a luxury," ONE News. November 14, 2014. http://
   tvnz.co.nz/national-news/concern-milk-moving-staple-luxury-6130538

"Descriptions, by the National Dairy Council. . . . part of a healthy lifestyle"

"Milk's Unique Nutrient Package: Benefits for Bones and Beyond," National Dairy Council.
   2009. http://www.nationaldairycouncil.org/SiteCollectionDocuments/education_
   materials/wic/MILKsUniqueNutrientPackage.pdf

"The USDA defines an 'essential nutrient' as 'a dietary substance required for healthy body functioning'"

"Dairy Makes Sense: 9 Essential Nutrients," Midwest Dairy Association. http://www
   .dairymakessense.com/nutrition/9-essential-nutrients/

*"For years Doctor David S. Ludwig. . . . have been challenging the U.S. Department of Agriculture's
   (USDA) dietary recommendations regarding milk. . . ."*

"Harvard researchers launch Healthy Eating Plate," Harvard School of Public Health.
   Released September 14, 2011. http://www.hsph.harvard.edu/news/press-releases/
   healthy-eating-plate/

Sole, Elise. "Harvard doctor refutes milk recommendations," Yahoo! Lifestyle. July 4, 2013.
   https://au.lifestyle.yahoo.com/health/diet-nutrition/article/-/17863803/harvard-
   doctor-refutes-milk-recommendations/

"These recommendations can be found at ChooseMyPlate.gov. . . . and everyone else, three cups per day"

"Food Pyramids and Plates: What Should You Really Eat?" Harvard School of Public Health.
   http://www.hsph.harvard.edu/nutritionsource/pyramid-full-story/

"Despite the dairy industry's repeated attempts. . . . 'two out of three adults just don't get enough milk products every day' "

"Drink your milk, mom!" Dairy Farmers of Canada. http://www.dairygoodness.ca/getenough/

"As it turns out, your average 6-ounce serving of flavored yogurt contains 170 calories and 26 grams of sugar"

"Calories in Yogurt, Fruit, Low Fat, 10 Grams Protein Per 8 Ounce," Calorie Count. http://caloriecount.about.com/calories-yogurt-fruit-low-fat-10-i1121

"Yoplait Original," Yoplait. http://www.yoplait.com/products/yoplait-original-style

"That's the equivalent of 6.5 teaspoons of sugar . . . the American Heart Association recommends no more than 6 teaspoons per day for women and no more than 9 for men"

"Frequently Asked Questions About Sugar," American Heart Association. Last modified May 19, 2014. http://www.heart.org/HEARTORG/GettingHealthy/NutritionCenter/HealthyEating/Frequently-Asked-Questions-About-Sugar_UCM_306725_Article.jsp

". . . which Governor Cuomo has made the official snack of New York State through legislation he signed in October, 2014 . . ."

Blain, Glenn. "Yogurt rules New York's snack world," Celeste Katz Daily Politics. October 15, 2014. http://www.nydailynews.com/blogs/dailypolitics/yogurt-rules-new-york-snack-world-blog-entry-1.1975086

"Now for the children nine years and older, let's say they choose low-fat chocolate milk. . . . a quarter of their daily caloric needs"

"Low-Fat Chocolate Milk (1% fat)," CalorieKing. http://www.calorieking.com/foods/calories-in-milk-flavored-milk-chocolate-low-fat-1_f-ZmlkPTExNjc0MA.html

"Looking at the numbers . . . glasses of Coca-Cola"

"Milk chocolate fluid commercial lowfat with added vitamin A and vitamin D," HealthAliciousNess.com. http://www.healthaliciousness.com/nutritionfacts/nutrition_facts.php?id=Milk%20chocolate%20fluid%20commercial%20lowfat%20with%20added%20vitamin%20A%20and%20vitamin%20D&idn=01104; To convert to cups go to: "Nutrition Facts Comparison Tool," HealthAliciousNess.com. http://www.healthaliciousness.com/nutritionfacts/nutrition-facts-compare.php

"Coca-Cola Nutrition Information," Coca-Cola Company. http://productnutrition.thecoca-colacompany.com/

"What we don't hear so much about is that milk is one of the most allergenic foods . . ."

"Children with Milk Allergy May be 'Allergic to School,'" HealthCanal. April 6, 2013. http://www.healthcanal.com/immune-system/39408-children-with-milk-allergy-may-be-%E2%80%98allergic-to-school%E2%80%99.html

". . . the majority of American adults can't digest it . . ."

Weise, Elizabeth. "Sixty percent of adults can't digest milk," *USA Today*. Last modified

September 15, 2009. http://usatoday30.usatoday.com/tech/science/2009-08-30-lactose-intolerance_N.htm

"Lactose Intolerance Statistics—Statistic Brain," 2013 Statistic Brain Research Institute. Last modified July 23, 2012. http://www.statisticbrain.com/lactose-intolerance-statistics/

"... animal studies have shown that the major type of protein in milk, casein, also promotes cancer"

Campbell, T. Colin. "Animal Protein as a Carcinogen," T. Colin Campbell Center for Nutrition Studies. October 29, 2012. http://www.tcolincampbell.org/courses-resources/article/animal-protein-as-a-carcinogen

"... lactose, the sugar in milk, breaks down during digestion into the highly inflammatory sugar, D-galactose, which has been proven to promote aging and disease in mice"

Michaëlsson, Karl et al. "Milk intake and risk of mortality and fractures in women and men: cohort studies," The BMJ. Published October 28, 2014. http://www.bmj.com/content/349/bmj.g6015

Coghlan, Andy. "Guzzling milk might boost your risk of breaking bones," NewScientist. October 28, 2014. http://www.newscientist.com/article/dn26469-guzzling-milk-might-boost-your-risk-of-breaking-bones.html#.VFGqVueh1xV

Kaplan, Karen. "Does milk do a body good? Maybe not, a new study suggests," Los Angeles Times. October 29, 2014. http://www.latimes.com/science/la-sci-sn-milk-health-risks-20141029-story.html#page=1

Mathews, Kevin. "Does Milk Really Improve Bone Health?" Care2. November 8, 2014 http://www.care2.com/causes/does-milk-really-improve-bone-health.html

"We are told to drink milk for strong bones"

"Calcium—Dietary Supplement Fact Sheet," U.S. Department of Health & Human Services National Institutes of Health. Reviewed November 21, 2013. http://ods.od.nih.gov/factsheets/Calcium-HealthProfessional/

"However, comparative studies show that countries. . . . lower bone-fracture rates than those that do"

Perry, Susan. "Milk-consumption guidelines questioned; scientists call for more evidence," MinnPost. July 9, 2013. http://www.minnpost.com/second-opinion/2013/07/milk-consumption-guidelines-questioned-scientists-call-more-evidence

"As Ron Schmid explains. . . . farm to city possible"

Schmid, Ron. The Untold Story of Milk, Revised and Updated: The History, Politics and Science of Nature's Perfect Food: Raw Milk from Pasture-Fed Cows. Rev. ed. (Washington, DC: Newtrends Publishing, 2009), 3–5.

"In her history, Nature's Perfect Food . . . now featured happy healthy infants"

Dupuis, Melanie. Nature's Perfect Food: How Milk Became America's Drink (New York: New York University Press, 2002), 51, 104

CHAPTER 1: THE DAIRY LANDSCAPE

"There are the variations on the same theme. . . . and added back to make it 'full' fat"

"Types of Milk and Their Fat Content," Food World News. September 12, 2014. http://www
.foodworldnews.com/articles/5993/20140912/types-milk-fat-content.htm

Gauri S. Mittal, ed., *Computerized Control Systems in the Food Industry* (New York, New York:
Marcel Dekker, 1996), 428–430. Available for viewing at http://books.google
.ca/books?id=RKi_eC7NPusC&pg=PA428&lpg=PA428&dq=milk+standardizer-
clarifier?&source=bl&ots=X4Rc6_Dylb&sig=h8j8kQNUXbeaeugsJ2OOqymIAc4&h
l=en&sa=X&ei=XPRwVJKtOrGwsAShvIGgBw&ved=0CD8Q6AEwBg#v=onepage
&q=milk%20standardizer-clarifier%3F&f=false

"Separators, Clarifiers," Schier Company, Inc. http://www.schiercompany.com/Page3.html

"To be called 'milk,' the Federal Food and Drug Administration (FDA) requires that it be pasteurized"

"Standards of Identity for Dairy Products, Section 131.110, Milk." Milk Facts. http://
milkfacts.info/Milk%20Processing/Standards%20of%20Identity.htm

"Subpart B—Requirements for Specific Standardized Milk and Cream," 21CFR131.110.
http://www.gpo.gov/fdsys/pkg/CFR-2006-title21-vol2/pdf/CFR-2006-title21-vol2-
sec131-110.pdf

*"Once milk has been pasteurized, most of the time it is homogenized . . . the issue of whether
homogenized milk is unhealthy remains live and an ongoing area of investigation"*

"Homogenization and Pasteurization," Dairy Farmers Today. http://www
.dairyfarmingtoday.org/Quality-And-Safety/FarmToFridge/Pages/
HomogenizationPasteurization.aspx

Ellis-Christensen, Tricia. "What is Homogenized Milk?" wiseGEEK. Last modified October
14, 2014. http://www.wisegeek.com/what-is-homogenized-milk.htm

"Homogenization: A Closer Look," Raw Milk Facts. Last modified June 21, 2012. http://
www.raw-milk-facts.com/homogenization_T3.html

Enig, Mary G. "Milk Homogenization and Heart Disease," A Campaign for Real Milk. Last
modified February 4, 2014. http://www.realmilk.com/health/milk-homogenization-
and-heart-disease/

Piscatello, Nancy. "Raw milk 101: The difference between raw/pasteurized milk (Part Three),"
Examiner. November 8, 2010. http://www.examiner.com/article/raw-milk-101-the-
difference-between-raw-pasteurized-milk-part-three

Weisbaum, Herb. "Non-homogenized milk health claims are 'nonsense,'" Komo News
Network. Last modified March 8, 2013. http://www.komonews.com/news/consumer/
Non-homogenized-milk-health-claims-are-nonsense-195627071.html

"Born in 1915 to, according to one dairy-industry history . . . of US agricultural commodities"

"History," Dairy Management Inc. http://www.dairy.org/about-dmi/history

Miller, G.D. et al. "Benefits of the National Dairy Council to the dairy processing industry," National Center for Biotechnology Information, PubMed. Published in the *Journal of Dairy Science* July 1994. http://www.ncbi.nlm.nih.gov/pubmed/7929954

Wiley, S. Andrea. *Re-Imagining Milk* (New York: Routledge, 2011), 51–52

"DMI, which incorporated in 1995 . . . '. . . and implemented in coordination with its members'"

"History," Dairy Management Inc. http://www.dairy.org/about-dmi/history

Dairy Management Inc. "Dairy Management Partnerships Set to Ignite Fluid Milk Innovation," PerishableNews.com. Posted October 31, 2014. http://www.perishablenews.com/index.php?article=0040438

"DMI and the Dairy Checkoff," Dairy Management Inc. http://www.dairy.org/about-dmi

"United Dairy Industry Association Board Members," Dairy Management Inc. http://www.dairycheckoff.com/AboutUs/Pages/UnitedDairyIndustryAssociationBoardMembers.aspx

"The California Milk Processor Board. . . . In 1994 milk sales in California increased for the first time in over a decade"

Holt, Douglas B., L'Oréal Professor of Marketing, University of Oxford. "got milk?", Advertising Educational Foundation. http://www.aef.com/on_campus/classroom/case_histories/3000

"With a 90 percent recognition rate . . . co-opted by dairy boards across the United States"

The California Milk Processor Board. "Got Milk? Expands communications in unique agency partnership," Dairy Herd Management. Last modified August 25, 2014. http://www.dairyherd.com/dairy-news/Got-Milk-Expands-Communications-In-Unique-Agency-Partnership-272556721.html

"History of Cow's Milk from the Ancient World to the Present, 8000 BC–63 BC," ProCon.org. Last modified July 10, 2013. http://milk.procon.org/view.resource.php?resourceID=000832

"The Mobile Dairy Classroom . . . where, and how behind dairy production"

"Mobile Dairy Classroom," Dairy Council of California. http://www.healthyeating.org/Schools/Mobile-Dairy-Classroom.aspx

"The list of agricultural commodities . . . 'Pork. The Other White Meat'"

"Commodity checkoff program," Wikipedia. Last modified July 4, 2014. http://en.wikipedia.org/wiki/Commodity_checkoff_program

"New videos depict break-dancing . . . 'Milk Life' is the new header"

Schultz, E.J. " 'Got Milk' Dropped as National Milk Industry Changes Tactics," AdvertisingAge. February 24, 2014. http://adage.com/article/news/milk-dropped-national-milk-industry-tactics/291819/

"Milk Life," America's Milk Companies. http://milklife.com/front?page=2&sort_
    by=created&sort_order=DESC

"Milk Life," America's Milk Companies. June 12, 2014. http://milklife.com/articles/fun/
    milk-life-3

CHAPTER 2: IRONED OUT

*"One nutrition student, Andy Bellatti . . . health benefits of, and differences among, super foods such
    as chia, hemp, and flaxseeds"*

Bellatti, Andy. "5 Ways the Nutrition Field Hinders Its Own Progress," Small Bites. July 18,
    2011. http://smallbites.andybellatti.com/5-ways-in-which-the-nutrition-field-hinders-
    its-own-progress/

"In answering the question . . . '. . . most common nutritional problem that I encounter in my clinic'"

Dickinson, Michael. "Is too much milk bad for my kid?" *The Globe and Mail.* Last modified
    Friday February 1, 2013. http://www.theglobeandmail.com/life/health-and-fitness/ask-
    a-health-expert/is-too-much-milk-bad-for-my-kid/article8093778/

"Enter little Miss Martin . . . 'Oh it sounds like she could be anemic'"

"How Much Milk: What Amount of Milk Meets Kids' Needs?" The Huffington Post Canada.
    Last modified February 15, 2013. http://www.huffingtonpost.ca/2012/12/17/how-
    much-milk_n_2313469.html

"'Just one 8-ounce serving of milk . . . other key nutrients'"

"Milk's Unique Nutrient Package: Benefits for Bones and Beyond," National Dairy Council. 2009.
    http://www.nationaldairycouncil.org/SiteCollectionDocuments/education_materials/
    wic/MILKsUniqueNutrientPackage.pdf

"Caroline Hunt, a nutritionist for the USDA . . . '. . . milk should make up a large part of the diet'"

Hunt, Caroline. "Food for Young Children," U.S. Department of Agriculture
    Farmer's Bulletin. March 4, 1916. Digitized by the Internet Archive in 2010 from
    Open Knowledge Commons, 1, 5. Available at http://archive.org/stream/
    foodforyoungchil00hunt#page/14/mode/2up/search/milk

"According to one dairy industry estimate. . . . '. . . calcium and protein for consumers'"

Yang, Jia Lynn. "Beverage of champions: Chocolate milk gets an Olympic-style makeover,"
    The Washington Post. January 31, 2014. http://www.washingtonpost.com/
    business/economy/beverage-of-champions-chocolate-milk-gets-an-olympic-style-
    makeover/2014/01/31/a13261b6-89c8-11e3-916e-e01534b1e132_story.html

"Health Benefits of Breakfast Cereal," Kellogg Company. http://www.kelloggcompany.com/
    en_US/health-benefits-of-breakfast-cereal.html

"Cereal: The Complete Story," Kellogg's Nutrition. https://www.kelloggsnutrition.com/
    en_worldwide/where_we_are/articles/Cereal_The_Complete_Story.html

"The Globe and Mail *thought the question sufficiently prevalent. . . . '. . . twelve months and three years of age'"*

Dickinson, Michael. "Is too much milk bad for my kid?" *The Globe and Mail*. Last modified Friday February 1, 2013. http://www.theglobeandmail.com/life/health-and-fitness/ask-a-health-expert/is-too-much-milk-bad-for-my-kid/article8093778/

"Clicking on Dairy . . . if they leave the dairy site with the impression that more is better"

"How Much Food from the Dairy Group Is Needed Daily?" U.S. Department of Agriculture, ChooseMyPlate.gov. http://www.choosemyplate.gov/food-groups/dairy-amount.html

"The results, which suggest . . . less milk than health experts in the United States and Canada have been advising . . ."

"Canada's Food Guide," Health Canada. Last modified May 23, 2012. http://www.hc-sc.gc.ca/fn-an/food-guide-aliment/order-commander/index-eng.php

"An article in the journal Pediatrics *. . . parents consider a vitamin D supplement"*

"Two cups of milk a day ideal for children's health, study shows," University of Toronto News. Posted December 17, 2012. http://www.news.utoronto.ca/two-cups-milk-day-ideal-children-health-study-shows

Maguire, Jonathon L. et al. "The Relationship Between Cow's Milk and Stores of Vitamin D and Iron in Early Childhood," American Academy of Pediatrics. Accepted August 14, 2012. http://pediatrics.aappublications.org/content/early/2012/12/12/peds.2012-1793.abstract?sid=9e0deaaa-2cac-42a4-bd62-3adde88c0cc8

"How Much Milk: What Amount of Milk Meets Kids' Needs?" The Huffington Post Canada. Last modified February 15, 2013. http://www.huffingtonpost.ca/2012/12/17/how-much-milk_n_2313469.html

Boyles, Salynn. "2 Cups of Milk a Day Optimal for Most Preschoolers," WebMD. December 17, 2012. http://children.webmd.com/news/20121213/cups-milk-preschoolers

"Iron and Iron Deficiency," MedicineNet.com. Medically reviewed by a doctor March 14, 2014. http://www.medicinenet.com/iron_and_iron_deficiency/article.htm

Abrams, Lindsay. "Study: Kids Should Drink Exactly Two Cups of Milk Per Day," *The Atlantic*. Last modified December 19, 2012. http://www.theatlantic.com/health/archive/2012/12/study-kids-should-drink-exactly-two-cups-of-milk-per-day/266437/

"It wouldn't be wise to interpret this advisory . . . or as simply two 8-ounce glasses of milk"

"What Counts as a Cup in the Dairy Group?" U.S. Department of Agriculture, ChooseMyPlate.gov. http://www.choosemyplate.gov/food-groups/dairy-counts.html

"The gap is more worrisome . . . those whose mothers consumed less milk"

Morton, Susan B. et al. "Maternal and perinatal predictors of newborn iron status," *The New Zealand Medical Journal*. Published in the *New Zealand Medical Journal* September 12,

2014. https://www.nzma.org.nz/journal/read-the-journal/all-issues/2010-2019/2014/vol-127-no-1402-12-september-2014/6293

"Why Pregnant Women Should Consume Less Milk," NDTV Cooks. Last modified September 13, 2014. http://cooks.ndtv.com/article/show/why-pregnant-women-should-consume-less-milk-591182

"Iron deficiency linked to milk intake," NZCity. September 12, 2014. http://home.nzcity.co.nz/news/article.aspx?id=193528&fm=psp,tst

"Milk drinking during pregnancy linked to infant iron deficiency: Research," IANS live. September 15, 2014. http://www.ianslive.in/index.php?param=news/Milk_drinking_during_pregnancy_linked_to_infant_iron_deficiency_Research-443867/Health%20&%20Travel/35

CHAPTER 3: A DATE WITH MYPLATE

"If you ever wondered . . . it isn't as colorful as the icon appears"
"ChooseMyPlate.gov," U.S. Department of Agriculture. http://www.choosemyplate.gov/

"So while I scrolled through . . . 'A little large and heavy on the dairy, but yummy overall'"
Satran, Joe. "My MyPlate Experiment, Day Two: The Dairy Problem," The Huffington Post. Last modified August 4, 2013. http://www.huffingtonpost.com/joe-satran/my-myplate-experiment-day_b_2627648.html#slide=more278777

"Greek yogurt contains twice the amount of protein . . . expand the program to four more states"
"After Meeting With Chobani, Gillbrand-Hanna Urge USDA to Reclassify Greek Yogurt in Nutrition Guidelines," Press Release, Kirsten Gillibrant United States Senator for New York. August 30, 2012. http://www.gillibrand.senate.gov/newsroom/press/release/after-meeting-with-chobani-gillibrand-hanna-urge-usda-to-reclassify-greek-yogurt-in-nutrition-guidelines

"Gillibrand, Hanna announce expansion of Greek yogurt pilot program in school lunches to four more states," WBNG News. January 9, 2014. http://www.wbng.com/news/state/Gillibrand-Hanna-announce-expansion-of-greek-yogurt-pilot-program-in-school-lunches-to-four-more-states-239483361.html

"To precisely understand how his breakfast . . . and seafood for the nutrient shortfall"
"Dietary Guidelines for Americans, 2010," U.S. Department of Agriculture, Center for Nutrition Policy and Promotion, xi, 34, 41-42. Available for downloading at http://www.cnpp.usda.gov/DGAs2010-PolicyDocument.htm

"All fluid milk products . . . (soy beverage) is also part of the Dairy Group"
"What Foods Are Included in the Dairy Food Group?" U.S. Department of Agriculture, ChooseMyPlate.gov. http://www.choosemyplate.gov/food-groups/dairy.html

"One comment succinctly . . . '. . . dairy and grains, above all'"

Satran, Joe. "My MyPlate Experiment Made Me a Little Neurotic, But Not That Healthy," The Huffington Post. Last modified April 17, 2013. http://www.huffingtonpost.com/joe-satran/my-myplate-experiment_b_2688083.html

"The Harvard School of Public Health has set out . . . blue liquid labeled 'water' therefore replaces MyPlate's blue dairy circle"

"Food Pyramids and Plates: What Should You Really Eat?" Harvard School of Public Health. http://www.hsph.harvard.edu/nutritionsource/pyramid-full-story/

"Harvard researchers launch Healthy Eating Plate," Harvard School of Public Health. For immediate release September 14, 2011. http://www.hsph.harvard.edu/news/press-releases/healthy-eating-plate/

"Satran completes his MyPlate food journal . . . '. . . But Not That Healthy'"

Satran, Joe. "My MyPlate Experiment Made Me a Little Neurotic, But Not That Healthy," The Huffington Post. Last modified April 17, 2013. http://www.huffingtonpost.com/joe-satran/my-myplate-experiment_b_2688083.html

"As the HSPH's Healthy Eating Plate website says . . . '. . . hasn't been able to compete'"

Ludwig, David S. and Walter C. Willett, "Three Daily Servings of Reduced-Fat Milk: An Evidence-Based Recommendation?", *JAMA Pediatrics* 167, no. 9 (2013): 788–789. Available for preview at http://archpedi.jamanetwork.com/article.aspx?articleid=1704826

Lees, Kathleen. "Got Milk? Look to Other Food Sources for Daily Calcium Intake," *Scienceworld Report*. First posted July 2, 2013. http://www.scienceworldreport.com/articles/7906/20130702/milk-look-food-sources-calcium-recommended-intake.htm

Sole, Elise. "Harvard doctor refutes milk recommendations," Yahoo! Lifestyle. July 4, 2013. https://au.lifestyle.yahoo.com/health/diet-nutrition/article/-/17863803/harvard-doctor-refutes-milk-recommendations/

". . . or for Canadian patriots . . . as fuel for a winning edge"

"Milk 2 Go Sport: A Champion's Choice, Fuel to Keep Your Body Going," Saputo. http://milk2gosport.ca/

CHAPTER 4: SCIENCE FACT OR SCIENCE FICTION?

"For instance, Andrew Hurdle. . . . science fact"

McDonald, Bob. "The Rising Seas, Hammerhead Vision, Birdfeeder Speciation, Science Fact or Fiction—Squinting," CBC Radio One, podcast audio, December 5, 2009. http://www.cbc.ca/quirks/episode/2009/12/05/the-rising-seas-hammerhead-vision-birdfeeder-speciation-science-fact-or-fiction---squinting/

"In one ad a man is freely flying . . . Mediterranean goddess"

Stanley, T.L. "Ad of the Day: Got Milk? Two new spots directed by Jeff Goodby explain why

milk is the drink of your dreams," ADWeek. April 2, 2013. http://www.adweek.com/
news/advertising-branding/ad-day-got-milk-148345

"Dr. Shapiro . . . '. . . which all have a positive impact on sleep quality'"

"Milk: The Bedtime Drink," PR Newswire. http://www.prnewswire.com/news-releases/
milk-the-bedtime-drink-201263871.html

*Arthur Spielman, PhD, an insomnia expert . . . '. . . other amino acids in those foods compete to get
into the brain'"*

"6 Sleep Myths Busted," Eating Well. http://www.eatingwell.com/nutrition_health/
nutrition_news_information/6_sleep_myths_busted?page=7

"On the website of the University of Arkansas . . . '. . . cause any real drowsiness'"

"Will drinking warm milk make you sleepy?" University of Arkansas for Medical Sciences
Health Library. http://www.uamshealth.com/?id=6752&sid=1

"What's more, low-fat milk contains about half the amount as whole milk"

"Nutrient Content of Milk Varieties," Milk Facts. www.milkfacts.info/Nutrition Facts/
Nutrient Content.htm

"In honor of Mother's Day . . . calming and therefore potentially sleep inducing"

Evans, Lisa. "Mothers' best health advice put to the test," *The Toronto Star.* May 10, 2013.
http://www.thestar.com/life/health_wellness/2013/05/10/mothers_best_health_
advice_put_to_the_test.html

"The first, a study published in the British Medical Journal *. . . '. . . the role of milk in mortality
needs to be established definitively now'"*

Michaëlsson, Karl et al. "Milk intake and risk of mortality and fractures in women and
men: cohort studies," *The BMJ.* Published October 28, 2014. http://www.bmj.com/
content/349/bmj.g6015

Coghlan, Andy. "Guzzling milk might boost your risk of breaking bones," *NewScientist.*
October 28, 2014. http://www.newscientist.com/article/dn26469-guzzling-milk-might-
boost-your-risk-of-breaking-bones.html#.VFGqVuehlxV

Kaplan, Karen. "Does milk do a body good? Maybe not, a new study suggests," *Los Angeles
Times.* October 29, 2014. http://www.latimes.com/science/la-sci-sn-milk-health-risks-
20141029-story.html#page=1

Mathews, Kevin. "Does Milk Really Improve Bone Health?" Care2. November 8, 2014.
http://www.care2.com/causes/does-milk-really-improve-bone-health.html

Schooling, C Mary. "Editorials: Milk and Mortality," *The BMJ.* Published October 28, 2014.
http://www.bmj.com/content/349/bmj.g6205

"The Harvard School of Public Health offers . . . '. . . does not increase one's fracture risk'"

"Calcium and Milk: What's Best for Your Bones and Health?" The Nutrition Source, Harvard

School of Public Health. http://www.hsph.harvard.edu/nutritionsource/calcium-full-story/

Subramanian, Courtney. "Milk-Off! The Real Skinny on Soy, Almond, and Rice," *Time*. February 26, 2014. http://healthland.time.com/2014/02/26/milk-soy-almond-rice/

"Manuals / Inspection Procedures: Dairy Vitamin Addition," Canadian Food Inspection Agency. Last modified September 5, 2013. http://www.inspection.gc.ca/food/dairy-products/manuals-inspection-procedures/dairy-vitamin-addition/eng/1378179097522/1378180040706

"Why else are we told to drink milk? Because it's a good source of protein . . . the tagline 'Milk Life'"

Schultz, E.J. " 'Got Milk' Dropped as National Milk Industry Changes Tactics," AdvertisingAge. February 24, 2014. http://adage.com/article/news/milk-dropped-national-milk-industry-tactics/291819/

Subramanian, Courtney. "Milk-Off! The Real Skinny on Soy, Almond, and Rice," *Time*. February 26, 2014. http://healthland.time.com/2014/02/26/milk-soy-almond-rice/

"In their book The China Study *. . . '. . . all stages of the cancer process'"*

Campbell, T. Colin and Thomas M. Campbell II. *The China Study: The Most Comprehensive Study of Nutrition Ever Conducted and the Startling Implications for Diet, Weight Loss, and Long-Term Health* (Dallas: BenBella Books, 2006), 6, 59, 65, 294

"Drink milk because it contains high concentrations. . . . recovering from strenuous workouts"

"The Benefits of Milk," Serious Powerlifting. http://www.seriouspowerlifting.com/2994/articles/the-benefits-of-milk

"Ask Dr. Andro: Are Colostrum and Milk Products in General Healthy Muscle Builders, a Waste of Money or Toxic Waste?" SuppVersity. August 21, 2011. http://suppversity.blogspot.ca/2011/08/ask-dr-andro-are-colostrum-and-milk.html

"Then again . . . as especially responsive to the hormone . . ."

Hyman, Mark. "Got Proof? Lack of Evidence for Milk's Benefits," The Huffington Post. Last modified September 20, 2013. http://www.huffingtonpost.com/dr-mark-hyman/milk-health-benefits_b_3551079.html

Herard, Cathy. "Dr. Oz: Symptoms of Milk Sensitivity & Does Milk Increase Cancer Risk?" Well Buzz. January 31, 2014. http://www.drozfans.com/dr-oz-cancer-2/dr-oz-non-dairy-milk-alternatives-milk-increase-cancer-risk/

"On the subject of hormones . . . milk will make you more fertile"

Knapton, Sarah. "Ice cream may help older women become pregnant, U.S. study claims," National Post Wire Services. Last modified October 23, 2014. http://news.nationalpost.com/2014/10/23/ice-cream-may-help-older-women-become-pregnant-u-s-study-claims/

"However, other research has identified . . . '. . . in commercial dairy products'"

Spiegel, Brett. "Milk and Cheese: Birth Control for Men?" Everyday Health. October 24, 2012. http://www.everydayhealth.com/sexual-health/1024/milk-and-cheese-birth-control-for-men.aspx

"Cheese Affects Fertility in Men," HerbsMed. December 19, 2012. http://herbsmed.net/cheese-affects-fertility-men/index.html

"Drink milk, some say. . . . skin against damage from environmental toxins"

"6 Health Benefits of Milk," Fitday. http://www.fitday.com/fitness-articles/nutrition/healthy-eating/6-health-benefits-of-milk.html#b

"Don't drink milk . . . skim milk was associated with more severe skin inflammations than milk that hasn't been stripped of its fat"

Reilly, Rachel. "Milk and sugary foods DO increase the risk of acne, say researchers who looked at 50 years of research," The Daily Mail. Last modified February 20, 2013. http://www.dailymail.co.uk/health/article-2281151/Milk-sugary-foods-DO-increase-risk-acne-say-researchers-looked-50-years-research.html?ito=feeds-newsxml

"Between 2003 and 2005 . . . weight control"

Warner, Melanie. "Chug Milk, Shed Pounds? Not So Fast," *The New York Times*. Published June 21, 2005. http://www.nytimes.com/2005/06/21/business/media/21adco.html?_r=1&pagewanted=all

"If the dairy industry was . . . ' . . . as a means of losing weight or trying to control weight'"

Berkey, C. S., H. R. Rockett, W. C. Willett, and G. A. Colditz, "Milk, dairy fat, dietary calcium, and weight gain: a longitudinal study of adolescents," *Archives of Pediatrics and Adolescent Medicine*, 159, no. 6 (June, 2005): 543–550. Available for preview at http://www.ncbi.nlm.nih.gov/pubmed/15939853

Stein, Rob. "Study: More Milk Means More Weight Gain," *The Washington Post*. June 7, 2005. http://www.washingtonpost.com/wp-dyn/content/article/2005/06/06/AR2005060601348.html

"Before deciding . . . fresh air and sunshine"

Sifferlin, Alexandra. "Drinking skim milk may not lower child obesity risk," CNN Health. March 20, 2013. http://www.cnn.com/2013/03/20/health/skim-milk-obesity

Adams, Stephen. "Skimmed milk 'makes kids fat,'" The Telegraph. March 19, 2013. http://www.telegraph.co.uk/health/healthnews/9938102/Skimmed-milk-makes-kids-fat.html

Hope, Jenny. "Skimmed milk 'doesn't stop toddlers getting fat': Children who drink whole milk actually gain fewer pounds," *The Daily Mail*. Last modified March 18, 2013. http://www.dailymail.co.uk/health/article-2295496/Skimmed-milk-doesnt-stop-toddlers-getting-fat-Children-drink-milk-actually-gain-fewer-pounds.html?ito=feeds-newsxml

Aubrey, Allison. "Whole Milk or Skim? Study Links Fattier Milk to Slimmer Kids," The Salt, National Public Radio. March 20, 2013. www.npr.org/blogs/

thesalt/2013/03/19/174739752/whole-milk-or-skim-study-links-fattier-milk-to-slimmer-kids

"Skimmed/Semi-Skimmed Milk Does Not Curb Excess Toddler Weight Gain," redOrbit. March 19, 2013. http://www.redorbit.com/news/health/1112806248/skimmedsemi-skimmed-milk-does-not-curb-excess-toddler-weight-gain/

For news—just breaking as this book was going to press—of a December 2014 study led by Dr. Mark DeBoer that focuses on the effects on children's body weight of the *quantity* rather than the *fat content* of the milk they drink, see: Lehman, Shereen. "Two cups of milk may be ideal for preschoolers," Reuters. December 30, 2014. http://www.reuters.com/article/2014/12/30/us-health-milk-child-obesity-iduskbn0k813h20141230. The study finds that of the almost 9,000 children observed, those who drank more than two cups of milk per day were more likely to be overweight or obese than the children who drank less.

"Two studies published subsequent . . . 'Switch to fat-free or low-fat (one percent) milk'"

"Key Consumer Message." U.S. Department of Agriculture, ChooseMyPlate.gov. http://www.choosemyplate.gov/food-groups/dairy.html

"The first, a meta-analysis . . . '. . . associated with obesity risk'"

Kratz, M., T. Baars and S. Guyenet. "The relationship between high-fat dairy consumption and obesity, cardiovascular, and metabolic disease." National Center for Biotechnology Information, PubMed. Published in the *European Journal of Nutrition*, February 2013. http://www.ncbi.nlm.nih.gov/pubmed/22810464

Holmberg, S. and A. Thelin. "High dairy fat intake related to less central obesity: a male cohort study with 12 years' follow-up." National Center for Biotechnology Information, PubMed. Published in the *Scandinavian Journal of Primary Health Care*, June 31, 2013. http://www.ncbi.nlm.nih.gov/pubmed/23320900

"When, in February 2014 . . . '. . . complicated and deserves further study'"

White, Jon. "Is full-fat milk best? The skinny on the dairy paradox," NewScientist Health. February 21, 2014. http://www.newscientist.com/article/dn25102-is-fullfat-milk-best-the-skinny-on-the-dairy-paradox.html#.UxKczV6eL4i

"Physicist Ursula Franklin . . . '. . . makes me an optimist'"

Powell, Marilyn. "A Word to the Wise, Part 2," CBC Radio One, podcast audio, December 27, 2013. http://www.cbc.ca/ideas/episodes/2013/12/27/a-word-to-the-wise-part-2-1/

CHAPTER 5: KNOW YOUR WEIGHTS AND MEASURES

"Milk, dietitians . . . in addition to calcium"

Ansel, Karen. "Milk: More important than you think!" Kids Eat Right. http://www.eatright.org/kids/article.aspx?id=6442467733

"The critical eight . . . phosphorus"

"Milk's Unique Nutrient Package: Benefits for Bones and Beyond," National Dairy Council. 2009. http://www.nationaldairycouncil.org/SiteCollectionDocuments/education_ materials/wic/MILKsUniqueNutrientPackage.pdf

"Each of these nutrients . . . protein is, well, 'protein'"

"Appendix D: Major Nutrients," U.S. Department of Agriculture's Food and Nutrition Service. www.fns.usda.gov/sites/default/files/appendd.pdf

"A cup of milk contains a substantial 13 grams of sugar . . . Hershey's Milk Chocolate Bar"

Magee, Elaine. "Sugar Shockers: Foods Surprisingly High in Sugar," WebMD. http://www .webmd.com/food-recipes/features/sugar-shockers-foods-surprisingly-high-in-sugar

"HERSHEY'S Milk Chocolate Bar, Nutrition Information," The Hershey Company. http:// www.hersheys.com/pure-products/details.aspx?id=3480

"Although the Daily Values . . . Dietary Reference Intakes (DRIs)"

"Commonly Asked Questions (FAQs)," Nutrition.gov. Last modified October 23, 2014. http://www.nutrition.gov/smart-nutrition-101/commonly-asked-questions-faqs

"The DRIs are the catchphrase . . . '. . . cause adverse health effects'"

"Calcium–Dietary Supplement Fact Sheet," U.S. Department of Health & Human Services National Institutes of Health. Reviewed November 21, 2013. http://ods.od.nih.gov/ factsheets/Calcium-HealthProfessional/

"Who sets the DRIs? . . . makers and the public"

"About the IOM," Institute of Medicine of the National Academies. http://www.iom.edu/ About-IOM.aspx

"There are no calcium RDAs . . . 1000 milligrams"

"Food and Nutrition, Questions & Answers, What are Dietary Reference Intakes?" Health Canada. Last modified January 23, 2006. http://www.hc-sc.gc.ca/fn-an/nutrition/ reference/dri_ques-ques_anref-eng.php

"Calcium – Dietary Supplement Fact Sheet," U.S. Department of Health & Human Services National Institutes of Health. Reviewed November 21, 2013. http://ods.od.nih.gov/ factsheets/Calcium-HealthProfessional/

"Jointly regulated . . . outdated nutrient recommendations"

"Reference Daily Intake," Wikipedia. Last modified September 24, 2014. http://en.wikipedia .org/wiki/Reference_Daily_Intake

"Daily Value (DV) Tables," U.S. Department of Health & Human Services National Institutes of Health. http://ods.od.nih.gov/HealthInformation/dailyvalues.aspx

Rowlett, Russ. "USFDA Daily Values." How Many? A Dictionary of Units of Measurement. University of North Carolina at Chapel Hill. Last modified June 19, 2001. http://www .unc.edu/~rowlett/units/scales/dailyvalues.htm

"Unlike the RDA ... 1,000 milligrams as the magic number"

"Guidance for Industry: A Food Labeling Guide (14. Appendix F: Calculate the Percent Daily Value for the Appropriate Nutrients," U.S. Food and Drug Administration. Last modified June 20, 2014. http://www.fda.gov/Food/GuidanceRegulation/ GuidanceDocumentsRegulatoryInformation/LabelingNutrition/ucm064928.htm

"The NDC's tribute to niacin ... '... Standard Release 21 (2008)'"

For an explanation of "Niacin Equivalents," see: Higdon, Jane ... Higdon, Jane. "Micronutrient Information Center–Niacin," Linus Pauling Institute, Oregon State University. Last modified July 2013. http://lpi.oregonstate.edu/infocenter/vitamins/niacin/

"Milk's Unique Nutrient Package: Benefits for Bones and Beyond," National Dairy Council. 2009. http://www.nationaldairycouncil.org/SiteCollectionDocuments/education_ materials/wic/MILKsUniqueNutrientPackage.pdf

"'Niacin (Niacin Equivalents) 10% Daily Value.'"

Higdon, Jane. "Micronutrient Information Center—Niacin," Linus Pauling Institute, Oregon State University. Last modified July 2013. http://lpi.oregonstate.edu/infocenter/ vitamins/niacin/

"The DV for niacin is 20 milligrams"

"Guidance for Industry: A Food Labeling Guide (14. Appendix F: Calculate the Percent Daily Value for the Appropriate Nutrients," U.S. Food and Drug Administration. Last modified June 20, 2014. http://www.fda.gov/Food/GuidanceRegulation/ GuidanceDocumentsRegulatoryInformation/LabelingNutrition/ucm064928.htm

"SR25–Reports by Single Nutrients," U.S. Department of Agriculture Agricultural Research Service. http://www.ars.usda.gov/Services/docs.htm?docid=22769

"Just to be sure ... 0.23 milligrams"

"Release 27, USDA National Nutrient Database for Standard Reference," U.S. Department of Agriculture Agricultural Research Service. http://www.ars.usda.gov/Services/docs .htm?docid=8964

"So I looked up the earlier Release 21 ... per 100 grams"

"Release 21, USDA National Nutrient Database for Standard Reference," U.S. Department of Agriculture Agricultural Research Service. http://www.ars.usda.gov/Services/docs .htm?docid=18880

"Thus, as of 2014 ... provides 10 percent of the DV for niacin"

"Milk's 9 Essential Nutrients," Washington Dairy Products Commission. Submitted April 3, 2013. http://www.wadairy.com/blog/milks-9-essential-nutrients

"All About Milk," Washington Dairy Products Commission. http://www.wadairy.com/all-about-milk/milk

"The Nutrition Facts ... 10 percent of the DV for niacin"

"Natrel Organic Skim Milk," Agropur Dairy Cooperative. http://natrel.ca/en/products/
    organic/natrel-organic-skim-milk
"In its fact-providing appendix . . . ' . . . carbohydrates, and fats'"
"Appendix D: Major Nutrients," U.S. Department of Agriculture's Food and Nutrition Service,
    3-5. Available for downloading at www.fns.usda.gov/sites/default/files/appendd.pdf
"Eat a broccoli spear . . . three times more vitamin B₆ than one cup of milk provides"
"Nutrition Facts Comparison Tool," HealthAliciousNess.com. http://www.healthaliciousness
    .com/nutritionfacts/nutrition-facts-compare.php
"Top 10 Foods Highest in Vitamin K," HealthAliciousNess.com http://www
    .healthaliciousness.com/articles/food-sources-of-vitamin-k.php
"Top 10 Foods Highest in Magnesium," HealthAliciousNess.com http://www
    .healthaliciousness.com/articles/foods-high-in-magnesium.php
"Top 10 Foods Highest in Vitamin B5 (Pantothenic Acid)," HealthAliciousNess.com http://
    www.healthaliciousness.com/articles/foods-high-in-pantothenic-acid-vitamin-B5.php
"Top 10 Foods Highest in Vitamin B6," HealthAliciousNess.com http://www
    .healthaliciousness.com/articles/foods-high-in-vitamin-B6.php

CHAPTER 6: OVERRATED

"We can also obtain . . . ultraviolet light"
Gray, Nathan. "Mushrooms provide as much vitamin D as supplements, researchers find,"
    NUTRAingredients.com. April 23, 2013. http://www.nutraingredients.com/Research/
    Mushrooms-provide-as-much-vitamin-D-as-supplements-researchers-find
"(A one-cup serving of Froot Loops contains just under 25 percent of the DV for each of these nutrients)"
"Nutrition Facts and Analysis for Cereals ready-to-eat, Kellogg, Kellogg's Froot Loops,"
    Nutrition Data. nutritiondata.self.com/facts/breakfast-cereals/1532/2
"You can watch it do so by viewing . . . added to soy-based milk"
Beltrone, Gabriel. "Ad of the Day: Got Milk? Iconic campaign pokes fun at 'imitation milk' in
    Goodby's faux-game-show spots," Adweek. May 22, 2012. http://www.adweek.com/
    news/advertising-branding/ad-day-got-milk-140699
"After the link was made . . . times have changed"
de Samaniego-Vaesken, Maria, Elena Alonso-Aperte and Gregorio Varela-Moreiras. "Vitamin
    food fortification today," National Center for Biotechnology Information, PMC. Published
    online April 2, 2012. http://www.ncbi.nlm.nih.gov/pmc/articles/PMC3319130/
"First, even though one 8-ounce glass of milk contains . . . recommending vitamin D intakes of over
    1000 IU"
Feldman, Rachel. "Benefits of Vitamin D." https://www.rachelswellness.com/2014/06/14/
    benefits-of-vitamin-d/

"Guidance for Industry: A Food Labeling Guide (14. Appendix F: Calculate the Percent Daily Value for the Appropriate Nutrients," U.S. Food and Drug Administration. Last modified June 20, 2014. http://www.fda.gov/Food/GuidanceRegulation/ GuidanceDocumentsRegulatoryInformation/LabelingNutrition/ucm064928.htm

Bischoff-Ferrari, Heike, and Walter Willett. "Comment on the IOM Vitamin D and Calcium Recommendations for Adult Bone Health, too Low on Vitamin D—and too Generous on Calcium," The Nutrition Source, Harvard School of Public Health. http://www.hsph .harvard.edu/nutritionsource/vitamin-d-fracture-prevention/

Weil, Andrew. "New Recommendation: Why You Need More Vitamin D," The Huffington Post. Last modified November 17, 2011. http://www.huffingtonpost.com/andrew-weil- md/new-recommendation-why-yo_b_446580.html

Nestle, Marion. "Transcript of our interview: Marion Nestle interview with Mark Hegsted, September 7, 2005." www.foodpolitics.com/wp-content/uploads/hegsted_ edited.doc

"Second, vitamin D fortification of breakfast cereal is now voluntary . . . popular processed foods"

Mills, Carys. "Kellogg given OK to add 'Sunshine Vitamin' to cereal," The Toronto Star. October 24, 2014. http://www.thestar.com/business/2013/08/24/kellogg_given_ok_ to_add_sunshine_vitamin_to_cereal.html

"There are plenty of natural sources . . . vitamin A in the North American food supply"

"Top 10 Foods Highest in Vitamin A," HealthAliciousNess.com. http://www .healthaliciousness.com/articles/food-sources-of-vitamin-A.php

"While the World Health Organization (WHO) . . . 114 grams"

Scott-Thomas, Caroline. "High protein trend to hit Europe – whether we need it or not," NUTRAingredients.com. August 2, 2013. http://www.nutraingredients.com/ Consumer-Trends/High-protein-trend-to-hit-Europe-whether-we-need-it-or-not

"Daily Protein Intake Per Capita," ChartsBin. http://chartsbin.com/view/1155

"A 2012 Food and Health Survey . . . trying to consume"

"2012 Food & Health Survey: Consumer Attitudes toward Food Safety, Nutrition and Health," International Food Information Council Foundation. Last modified May 23, 2014. http:// www.foodinsight.org/2012_Food_Health_Survey_Consumer_Attitudes_toward_ Food_Safety_Nutrition_and_Health

Watson, Elaine. "From Chobani to Special K: Are we on the cusp of a protein renaissance?" Food Navigator USA. Last modified January 25, 2013. http://www.foodnavigator-usa.com/ Markets/From-Chobani-to-Special-K-Are-we-on-the-cusp-of-a-protein-renaissance

"The big-name food manufacturers . . . to Greek yogurt"

Watrous, Monica. "Beyond whey: Emerging sources of protein," Food Business News. March 10, 2014. http://www.foodbusinessnews.net/articles/news_home/New-Product-

Launches/2014/03/Beyond_whey_Emerging_sources_o.aspx?ID={212DA70C-4362-
4A6A-8BE0-E78E59001ECl}&cck=1

"A study published in March 2014 . . . three times more protein than they should be"

Levine, Morgan E., Suarez, Jorge A., et al. "Low Protein Intake Is Associated with a Major
    Reduction in IGF-1, Cancer, and Overall Mortality in the 65 and Younger but Not Older
    Population," Cell Metabolism. Published in the journal *Cell Metabolism* March 4, 2014.
    http://www.cell.com/cell-metabolism/fulltext/S1550-4131%2814%2900062-X

Dennis, Brady. "Too much protein could lead to early death, study says," *The Washington Post*.
    March 4, 2014. http://www.washingtonpost.com/national/health-science/too-much-
    protein-could-lead-to-early-death-study-says/2014/03/04/0af0603e-a3b5-11e3-8466-
    d34c451760b9_story.html

"The exact amount . . . '. . . while staying within calorie needs'"

"What Counts As an Ounce Equivalent in the Protein Foods Group?" U.S. Department
    of Agriculture, ChooseMyPlate.gov. http://www.choosemyplate.gov/food-groups/
    protein-foods-counts.html

"How Much Food from the Protein Foods Group is Needed Daily?" U.S. Department of
    Agriculture, ChooseMyPlate.gov. http://www.choosemyplate.gov/food-groups/
    protein-foods-amount.html

"Time to revisit . . . excessive amounts of protein"

"How Much Food from the Dairy Group is Needed Daily?' U.S. Department of Agriculture,
    ChooseMyPlate.gov. http://www.choosemyplate.gov/food-groups/dairy-amount.html

"It's clear that Americans have no intention of putting the brakes on their protein intake . . ."

Watson, Elaine. "From Chobani to Special K: Are we on the cusp of a protein renaissance?" *Food
    Navigator USA*. Last modified January 25, 2013. http://www.foodnavigator-usa.com/
    Markets/From-Chobani-to-Special-K-Are-we-on-the-cusp-of-a-protein-renaissance

"In partnership with Kellogg's, the Milk Processor Education Program (MilkPEP) . . . fiber and protein"

Kelloggs Share Breakfast Campaign. http://www.kelloggs.com/en_US/share-breakfast.html

"In 2013 actor Taye Diggs . . . '. . . to start every day'"

"Actor and Father Taye Diggs Highlights How Milk's High-Quality Protein At Breakfast
    Helps His Family Start Every Day," PRNewswire. March 5, 2013. http://www
    .prnewswire.com/news-releases/actor-and-father-taye-diggs-highlights-how-milks-
    high-quality-protein-at-breakfast-helps-his-family-start-every-day-195308911.html

"The World Health Organization, which has made a point . . . one-gram rise in protein intake"

Scott-Thomas, Caroline. "High protein trend to hit Europe—whether we need it or not,"
    NUTRAingredients.com. August 2, 2013. http://www.nutraingredients.com/
    Consumer-Trends/High-protein-trend-to-hit-Europe-whether-we-need-it-or-not

"Population nutrient intake goals for preventing diet-related chronic diseases," World Health

Organization. http://www.who.int/nutrition/topics/5_population_nutrient/en/
index25.html

"Human Vitamin and Mineral Requirements, Chapter 11: Calcium – Determinants of calcium
balance," Food and Agriculture Organization of the United States Corporate Document
Repository. http://www.fao.org/docrep/004/y2809e/y2809e0h.htm#bm17.3

"In a 2013 New Zealand Herald article . . . '. . . buffering agent'"

Shaw, Dave. "Factors that could be bad for your bones," *The New Zealand Herald.*
October 7, 2013. http://www.nzherald.co.nz/lifestyle/news/article.cfm?c_
id=6&objectid=11136149

"Even before the 2010 Dietary Guidelines for Americans . . . '. . . for Americans in all age groups'"

"Potassium Recommendation Fact Sheet," National Dairy Council. http://www
.nationaldairycouncil.org/SiteCollectionDocuments/health_wellness/dairy_nutrients/
PotassiumRecommendationFactSheetFINAL.pdf

"There are so many fruits and vegetables . . . or 15 percent of the DV"

"Top 10 Foods Highest in Potassium," HealthAliciousNess.com. http://www
.healthaliciousness.com/articles/food-sources-of-potassium.php

"The website of the Dairy Farmers of Ontario . . . only a 'good' source of vitamin B₁₂ . . ."

"FAQ – Pasteurization," Dairy Farmers of Ontario. Last modified May 17, 2012. http://www
.milk.org/corporate/view.aspx?content=Faq/Pasteurization

"The NDC's answer for B₁₂ is 22 percent of the DV"

"Milk's Unique Nutrient Package: Benefits for Bones and Beyond," National Dairy Council.
2009. http://www.nationaldairycouncil.org/SiteCollectionDocuments/education_
materials/wic/MILKsUniqueNutrientPackage.pdf

"Take Ultra High Temperature (UHT) pasteurized milk . . . helping to protect the environment"

"Milk Nutrition Facts," Tetra Pak Milk Unleashed. http://www.milkunleashed.com/shelf-
safe-milk/nutrition-facts.html

"Questions About Milk Unleashed?" Tetra Pak Inc. http://www.milkunleashed.com/shelf-
safe-milk/faq.html

"Protect What's Good," Tetra Pak Inc. http://www.milkunleashed.com/shelf-safe-milk/
tetra-pak-aseptic-packaging.html

"According to the USDA, riboflavin . . . '. . . mouth and nose healthy'"

"Appendix D: Major Nutrients," U.S. Department of Agriculture's Food and Nutrition Service,
3. Available for downloading at www.fns.usda.gov/sites/default/files/appendd.pdf

"Vegemite . . . in one 3-ounce piece"

"Top 10 Foods Highest in Vitamin B2 (Riboflavin), HealthAliciousNess.com http://www
.healthaliciousness.com/articles/foods-high-in-riboflavin-vitamin-B2.php

"The FDA allows foods that contain . . . of the nutrient"

"Daily Values," Vegan Peace. http://www.veganpeace.com/nutrient_information/
    recommended_values/daily_values.htm

"But do you know what else . . . additives such as phosphoric acid"

Bone, Muscle and Joint Team. "Sodas, Tea and Coffee: Which Can Lower Your Bone
    Density?" Cleveland Clinic. September 24, 2014. http://health.clevelandclinic
    .org/2014/09/sodas-tea-and-coffee-which-can-lower-your-bone-density/

Gutekunst, Lisa. "Hidden Phosphorus in Your Diet and How to Control It," DaVita
    HealthCare Partners Inc. http://www.davita.com/kidney-disease/diet-and-nutrition/
    diet-basics/hidden-phosphorus-in-your-diet-and-how-to-control-it/e/5322

"It is in everything . . . my new favorite, watermelon seeds"

"Top 10 Foods Highest in Phosphorus," HealthAliciousNess.com http://www
    .healthaliciousness.com/articles/high-phosphorus-foods.php

"Seeds watermelon seed kernels dried," HealthAliciousNess.com. http://www
    .healthaliciousness.com/nutritionfacts/nutrition_facts.php?id=Seeds%20
    watermelon%20seed%20kernels%20dried&idn=12174; To convert to ounces go to:
    "Nutrition Facts Comparison Tool," HealthAliciousNess.com. http://www
    .healthaliciousness.com/nutritionfacts/nutrition-facts-compare.php

CHAPTER 7: THE SEEDS OF STRONG BONES

"The upshot, as Dr. David S. Ludwig of Harvard . . . '. . . would crumble without them'"

Ludwig, David S. and Walter C. Willett, "Three Daily Servings of Reduced-Fat Milk: An
    Evidence-Based Recommendation?", *JAMA Pediatrics* 167, no. 9 (2013): 788–789.
    Available for preview at http://archpedi.jamanetwork.com/article
    .aspx?articleid=1704826

Gorman, Ryan. "Milk might NOT be good for you: Harvard scientist claims sweeteners added
    to cartons cancel out health benefits," *The Daily Mail*. Last modified July 2, 2013. http://
    www.dailymail.co.uk/news/article-2353336/Got-milk-Better-make-sure-its-low-fat-
    sugar-free.html

Dahl, Melissa. "Milk does a body good? Maybe not always, Harvard doc argues," *Today*.
    July 1, 2013. http://www.today.com/health/milk-does-body-good-maybe-not-always-
    harvard-doc-argues-6C10505414

"His colleague, Dr. Walter Willett . . . '. . . with this level it is fine to be full fat'"

White, Jon. "Is full-fat milk best? The skinny on the dairy paradox," *NewScientist Health*.
    February 21, 2014. http://www.newscientist.com/article/dn25102-is-fullfat-milk-best-
    the-skinny-on-the-dairy-paradox.html#.UxKczV6eL4i

"Milk is high in calcium and phosphorus . . . 7 percent of the DV for magnesium per cup"

"Milk lowfat fluid 1% milkfat with added vitamin A and vitamin D," HealthAliciousNess.com.

http://www.healthaliciousness.com/nutritionfacts/nutrition_facts.php?id=Milk%20
lowfat%20fluid%201%%20milkfat%20with%20added%20vitamin%20A%20and%20
vitamin%20D&idn=01082; To convert to cups go to: "Nutrition Facts Comparison
Tool," HealthAliciousNess.com. http://www.healthaliciousness.com/nutritionfacts/
nutrition-facts-compare.php

"And yet dried basil . . . a bone-building superfood"

"Spices basil dried," HealthAliciousNess.com. http://www.healthaliciousness.com/
nutritionfacts/nutrition_facts.php?id=Spices%20basil%20dried&idn=02003; To convert
to tablespoons go to: "Nutrition Facts Comparison Tool," HealthAliciousNess.com.
http://www.healthaliciousness.com/nutritionfacts/nutrition-facts-compare.php

"Calcium is in a class of its own, they say . . . nutrient 'of concern'"

Rude, Cheryl. "June Is Dairy Month," Marshall Independent. June 12, 2013. http://www
.marshallindependent.com/page/content.detail/id/540172/June-is-Dairy-Month.
html?nav=5007

"The American Dairy Association (IDFA), falls apart under scrutiny"

Sole, Elise. "Harvard doctor refutes milk recommendations," Yahoo! Lifestyle. July 4, 2013.
https://au.lifestyle.yahoo.com/health/diet-nutrition/article/-/17863803/harvard-
doctor-refutes-milk-recommendations/

"Industry Facts: The Importance of Milk in the Diet," International Dairy Foods Association.
http://www.idfa.org/resource-center/industry-facts/

"In 1990, the year my grandfather died . . . his best year of track competition"

"Carl Lewis, vegan olympic sprinter," Great Vegan Athletes. www.greatveganathletes.com/
vegan_athlete_carl_lewis

"Muscleman Mac Danzig . . . 100 percent vegan"

"50 Famous Vegetarians: Mac Danzig," Pros and Cons. Last modified February 11, 2013.
http://vegetarian.procon.org/view.resource.php?resourceID=004527#Danzig

"Three-time Rolex Grand Am Champion Andy Lally . . . meat-and-potatoes folk"

"Andy Lally, vegan racing driver," Great Vegan Athletes. http://www.greatveganathletes
.com/vegan_athlete_andy-lally-vegan-racing-driver

"Bodybuilding champion Kenneth Williams . . . proud vegan since 2000"

"Kenneth G. Williams, vegan bodybuilder," Great Vegan Athletes. http://www
.greatveganathletes.com/vegan_athlete_kenneth-g-williams-vegan-bodybuilder

"Mike Tyson says . . . power from greens"

"Mike Tyson: 'I Became a Vegan'–Where They Are Now – Oprah Winfrey Network,"
YouTube video, 3:32, posted by "OWN TV, " April 9, 2013. http://www.youtube.com/
watch?v=Vc-DeGEXAmM

"the tatsoi . . . magnesium in just one cup of raw greens"

"Tatsoi," Mr. McGregor's Greens and Herbs. http://arcgreenhouses.com/baby-greens/tatsoi

"Turnip greens . . . and 13 percent of the DV for vitamin B6"

"Turnip greens," The World's Healthiest Foods. http://www.whfoods.com/genpage
.php?tname=foodspice&dbid=144

" 'Because 73 percent of the calcium available . . . non-dairy sources' "

Sole, Elise. "Harvard doctor refutes milk recommendations," Yahoo! Lifestyle. July 4, 2013.
https://au.lifestyle.yahoo.com/health/diet-nutrition/article/-/17863803/harvard-
doctor-refutes-milk-recommendations/

*"Calcium is on its way to becoming even more available . . . a go-to for bakers of gluten-free goods in
particular"*

"Amaranth grain cooked," HealthAliciousNess.com. http://www.healthaliciousness.com/
nutritionfacts/nutrition_facts.php?id=Amaranth%20grain%20cooked&idn=20002; To
convert to cups go to: "Nutrition Facts Comparison Tool," HealthAliciousNess.com.
http://www.healthaliciousness.com/nutritionfacts/nutrition-facts-compare.php

Culliney, Kacey. "Fiber, whole grains and seeds: Packing nutritional punch into gluten-free,"
Bakery and snacks.com. Last modified October 14, 2013. http://www.bakeryandsnacks.com/
Ingredients/Fiber-whole-grains-and-seeds-Packing-nutritional-punch-into-gluten-free

"If calcium is what you're after . . . every health-significant way"

Ward, Jennifer. "Chia Seeds: The latest superfood," Culinate. January 11, 2012. http://www
.culinate.com/articles/produce_dairies/chia_seeds

Duncan, Lindsey. "Chia: Ancient Super-Seed Secret," *The Dr. Oz Show*. Posted October 14,
2011. http://www.doctoroz.com/blog/lindsey-duncan-nd-cn/chia-ancient-super-secret

"Chia seeds are going mainstream . . . over one billion dollars by 2020"

Latif, Ray. "Video: Chia\Vie Aiming for Growth in Grocery, Club Channels," Bevnet. Posted
October 23, 2013. http://www.bevnet.com/news/2013/video-chiavie-aiming-for-
growth-in-grocery-club-channels

Rothman, Max. "Target Identifies Emerging Brands, Begins Four-Wave Test," Bevnet. Posted
November 6, 2013. http://www.bevnet.com/news/2013/target-identifies-emerging-
brands-begins-four-wave-test

Klineman, Jeffrey. "The Battle for Breakfast," Bevnet. Posted October 17, 2013. http://www
.bevnet.com/magazine/issue/2013/the-battle-for-breakfast

Watson, Elaine. "Chia and quinoa lead the field—by miles—when it comes to product launches
with ancient grains and seeds, says Datamonitor," Bakery and snacks.com. Last modified
November 20, 2013. http://www.bakeryandsnacks.com/Trends/Health/Chia-and-
quinoa-lead-the-field-by-miles-when-it-comes-to-product-launches-with-ancient-
grains-and-seeds-says-Datamonitor

"Meet your team; Analyst and research team; Tom Vierhile: Innovation Insights Director," Datamonitor Consumer. http://www.datamonitorconsumer.com/meetyourteam/

Daniells, Stephen. "Chia boom: With 239% growth, chia category set to hit $1 bn by 2020," Bakery and snacks.com. Last modified November 22, 2013. http://www.bakeryandsnacks.com/Trends/Ancient-Grains/Chia-boom-With-239-growth-chia-category-set-to-hit-1-bn-by-2020

"Creating a new chain . . . as plain and white as the dairy industry paints it"

Deniells, Stephen. "Latin American suppliers plan 'Chia Council' to develop business," Food Navigator USA. Last modified August 29, 2012. http://www.foodnavigator-usa.com/Markets/Latin-American-suppliers-plan-Chia-Council-to-develop-business

CHAPTER 8: MILKING CALCIUM

"To each other they say the opposite. In the words of Tom Gallagher . . . '. . . an irrelevant beverage at some point'"

Barret, Rick. "U.S. milk sales reach lowest level in decades," *Milwaukee-Wisconsin Journal Sentinel*. September 3, 2012. http://www.jsonline.com/business/us-milk-sales-reach-lowest-level-in-decades-4m6mnqa-168400516.html

"The storm of plants and now insects . . . to keep milk alive"

Watrous, Monica. "Beyond whey: Emerging sources of protein," Food Business News. March 10, 2014. http://www.foodbusinessnews.net/articles/news_home/New-Product-Launches/2014/03/Beyond_whey_Emerging_sources_o.aspx?ID={212DA70C-4362-4A6A-8BE0-E78E59001EC1}&cck=1

Sifferlin, Alexandra. "What's In a Bug? Lots of Healthy Nutrients: Crickets," *Time*. August 21, 2013.http://healthland.time.com/2013/08/21/why-eating-bugs-is-good-for-you-its-about-the-nutrients/

"Gallagher's announcement in October 2014 . . . '. . . relevant to consumers at every stage of life'"

Dickrell, Jim. "DMI Announces More Than $500 Million in Fluid Milk Partnerships," *Farm Journal*. October 30, 2014. http://www.agweb.com/article/dmi-announces-more-than-500-million-in-fluid-milk-partnerships-jim-dickrell/

Dairy Management Inc. "Dairy Management Partnerships Set to Ignite Fluid Milk Innovation," PerishableNews.com. Posted October 31, 2014. http://www.perishablenews.com/index.php?article=0040438

Peterson, Kim. "Coca-Cola's latest gambit: A new kind of milk," CBS Moneywatch. November 24, 2014. http://www.cbsnews.com/news/coca-cola-is-introducing-fairlife-milk/

"Look at the other four groups with which milk shares space . . . group of plants and animals"

"Welcome to the Five Food Groups," U.S. Department of Agriculture, ChooseMyPlate.gov. http://www.choosemyplate.gov/food-groups/

"The dairy group, in contrast . . . processed forms of cow's milk"

"What Foods Are Included in the Dairy Group?" U.S. Department of Agriculture, ChooseMyPlate.gov. http://www.choosemyplate.gov/food-groups/dairy.html

"Go to the dairy section . . . '. . . calcium that can be absorbed from these foods varies'"

"Tips for Making Wise Choices in the Dairy Group," U.S. Department of Agriculture, ChooseMyPlate.gov. http://www.choosemyplate.gov/food-groups/dairy-tip.html#nomilk

"However, some plants contain sufficiently high levels of calcium to compensate"

"Top 10 Foods Highest in Calcium," HealthAliciousNess.com.http://www.healthaliciousness .com/articles/foods-high-in-calcium.php

"Hence Dr. David Ludwig's pointed effort . . . '. . . seeds and perhaps fish'"

Lee, Kathleen. "Got Milk? Look to Other Food Sources for Daily Calcium," *Science World Report*. First posted July 2, 2013. http://www.scienceworldreport.com/ articles/7906/20130702/milk-look-food-sources-calcium-recommended-intake.htm

Sole, Elise. "Harvard doctor refutes milk recommendations," Yahoo! Lifestyle. July 4, 2013. https://au.lifestyle.yahoo.com/health/diet-nutrition/article/-/17863803/harvard-doctor-refutes-milk-recommendations/

"As an article in the Chicago Tribune *. . . and 49.3 percent respectively"*

Deardorff, Julie. "not milk? If you can't imagine life without a daily dose of dairy, consider new research that questions the value—if not the safety—of this dietary staple," *Chicago Tribune*. February 5, 2006. http://articles.chicagotribune.com/2006-02-05/ features/0602050428_1_calcium-intake-dairy-products-milk

"Table 2: Comparison of Food Sources of Absorbable Calcium," National Dairy Council. http://www.nationaldairycouncil.org/SiteCollectionDocuments/health_wellness/ dairy_nutrients/CalciumAbsorptionpdf.pdf, 2.

"When I was in Florida . . . '. . . other misinformation that's out there, it's incredible'"

April 15, 2004 interview of Allen Morris, former Associate Extension Scientist and Economist at the University of Florida's Citrus Research and Education Center, Lake Alfred, Florida.

"The Recommended Dietary Allowances . . . '. . . where it supports their structure'"

"Vitamin D and Calcium: Updated Dietary Reference Intakes," Health Canada. Last modified March 22, 2012. http://www.hc-sc.gc.ca/fn-an/nutrition/vitamin/vita-d-eng.php#a7

"Calcium–Dietary Supplement Fact Sheet," U.S. Department of Health & Human Services, National Institutes of Health. Last modified November 21, 2013. http://ods.od.nih.gov/ factsheets/Calcium-HealthProfessional/

"We may not know offhand why . . . and 310 milligrams respectively"

"Magnesium–Dietary Supplement Fact Sheet," U.S. Department of Health & Human

Services, National Institutes of Health. Reviewed November 4, 2013. http://ods.od.nih.
gov/factsheets/Magnesium-HealthProfessional/

"In 2011 Time *magazine's . . . '. . . our recommendations for calcium intake'"*

Park, Alice. "Study: U.S. Calcium Guidelines May Be too High," *Time.* May 25, 2011. http://
healthland.time.com/2011/05/25/study-u-s-calcium-guidelines-may-be-too-high/

"If Warensjo's study undermines . . . '. . . calcium and phosphorus content'"

Chan, June M. and Edward L. Giovannucci. "Dairy Products, Calcium, and Vitamin D and Risk
of Prostate Cancer," *Epidemiologic Reviews* 23, no. 1 (2001): 87–92, as cited in *The China
Study: The Most Comprehensive Study of Nutrition Ever Conducted and the Startling Implications
for Diet, Weight Loss, and Long-term Health* (Dallas: BenBella Books, 2006), 178.

Giovannucci, Edward. "Dietary Influences of 1,25 (OH)$_2$ Vitamin D in Relation to Prostate
Cancer: A Hypothesis," *Cancer Causes and Control 9*, no. 6 (December 1998): 567–582, as
cited in *The China Study: The Most Comprehensive Study of Nutrition Ever Conducted and
the Startling Implications for Diet, Weight Loss, and Long-Term Health* (Dallas: BenBella
Books, 2006), 178.

"As Dr. Neville Golden . . . '. . . don't have enough vitamin D, you're not going to absorb it'"

Neighmond, Patti. "Recipe for Strong Teen Bones: Exercise, Calcium and Vitamin D,"
Shots, Health News from NPR. October 28, 2013. http://www.npr.org/blogs/
health/2013/10/28/240553878/the-recipe-for-strong-teenage-bones-exercise-calcium-and-d

"The Campbells explain the process . . . susceptible to an untold number of diseases"

Campbell and Campbell, *The China Study*, 180–181.

Sneider, Mary Catharine. "Health Talk: D, the heavyweight vitamin," *The Sentinel.* October
26, 2013. http://cumberlink.com/news/local/health-talk-d-the-heavy-weight-vitamin/
article_cacf3f78-3e76-11e3-8017-0019bb2963f4.html

"The Campbells note . . . United States than in Singapore"

Campbell and Campbell, *The China Study*, 208–209

"D. Mark Hegsted, Biography," Wikipedia. Last modified October 12, 2014. http://
en.wikipedia.org/wiki/D._Mark_Hegsted

"Dietitians like to remind us . . . scare us into consuming more milk and dairy"

Rude, Cheryl. "June Is Dairy Month," Marshall Independent. June 12, 2013. http://www
.marshallindependent.com/page/content.detail/id/540172/June-is-Dairy-Month
.html?nav=500

"Yet even the World Health Organization . . . '. . . is required to prevent osteoporosis'"

"Population nutrient intake goals for preventing diet-related chronic disease:
Recommendations for preventing osteoporosis," World Health Organization. http://
www.who.int/nutrition/topics/5_population_nutrient/en/index25.html

"The UK's recommendations are more in line . . . '. . . the needs of most individuals'"

Theobald, H. E. "Briefing Paper: Dietary calcium and health," *Nutrition Bulletin*, 30 (British Nutrition Foundation, 2005), 237–277, 252

"First, the age-adjusted rates for incidence . . . '. . . fracture rates in recent decades'"

"Population nutrient intake goals for preventing diet-related chronic disease: Recommendations for preventing osteoporosis," World Health Organization. http://www.who.int/nutrition/topics/5_population_nutrient/en/index25.html

"Remember WHO's suggestion . . . '. . . calcium intake on calcium balance'"

"Population nutrient intake goals for preventing diet-related chronic disease: Recommendations for preventing osteoporosis," World Health Organization. http://www.who.int/nutrition/topics/5_population_nutrient/en/index25.html

"The Physicians Committee for Responsible Medicine . . . interfere with calcium uptake"

"New PCRM Study Shatters Milk Myth: Children's Bone Health Tied to Exercise, Not Dairy," Physicians Committee for Responsible Medicine. http://www.pcrm.org/search/?cid=1202

Lanou, A. J., S. E. Berkow, and N. D. Barnard. "Calcium, Dairy Products, and Bone Health in Children and Young Adults: A Reevaluation of the Evidence," *Pediatrics* 115, no. 3 (March 1, 2005), 736–743.

"More recently . . . '. . . better evidence for our dietary recommendations'"

"Drinking milk in teen years questioned for bone benefits," CBC News. Last modified November 18, 2013. http://www.cbc.ca/news/health/drinking-milk-in-teen-years-questioned-for-bone-benefits-1.2431015

Mozes, Alan. "Drinking Milk as Teens Might Not Protect Men's Bones, Study Suggests," *U.S., News & World Report*, HealthDay. November 19. 2013. http://health.usnews.com/health-news/news/articles/2013/11/19/drinking-milk-as-teens-might-not-protect-mens-bones-study-suggests

"Anchor: 'Can't imagine . . .' . . . Reporter: 'Neither can I'"

"Milk may not be as good for your bones as you thought," CTVNews Video, posted by *The Globe and Mail*, November 19, 2013. http://www.theglobeandmail.com/life/life-video/video-ctv-ottawa-milk-benefits-exaggerated/article15515794/

CHAPTER 9: "D" IS NOT FOR DAIRY

"Although rickets all but disappeared . . . lifestyles sheltered from the sun"

Cheng, Maria. "Rickets bone disease making a comeback in U.K., doctors say," CTV News. Published November 8, 2013. http://www.ctvnews.ca/health/health-headlines/rickets-bone-disease-making-a-comeback-in-u-k-doctors-say-1.1533498

"One hour of exposure to the summer . . . when I last checked was 400 international units (IU)"

Weil, Andrew. "New Recommendation: Why You Need More Vitamin D," The Huffington

Post. Last modified November 17, 2011. http://www.huffingtonpost.com/andrew-weil-md/new-recommendation-why-yo_b_446580.html

"Guidance for Industry: A Food Labeling Guide (14. Appendix F: Calculate the Percent Daily Value for the Appropriate Nutrients," U.S. Food and Drug Administration. Last modified June 20, 2014. http://www.fda.gov/Food/GuidanceRegulation/GuidanceDocumentsRegulatoryInformation/LabelingNutrition/ucm064928.htm

"Despite the capacity . . . 4,000 IU for everyone older than nine"

Bischoff-Ferrari, Heike, and Walter Willett. "Comment on the IOM Vitamin D and Calcium Recommendations for Adult Bone Health, too Low on Vitamin D—and too Generous on Calcium," The Nutrition Source, Harvard School of Public Health. http://www.hsph.harvard.edu/nutritionsource/vitamin-d-fracture-prevention/

"In the spring of 2009 Scientific American . . . '. . . reality right now in the U.S.'"

Lite, Jordan. "Vitamin D deficiency soars in the U.S., study says," *Scientific American*. March 23, 2009. http://www.scientificamerican.com/article.cfm?id=vitamin-d-deficiency-united-states

"The Mayo Clinic's website once contained . . . of vitamin D, which is the RDA for everyone between the ages of one and seventy, is insufficient"

Feldman, Rachel. "Benefits of Vitamin D." https://www.rachelswellness.com/2014/06/14/benefits-of-vitamin-d/

"Drugs and Supplements, Vitamin D Dosing," The Mayo Clinic. http://www.mayoclinic.org/drugs-supplements/vitamin-d/dosing/hrb-20060400

"In 2005 Dr. Andrew Weil . . . advise we all get that much"

Weil, Andrew. "New Recommendation: Why You Need More Vitamin D," The Huffington Post. Last modified November 17, 2011. http://www.huffingtonpost.com/andrew-weil-md/new-recommendation-why-yo_b_446580.html

"In 2005 David Mark Hegsted . . . '. . . two thousand and four thousand units'"

Nestle, Marion. "Transcript of our interview: Marion Nestle interview with Mark Hegsted, September 7, 2005." www.foodpolitics.com/wp-content/uploads/hegsted_edited.doc

"The website of the Harvard School of Public Health has posted . . . '. . . for safety reasons'"

Bischoff-Ferrari, Heike, and Walter Willett. "Comment on the IOM Vitamin D and Calcium Recommendations for Adult Bone Health, too Low on Vitamin D—and too Generous on Calcium," The Nutrition Source, Harvard School of Public Health. http://www.hsph.harvard.edu/nutritionsource/vitamin-d-fracture-prevention/

Mann, Denise. "Guidelines Call for Increase in Vitamin D: Institute of Medicine Wants to Raise the Recommended Dietary Allowance of Vitamin D and Calcium," WebMD. November 30, 2010. http://www.webmd.com/diet/news/20101129/guidelines-increase-vitamin-d

"In its report on Human Vitamin . . . '. . . or compensate for a low one'"

"Human Vitamin and Mineral Requirements, Chapter 11: Calcium–Determinants of Calcium Balance," Food and Agriculture Organization of the U.S. Corporate Document Repository. http://www.fao.org/docrep/004/y2809e/y2809e0h.htm#bm17

"In a paper he wrote reviewing . . . '. . . western-style diets'"

Hegsted, D. M. "From Chick Nutrition to Nutrition Policy," *Annual Review of Nutrition* 20 (2000): 1–19, 1

"Magnesium, like calcium . . . the 400 milligram DV for magnesium"

"Top 10 Foods Highest in Magnesium," HealthAliciousNess.com http://www.healthaliciousness.com/articles/foods-high-in-magnesium.php

King, D. E., A. G. Mainous 3rd, M. E. Gessey, and R. F. Woolson. "Dietary Magnesium and C-Reactive Protein Levels," *Journal of the American College of Nutrition* 24, no. 3 (June 2005): 166–171, as cited at http://www.ncbi.nlm.nih.gov/pubmed/15930481, National Center for Biotechnology Information, PubMed

"As Dr. David Ludwig states, 'Indeed, the recommended . . . a recent meta-analysis'"

Perry, Susan. "milk-consumption guidelines questioned; scientists call for more evidence," *MinnPost*. July 9, 2013. http://www.minnpost.com/second-opinion/2013/07/milk-consumption-guidelines-questioned-scientists-call-more-evidence

"The United States and Canada could learn from the United Kingdom, which speaks the same 'drink your milk for calcium' language . . ."

"Wirral MP celebrates free milk in schools," *Wirral Globe*. Last modified September 27, 2013. http://www.wirralglobe.co.uk/news/10703947. Wirral_MP_celebrates_free_milk_in_schools/

"In her briefing paper . . . and both men and women older than seventy"

Theobald, H.E., 2005 British Nutrition Foundation, Nutrition Bulletin 30, 237–277, 257

"Calcium – Dietary Supplement Fact Sheet," U.S. Department of Health & Human Services National Institutes of Health. Reviewed November 21, 2013. http://ods.od.nih.gov/factsheets/Calcium-HealthProfessional/

"The lack of science behind the calcium RDAs . . . '. . . pretty much the way we wrote them'"

Nestle, Marion. "Transcript of our interview: Marion Nestle interview with Mark Hegsted, September 7, 2005." www.foodpolitics.com/wp-content/uploads/hegsted_edited.doc

"Imagine for a minute if the USDA joined WHO . . . is sufficient to prevent osteoporosis"

"Population nutrient intake goals for preventing diet-related chronic disease: Recommendations for preventing osteoporosis," World Health Organization. http://www.who.int/nutrition/topics/5_population_nutrient/en/index25.html

"Say the USDA also heeded the findings of the Swedish studies . . . they are hazardous to our health"

Park, Alice. "Study: U.S. Calcium Guidelines May Be too High," *Time*. May 25, 2011. http://healthland.time.com/2011/05/25/study-u-s-calcium-guidelines-may-be-too-high/

Michaëlsson, Karl et al. "Milk intake and risk of mortality and fractures in women and men: cohort studies," *The BMJ*. Published October 28, 2014. http://www.bmj.com/content/349/bmj.g6015

". . . three tablespoons of dried basil . . . red blood cell, heart, and colon health"

"Spices basil dried," HealthAliciousNess.com. http://www.healthaliciousness.com/nutritionfacts/nutrition_facts.php?id=Spices%20basil%20dried&idn=02003; To convert to tablespoons go to: "Nutrition Facts Comparison Tool," HealthAliciousNess.com. http://www.healthaliciousness.com/nutritionfacts/nutrition-facts-compare.php

"Milk lowfat fluid 1% milkfat with added vitamin A and vitamin D," HealthAliciousNess.com. http://www.healthaliciousness.com/nutritionfacts/nutrition_facts.php?id=Milk%20lowfat%20fluid%201%%20milkfat%20with%20added%20vitamin%20A%20and%20vitamin%20D&idn=01082; To convert to cups and compare to tablespoons of basil go to: "Nutrition Facts Comparison Tool," HealthAliciousNess.com. http://www.healthaliciousness.com/nutritionfacts/nutrition-facts-compare.php

"Dietary Guidelines for Americans, 2010," U.S. Department of Agriculture, Center for Nutrition Policy and Promotion, 40-41. Available for downloading at http://www.cnpp.usda.gov/DGAs2010-PolicyDocument.htm

"Appendix D: Major Nutrients," U.S. Department of Agriculture's Food and Nutrition Service. www.fns.usda.gov/sites/default/files/appendd.pdf

"Remember that even the National Dairy Council . . . better absorbed than the calcium in milk"

"Table 2: Comparison of Food Sources of Absorbable Calcium," National Dairy Council. http://www.nationaldairycouncil.org/SiteCollectionDocuments/health_wellness/dairy_nutrients/CalciumAbsorptionpdf.pdf, 2

"If your palate is more like that of George H. W. Bush . . . in the White House garden, don't worry"

Dowd, Maureen. " 'I'm President,' So No More Broccoli!", *New York Times*. Published March 23, 1990. http://www.nytimes.com/1990/03/23/us/i-m-president-so-no-more-broccoli.html

"Doctors David Ludwig and Walter Willett call on . . . '. . . a universal minimum requirement'"

Perry, Susan. "Milk-consumption guidelines questioned; scientists call for more evidence," *MinnPost*. July 9, 2013. http://www.minnpost.com/second-opinion/2013/07/milk-consumption-guidelines-questioned-scientists-call-more-evidence

"The USDA has done the same for alcohol . . . ages of nineteen and thirty"

"Dietary Guidelines for Americans, 2010," U.S. Department of Agriculture, Center for Nutrition Policy and Promotion, 21. Available for downloading at http://www.cnpp.usda.gov/DGAs2010-PolicyDocument.htm

"Calories: How Many Can I Have?", U.S. Department of Agriculture, ChooseMyPlate.gov.

http://www.choosemyplate.gov/weight-management-calories/calories/empty-calories-amount.html

"Doctors such as David Ludwig . . . one giant experiment"

Deardorff, Julie. "not milk? If you can't imagine life without a daily dose of dairy, consider new research that questions the value—if not the safety—of this dietary staple," *Chicago Tribune*. February 5, 2006. http://articles.chicagotribune.com/2006-02-05/features/0602050428_1_calcium-intake-dairy-products-milk

Ludwig, David S. and Walter C. Willett. "Three Daily Servings of Reduced-Fat Milk: An Evidence-Based Recommendation?", *JAMA Pediatrics* 167, no. 9 (2013): 788–789. Available for preview at http://archpedi.jamanetwork.com/article.aspx?articleid=1704826

CHAPTER 10: A-NOT-OKAY

"In November 2012 Barbara O'Brien . . . to 195 pounds"

Quaife, Tom. "Commentary: Let's solve the fluid milk crisis," Dairy Herd Management. Last modified November 2, 2012. http://www.dairyherd.com/dairy-news/latest/Lets-solve-the-fluid-milk-crisis-176910041.html

Wyche, Paul. "Competition gulps market of cow's milk," *The Journal Gazette*. Last modified April 5, 2014. http://www.journalgazette.net/article/20140405/BIZ/304059967

"In his editorial, Quaife identified . . . '. . . cold milk in accessible places in convenient packaging in a variety of flavors'"

Quaife, Tom. "Commentary: Let's solve the fluid milk crisis," Dairy Herd Management. Last modified November 2, 2012. http://www.dairyherd.com/dairy-news/latest/Lets-solve-the-fluid-milk-crisis-176910041.html

"As Ruslan Medzhitov, an immunobiologist at Yale School of Medicine . . . '. . . Get out'"

"Noted," *Yale Alumni Magazine*. July/August 2012, 26. https://www.yalealumnimagazine.com/articles/3479

"In his book Wheat Belly *. . . rather than sugar content is the culprit"*

Frid, H., M. Nilsson, J. J. Holst, and I. M. Bjork. "Effect of whey on blood glucose and insulin responses to composite breakfast and lunch meals in type 2 diabetic subjects," *American Journal of Clinical Nutrition* 82, no. 1 (July 2005): 69–75 as cited in William Davis, *Wheat Belly: Lose the Wheat, Lose the Weight, and Find Your Path Back to Health* (Toronto: Collins, 2011), 180

Adebamowo, C. A., D. Spiegelman, F. W. Danby, et al. "High School Dietary Dairy Intake and Teenage Acne," *Journal of the American Academy of Dermatology* 52, no. 2 (February 2005): 207–14, as cited in Davis, *Wheat Belly*, 180

"He notes that . . . and Zulus, so is dairy"

Davis, *Wheat Belly*, 178–179

"The website learnstuff.com . . . '. . . infants and children'"

"Got Milk? Infographic," Learn Stuff. Last modified October 5, 2012. http://www.learnstuff
.com/got-milk/

"That's why Canada has decided to require 'common allergens,' . . . finally sulphites"

Gagné, Claire. "Food Labelling: How to Choose Products When You Have Allergies,"
Huffington Post. Last modified January 25, 2014. http://www.huffingtonpost
.ca/2014/01/16/food-labelling-canada_n_4609972.html

"The tension between the push for . . . a 'natural' lactation"

Morton, James. "Daisy's modified milk proves divisive," *The New Zealand Herald*.
October 3, 2012. http://www.nzherald.co.nz/health/news/article.cfm?c_
id=204&objectid=10838017

Tocker, Ali. "Strong Opposition to GE Milk," *NZ Farmer*. Last modified February 10, 2012.
http://www.stuff.co.nz/business/farming/7757038/Strong-opposition-to-GE-milk

"The Oxford dictionary defines 'natural' as 'established by nature'"

The Concise Oxford Dictionary, seventh edition (Oxford: Clarendon Press)

"'Name the Ingredients'" . . . 'Real. Simple. Got Milk?'"

"Got Milk Commercial—Name the Ingredients-Name the Ingredients-Got Milk?-Goodby,
Silverstein & Partners," AdWeek. Last modified July 31, 2012. http://www.adweek.com/
video/got-milk-commercial-name-ingredients-got-milk-goodby-silverstein-partners-142354

"got milk? 'Name the Ingredients,' " Vimeo. June 4, 2012. http://vimeo.com/43433385

"It's called a2 milk and it's sold by the a2 Milk Company . . . is messing with people's health"

Harkinson, Josh. "You're Drinking the Wrong Kind of Milk," *Mother Jones*. March 12, 2014.
http://www.motherjones.com/environment/2014/03/a1-milk-a2-milk-america

"Our History," a2 Nutrition. http://a2nutrition.com.au/our-expertise/our-history/

Lewis, Roz. "What is the truth about Dannii's designer milk? Star says new product helps beat
her dairy sensitivity," The Daily Mail. Last modified November 20, 2012. http://www
.dailymail.co.uk/health/article-2234532/Dannii-Minogue-Star-says-new-product-
helps-beat-dairy-sensitivity.html

"The company received another boost . . . call for larger, more detailed studies"

Hayes, Jessica. "A2 milk drinkers may get less gut aches," *Farm Weekly*. August 11, 2014.
http://www.farmweekly.com.au/news/agriculture/cattle/dairy/a2-milk-drinkers-may-
get-less-gut-aches/2708166.aspx?storypage=0

"Switching to A2 milk can bring digestive health benefits," *The Weekly Times*. August 15, 2014.
http://www.weeklytimesnow.com.au/business/dairy/switching-to-a2-milk-can-bring-
digestive-health-benefits/story-fnkeqg0i-1227024011714

"Some health experts have dismissed a2 milk . . . '. . . we eat most—dairy and wheat'"

Lynch, Jared. "Leading nutritionist Rosemary Stanton questions a2 Milk's health claims," *The Sydney Morning Herald*. September 10, 2014. http://www.smh.com.au/business/retail/leading-nutritionist-rosemary-stanton-questions-a2-milks-health-claims-20140909-10cxhb.html

Lewis, Roz. "What is the truth about Dannii's designer milk? Star says new product helps beat her dairy sensitivity," *The Daily Mail*. Last modified November 20, 2012. http://www.dailymail.co.uk/health/article-2234532/Dannii-Minogue-Star-says-new-product-helps-beat-dairy-sensitivity.html

"In his July 7, 2012 Opinionator column . . . he was 'treated as a neurotic'"

Bittman, Mark. "Got Milk? You Don't Need It," *The New York Times*. July 7, 2012. http://opinionator.blogs.nytimes.com/2012/07/07/got-milk-you-dont-need-it/

"Mark Bittman's ordeal seems . . . his favorite flavor wintergreen"

Bittman, Mark. "Got Milk? You Don't Need It," *The New York Times*. July 7, 2012. http://opinionator.blogs.nytimes.com/2012/07/07/got-milk-you-dont-need-it/

"In 2004 the Queensland Health Department . . . for a2 milk's growing market share"

Binsted, Tim. "Parmalat boss hits out at a2 milk," *NZ Farmer*. Last modified March 18, 2014. http://www.stuff.co.nz/business/farming/dairy/9840448/Parmalat-boss-hits-out-at-a2-milk

Lynch, Jared. "Leading nutritionist Rosemary Stanton questions a2 Milk's health claims," *The Sydney Morning Herald*. September 10, 2014. http://www.smh.com.au/business/retail/leading-nutritionist-rosemary-stanton-questions-a2-milks-health-claims-20140909-10cxhb.html

Astley, Mark. "a2 milk not confusing Australian consumers: A2DPA," *Dairy Reporter*. Last modified March 25, 2014. http://www.dairyreporter.com/Manufacturers/a2-milk-concept-not-confusing-Australian-consumers-A2DPA

Katz, Bella. "A2 milk story wins greater market share," stuff.co.nz Business Unlimited. Last modified March 25, 2014. http://www.stuff.co.nz/business/unlimited/entrepreneurs/9862110/A2-milk-story-wins-greater-market-share

"A2 sales up 22 per cent, targets US," The Australian. February 26, 2014. http://www.theaustralian.com.au/news/latest-news/a2-sales-up-22-per-cent-targets-us/story-fn3dxity-1226837967071

"A2 Corp to take over NZ marketing, enter North America, Europe," *The National Business Review*. October 31, 2012. http://www.nbr.co.nz/article/A2-corp-take-control-nz-marketing-enter-north-america-europe-bd-131559

"Since the 2012 meeting between the National Milk Producers Federation . . . 'ignite fluid milk innovation'"

Dairy Management Inc. "Dairy Management Partnerships Set to Ignite Fluid Milk
Innovation," PerishableNews.com. Posted October 31, 2014. http://www
.perishablenews.com/index.php?article=0040438

"Still others with more radical ideas . . . have stepped up to the plate"

Weston, Shaun. "Meiji New Style Milk fragrances milk," FoodBev.com. September 23, 2014.
http://www.foodbev.com/news/meiji-new-style-milk-fragranced-milk#
.VCNKiueeL4g

Astley, Mark. "Meiji fragranced milk a 'new type of milk': Datamonitor," *Dairy Reporter.* Last
modified September 29, 2014. http://www.dairyreporter.com/Manufacturers/Meiji-
fragranced-milk-a-new-type-of-milk-Datamonitor

"Dr. Scott Spies . . . '. . . very healthy lifestyle without milk' "

Martinez, Astrid. "How can you lead a healthy life if you can't drink milk?" WBTV. Last
modified September 28, 2012. http://www.wbtv.com/story/19652161/moo-ving-
presentation

CHAPTER 11: A HISTORY OF INTOLERANCE

"A National Institutes of Health webpage . . . '. . . lactose after infancy' "

"Lactose intolerance," Genetics Home Reference. Reviewed May 2010. http://ghr.nlm.nih
.gov/condition/lactose-intolerance

Porras, Paul. "Milk has no place in school lunches," The Hill. July 9, 2014. http://thehill
.com/blogs/congress-blog/healthcare/211645-milk-has-no-place-in-school-
lunches#ixzz376hNei26

"A 2006 clinical report published . . . as few as 2 percent can't"

Heyman, Melvin B. for the Committee on Nutrition. "Lactose Intolerance in Infants, Children,
and Adolescents," *Pediatrics* 118, no. 3 (September 2006): 1279–1286, 1280, as cited in
W. Andrea Wiley, *Re-Imagining Milk* (New York: Routledge, 2011), 29

"However, these people make up a minority . . . '. . . institutionalized government sponsored racism' "

Mills, Milton testifying before the 2015 Dietary Guidelines Advisory Committee. "Second
Meeting-Day 2, Public Oral Testimony," U.S. Department of Health and Human Services, at 2hrs 22 min into the videocast. http://videocast.nih.gov/summary
.asp?Live=13448&bhcp=1

"It all began 8,000 to 10,000 years ago . . . was domesticated in the Near East"

"History of Cow's Milk from the Ancient World to the Present, 8000 BC–63 BC," ProCon.
org. Last modified July 10, 2013. http://milk.procon.org/view.resource
.php?resourceID=000832

"In Northern Europe in the 1970s . . . break down the sugar, lactose, in milk"

Thompson, Helen and Adam Cole. "Archaeologists Find Ancient Evidence of

Cheese-Making," NPR. December 13, 2012. http://www.npr.org/blogs/
thesalt/2012/12/13/167034734/archaeologists-find-ancient-evidence-of-cheese-making

Bogucki, P.I. "Ceramic sieves of the Linear Pottery culture and their economic implications,"
Oxford Journal of Archaeology 3, no.1 (1984): 15–30, at 15. For preview go to http://www
.readcube.com/articles/10.1111%2Fj.1468-0092.1984.tb00113.x?r3_referer=wol&show_
checkout=1

"Today, government, the dairy industry, and health experts . . . is the most mindbending"

"Milk for Kids With Lactose Intolerance," *Nibbles for Health: Nutrition Newsletters for Parents of
Young Children* 27 (USDA, Food and Nutrition Service, 2013), 2. Available at www.fns
.usda.gov/sites/default/files/Nibbles_Newsletter_27.pdf

"Health Tip: If You're Lactose Intolerant," HealthDay. October 2, 2012. http://health.usnews
.com/health-news/news/articles/2012/10/02/health-tip-if-youre-lactose-intolerant

"Besides containing significant levels of oxalic acid . . . urinary and fecal calcium loss"

Lagemann, M. et al. "Effect of cocoa on excretion of oxalate, citrate, magnesium and calcium in
the urine of children," National Center for BiotechnologyInformation, PubMed. http://
www.ncbi.nlm.nih.gov/pubmed/4069117

Zeratsky, Katherine. "A friend told me that chocolate impairs absorption of calcium. Is this
true?" Nutrition and Healthy Eating, Mayo Clinic. September 27, 2012. http://www
.mayoclinic.com/health/calcium/AN01294

"Advanced Orthomolecular Research 2012 catalogue," 37, AOR. Available for download at
www.aor.ca/catalogues/2014-2/

"The USDA is counting on this theory working . . . '. . . to drink it'"

"Milk for Kids With Lactose Intolerance," *Nibbles for Health: Nutrition Newsletters for Parents of
Young Children* 27 (USDA, Food and Nutrition Service, 2013), 2. Available at www.fns
.usda.gov/sites/default/files/Nibbles_Newsletter_27.pdf

"'Offer cheese' is the . . . fluid milk options fail"

"Milk for Kids With Lactose Intolerance," *Nibbles for Health: Nutrition Newsletters for Parents of
Young Children* 27 (USDA, Food and Nutrition Service, 2013), 2. Available at www.fns
.usda.gov/sites/default/files/Nibbles_Newsletter_27.pdf

"Mark Thomas, the evolutionary geneticist . . . can't identify the first instance of lactase persistence"

Thompson, Helen. "An Evolutionary Whodunit: How Did Humans Develop
Lactose Tolerance?" NPR. December 28, 2012. http://www.npr.org/blogs/
thesalt/2012/12/27/168144785/an-evolutionary-whodunit-how-did-humans-develop-
lactose-tolerance

"Some have postulated that the gene was first selected for in 5,500 BC"

Itan, Y. et al. "The origins of lactase persistence in Europe," PLoS Comput. Biol. 5,
e1000491 (2009) as cited in Gamba, Cristina et al. "Genome flux and stasis in a five

millennium transect of European prehistory," Nature Communications. Published
October 21, 2014. http://www.nature.com/ncomms/2014/141021/ncomms6257/abs/
ncomms6257.html

"Ron Pinhasi, PhD, an archaeologist at University College Dublin . . . 10 percent more they say"

Zimmer, Carl. "From Ancient DNA, a Clearer Picture of Europeans Today," *The New York
Times*. October 30, 2014. http://www.nytimes.com/2014/10/30/science/from-ancient-
dna-a-clearer-picture-of-europeans-today.html

Thompson, Helen. "An Evolutionary Whodunit: How Did Humans Develop
Lactose Tolerance?" NPR. December 28, 2012. http://www.npr.org/blogs/
thesalt/2012/12/27/168144785/an-evolutionary-whodunit-how-did-humans-develop-
lactose-tolerance

"Thus, upon visiting the Guru Angad Dev Veterinary . . . '. . . to sustain the white revolution'"

Goyal, Divya. "GADVASU focuses on value addition; Tota Singh says milk adulteration will
be stopped," *The Indian Express*. Posted September 13, 2014. http://indianexpress
.com/article/cities/ludhiana/gadvasu-focuses-on-value-addition-tota-singh-says-milk-
adulteration-will-be-stopped/#sthash.oOuHX2EK.dpuf

"Andrea Wiley, PhD, professor of anthropology . . . '. . . sufficient milk each day'"

Wiley, S. Andrea. *Re-Imagining Milk* (New York: Routledge, 2011), 58, 93–94

"Shanghai Bright Dairy and Food Corporation . . . 'One cup of milk can strengthen a nation'"

"Bright Dairy and Food Co., Ltd. Company Information," Hoovers. http://www.hoovers
.com/company-information/cs/company-profile.Shanghai_Bright_Dairy__Food_Co_
Ltd_.aa4f78fab1ec020d.html

Chen, Kathy. "Got Milk? The New Craze In China Is Dairy Drinks," *The Wall Street
Journal*. Last modified February 28, 2003. http://online.wsj.com/article/0,,
SB1046383693546800623,00.html

"In Canada, for instance, the Nutrition Services division . . . dairy in their diets and 'thinness'"

Mosby, Ian. " 'Food Will Win the War' ": The Politics and Culture of Food and Nutrition
During the Second World War" (PhD diss., York University, 2011), 92–93

"In 1943 Winston Churchill declared: 'Milk in babies is the best investment'"

Valenze, Deborah. *Milk: A Local & Global History* (New Haven, CT: Yale University Press,
2011), 254

"Back in the United States, a brochure . . . '. . . only a small part of that market is being tapped'"

More Milk for More Children (Marketing Administration, U.S. Department of Agriculture,
Miscellaneous Publication No. 493: 1942), 3–4. Available as a Google eBook at http://
books.google.ca/books?id=siQuAAAAYAAJ&printsec=frontcover#v=onepage&q&
f=false

"So many countries are buying in that in 2000 . . . last Wednesday of every September"

"School milk," Food and Agriculture Organization of the United Nations. http://www.fao
.org/economic/est/est-commodities/dairy/school-milk/en/

"15th World School Milk Day, 24 September 2014," Food and Agriculture Organization of
the United Nations. http://www.fao.org/economic/est/est-commodities/dairy/school-
milk/15th-world-school-milk-day-wsmd/en/

"The method in the madness . . . '. . . and improve social inclusion'"

"MP celebrates School Milk Day," *Retford Guardian*. Published on October 19, 2012. http://
www.retfordtoday.co.uk/news/local-news/mp-celebrates-school-milk-day-1-5043040

"In 2013 Vietnam's deputy director . . . average height of children by two centimeters"

"Milk programme seeks to improve children's health," Vietmaz. June 12, 2013. http://www
.vietmaz.com/2013/06/milk-programme-seeks-to-improve-childrens-health/

Astley, Mark. "Vietnam height initiatives drive drinking milk sales growth: Euromonitor,"
Dairy Reporter. Last modified April 28, 2014. http://www.dairyreporter.com/Markets/
Vietnam-height-initiatives-drive-drinking-milk-sales-growth-Euromonitor

"Thailand also has a plan . . . '. . . they want taller children with stronger bones'"

"Thais drink little milk, stay short," *Bangkok Post*. Published September 26, 2013. http://
www.bangkokpost.com/news/health/371607/health-minister-says-thai-children-must-
drink-more-milk

Hodal, Kate. "Thais told to drink milk to boost height," *The Guardian*. June 3, 2013. http://
www.theguardian.com/world/2013/jun/03/thais-told-drink-milk-boost-height

DeFraia, Daniel. "Thailand's 'Got Milk' campaign aims to make citizens taller," *Global Post*.
June 4, 2013. http://www.globalpost.com/dispatch/news/regions/asia-pacific/130604/
thailands-got-milk-campaign-aims-make-citizens-taller

*"A 'Concerned Taiwanese,' who had heard Wisconsin Public Radio's . . . '. . . Please correct your
awful advice'"*

Paster, Zorba. "Dr. Zorba Paster: Test yourself to see if you are dairy intolerant," *The Buffalo
News*. July 5, 2014. http://www.buffalonews.com/columns/dr-zorba-paster/dr-zorba-
paster-test-yourself-to-see-if-you-are-dairy-intolerant-20140705

"Thus MP Kevin Barron . . . '. . . develop our social skills'"

"MP hands out the milk for health," *Isle of Thanet Gazette*. Posted October 19, 2012. http://
www.thanetgazette.co.uk/MP-hands-milk-health/story-17124712-detail/story.html

"MP celebrates School Milk Day," *Retford Guardian*. Last modified October 19, 2012. http://
www.retfordtoday.co.uk/news/local-news/mp-celebrates-school-milk-day-1-5043040

*"Health Canada publishes safety fact sheets with titles like . . . 'Milk—One of the ten priority food
allergens'"*

"Milk—One of the ten priority food allergens," Health Canada. http://www.hc-sc.gc.ca/fn-
an/pubs/securit/2012-allergen_milk-lait/index-eng.php

"Consider the following hypothetical . . . '. . . development of all [emphasis added] children'"

"Sherwood MP helps Blidworth children celebrate milk day," Chad. October 15, 2012. http://www.chad.co.uk/news/council/education/sherwood-mp-helps-blidworth-children-celebrate-milk-day-1-5024438

"Despite all the Sukos . . . 'offers a variety of social opportunities'"

"MPs to celebrate school milk with a glass of the white stuff," Children's Food Trust. September 17, 2012. http://www.childrensfoodtrust.org.uk/news-and-events/news/mps-to-celebrate-school-milk-with-a-glass-of-the-white-stuff

"A 2010 survey of 350 parents of children . . . deadly poison"

"Personal Health: News and Notes," Philly.com. Posted November 5, 2012. http://articles.philly.com/2012-11-05/news/34931502_1_ivermectin-food-allergies-lice-infestations

"When Alex Ohlendorf was a junior . . . which he donated to his football team"

"got milk? backing you up," PRNewswire. http://photos.prnewswire.com/prnfull/20121129/LA18814

"Bonita Vista High School student wins Got Milk? Contest," CBS 8. Last modified November 30, 2012. http://www.cbs8.com/story/20227930/bonita-vista-high-school-student-wins-got-milk-contest

"Read the headline of one story . . . '. . . Imagine if the same result was achieved in China?'"

"World School Milk Day 2011, Elopak company magazine article: Building foundations for future dairy markets," Mleczarstwo. September 14, 2011. www.mleczarstwo.com/a7561,world_school_milk_day_2011_elopak_company_magazine_article.html

CHAPTER 12: THE BIG MISTAKE

"The tabled rules, which were presented in February . . . and limited to 200 calories"

Heavey, Susan and Charles Abbott. "Rules call for swing to healthier snacks in schools," Reuters. February 1, 2013. http://www.reuters.com/article/2013/02/01/us-usa-schools-snacks-idUSBRE91019720130201

"Hailed by many as a long-overdue . . . Afghanistan than combat wounds"

Viebeck, Elise. "Retired military chiefs: Obesity levels mean US is 'too fat to fight,'" The Hill. September 25, 2012. http://thehill.com/blogs/defcon-hill/army/258631-retired-military-chiefs-call-us-kids-still-too-fat-to-fight

"Those who have been most vocal . . . are killers for some humans"

"Want Milk? Is Cow's Milk Meant for Human Consumption? (Part 1)," One Green Planet. October 1, 2011. http://www.onegreenplanet.org/lifestyle/is-cows-milk-meant-for-human-consumption-part-1/

"According to the Centers for Disease Control and Prevention . . . one-third of Americans are obese"

"Adult Obesity Facts," Centers for Disease Control and Prevention. Last modified September 9, 2014. http://www.cdc.gov/obesity/data/adult.html

"Just ask Alice . . . a week to skim off one pound"

"How many calories does it take to lose one pound," Go Ask Alice! Columbia Health. Last modified November 19, 2007. http://goaskalice.columbia.edu/how-many-calories-does-it-take-to-lose-one-pound

"Assuming, as the balance of estimates say, about 60 percent . . . 250,000 to be exact"

Weise, Elizabeth. "Sixty percent of adults can't digest milk," *USA Today*. Last modified September 15, 2009. http://usatoday30.usatoday.com/tech/science/2009-08-30-lactose-intolerance_N.htm

"Lactose Intolerance Statistics–Statistic Brain," 2013 Statistic Brain Research Institute. Date verified July 23, 2012. http://www.statisticbrain.com/lactose-intolerance-statistics/

"State & County QuickFacts: USA," U.S. Census Bureau. Last modified July 8, 2014. http://quickfacts.census.gov/qfd/states/00000.html

"Elephant," Wikipedia. Last modified October 20, 2014. http://en.wikipedia.org/wiki/Elephant

"The USDA, along with the Academy of Nutrition and Dietetics and its graduates . . . to convert the lactase impersistent into milk drinkers"

Hayes, Dayle. "5 Smart Ways to Enjoy Dairy if Lactose is a Concern," Billings Clinic. http://www.billingsclinic.com/body.cfm?id=959

"They do so by offering tips such as full-fat . . . '. . . milk provides to stay strong and healthy'"

"Milk for Kids With Lactose Intolerance," *Nibbles for Health: Nutrition Newsletters for Parents of Young Children* 27 (USDA, Food and Nutrition Service, 2013), 2. Available at www.fns.usda.gov/sites/default/files/Nibbles_Newsletter_27.pdf

"The members of the calcium-rich class of plants . . . with green sources of calcium"

"Top 10 Foods Highest in Calcium," HealthAliciousNess.com. http://www.healthaliciousness.com/articles/foods-high-in-calcium.php

"The Nutrition of Mint," FitDay. http://www.fitday.com/fitness-articles/nutrition/healthy-eating/the-nutrition-of-mint.html

"Nutritional Info: Spices, savory, ground," SkipThePie.org. http://skipthepie.org/spices-and-herbs/spices-savory-ground/?weight=100

"Nutrition Info For: Spices, savory, ground," FitDay. http://www.fitday.com/webfit/nutrition/All_Foods/savory_ground.html

"In 1995, the New Yorker *reported . . . 50 million Americans were lactose intolerant"*

Rose, Alison. "Intolerance," The New Yorker. April 3, 1995, 35. Available at http://www.newyorker.com/archive/1995/04/03/1995_04_03_035_TNY_CARDS_000371131

"More recent statistics . . . broaching the 150 million mark"

Weise, Elizabeth. "Sixty percent of adults can't digest milk," *USA TODAY*. Last modified September 15, 2009. http://usatoday30.usatoday.com/tech/science/2009-08-30-lactose-intolerance_N.htm

CHAPTER 13: WHOLE TRUTH

"That's what the USDA and FDA say, albeit indirectly . . . '. . . or low-fat (one percent) milk'"

"What Foods Are Included in the Dairy Group? Key Consumer Message" U.S. Department of Agriculture, ChooseMyPlate.gov. http://www.choosemyplate.gov/food-groups/dairy.html

"According to FDA regulations . . . 'disease or health-related condition'"

"Health Claims: general requirements," 21CFR101.14. U.S. Food and Drug Administration. http://www.accessdata.fda.gov/scripts/cdrh/cfdocs/cfcfr/CFRSearch.cfm?fr=101.14

"The FDA has specific requirements for using . . . 15 percent of calories from saturated fat"

"General nutritional claims," 21CFR101.65(d)(2)(i), 21CFR101.65(d)(2). U.S. Food and Drug Administration. http://www.accessdata.fda.gov/scripts/cdrh/cfdocs/cfcfr/CFRSearch.cfm?fr=101.65

"Fat content claims," 21CFR101.62(b)(2). U.S. Food and Drug Administration. http://www.accessdata.fda.gov/scripts/cdrh/cfdocs/cfcfr/CFRSearch.cfm?fr=101.62

"Fatty acid content claims," 21CFR101.62(c)(2). U.S. Food and Drug Administration. http://www.accessdata.fda.gov/scripts/cdrh/cfdocs/cfcfr/CFRSearch.cfm?fr=101.62

"CytoSport, with its line of Muscle Milk . . . $85,000 to the American Heart Association"

Watson, Elaine. "Judge gives provisional thumbs up to $5.3m settlement over 'healthy' claims on Muscle Milk," Food Navigator-USA. Last modified November 22, 2013. http://www.foodnavigator-usa.com/Regulation/Judge-gives-provisional-thumbs-up-to-5.3m-settlement-over-healthy-claims-on-Muscle-Milk

Ford, Richard. "Cytosport's Muscle Milk hits UK mults in £40m sales drive," The Grocer. October 27, 2013. http://www.thegrocer.co.uk/fmcg/fresh/cytosports-muscle-milk-hits-uk-mults-in-40m-sales-drive/350903.article?utm_source=RSS_Feed&utm_medium=RSS&utm_campaign=rss

"In delineating the food group . . . second-class dairy citizen"

"What Foods Are Included in the Dairy Group?" U.S. Department of Agriculture, ChooseMyPlate.gov. http://www.choosemyplate.gov/food-groups/dairy.html

"In the days when milk . . . and whole milk the form"

Dupuis, Melanie . *Nature's Perfect Food: How Milk Became America's Drink* (New York: New York University Press, 2002), 78–81

"Sales of low-fat and skim milk combined didn't surpass sales of whole milk until 1988"

"Milestones," International Dairy Association. http://www.idfa.org/news--views/media-kits/milk/milestones/

"The USDA's website describes the Guidelines . . . '. . . and nutrition education activities'"

"Dietary Guidelines for Americans," U.S. Department of Agriculture, Center for Nutrition Policy and Promotion. www.cnpp.usda.gov/DietaryGuidelines

"Page one of the 1980 Guidelines reveals . . . '. . . your intake of fats from foods other than milk'"

"Dietary Guidelines for Americans, 1980," U.S. Department of Agriculture, Center for Nutrition Policy and Promotion, 1, 11–12. Available for downloading at http://www.cnpp.usda.gov/Dietary-Guidelines-1980

"Becker's, a chain of convenience stores that had over 90 franchises throughout Ontario . . ."

"Becker's, Convenience Stores," Wikipedia. Last modified November 7, 2014. http://en.wikipedia.org/wiki/Becker%27s

"Side by side, the 1985 Guidelines seem light-years . . . '. . . low-fat milk and milk products'"

"Dietary Guidelines for Americans, 1985," U.S. Department of Agriculture, Center for Nutrition Policy and Promotion, 1, 16. Last modified May 28, 2014. Available for downloading at http://www.cnpp.usda.gov/DGAs1985Guidelines.htm

"In 1990, the Guidelines stopped speaking . . . '. . . (less than twenty-two grams at two thousand calories per day) is suggested"

"Dietary Guidelines for Americans, 1990," U.S. Department of Agriculture, Center for Nutrition Policy and Promotion, 16. Last modified August 15, 2013. Available for downloading at http://www.cnpp.usda.gov/DGAs1990Guidelines.htm

"Finally in 2000, whole milk was lumped together . . . 'Keep your intake of these foods low'"

"Dietary Guidelines for Americans, 2000," U.S. Department of Agriculture, Center for Nutrition Policy and Promotion. Last modified August 15, 2013, 28. Available for downloading at http://www.cnpp.usda.gov/DGAs2000Guidelines.htm

"On May 27, 2000, President Bill Clinton . . . '. . . million of our children every day in school'"

"Radio Address by the President to the Nation," The White House, Office of the Press Secretary. May 27, 2000. http://www.health.gov/dietaryguidelines/dga2000/president.txt

"The lunch lady who . . . '. . . to meet recommended intake rather than relying on supplements'"

"Dietary Guidelines for Americans, 2010," U.S. Department of Agriculture, Center for Nutrition Policy and Promotion, 55, 34, xi, 9, 52, 68, 40. Available for downloading at http://www.cnpp.usda.gov/dietary-guidelines-2010

"The Healthy, Hunger-Free Kids Act . . . 'Fluid milk must be low-fat (one percent milk fat or less, unflavored) or fat-free (unflavored or flavored)'"

"Summary of the Healthy, Hunger-Free Kids Act of 2010 (By Program), Sec. 202 'Fluid Milk,'" U.S. Department of Agriculture, Food and Nutrition Service, 2. Available for downloading at www.fns.usda.gov/sites/default/files/PL111-296_Summary.pdf

"School Lunch Programs, Program requirements, Nutritional requirements, Fluid Milk,"
Richard B. Russell National School Lunch Act, 42 U.S.C. 1758(a)(2)(A). U.S. Government
Printing Office. http://www.gpo.gov/fdsys/pkg/USCODE-2010-title42/html/
USCODE-2010-title42-chap13-sec1758.htm

"Nutrition Standards in the National School Lunch and School Breakfast Programs," U.S.
Department of Agriculture, Food and Nutrition Service, Final rule. 7 CFR Parts 210 and
220, 4111, footnote "i." Available for downloading at http://www.fns.usda.gov/sites/
default/files/01-26-12_CND.pdf

*"In 1997 the USDA's Economic Research Service (ERS) published a report . . . in 1995, 17,431
million pounds were lost"*

Kantor, Linda Scott, Kathryn Lipton, Alden Manchester, and Victor Oliveira. "Estimating and
Addressing America's Food Losses," *FoodReview* 20, 1(January–April 1997), 7

"If the ERS report is correct . . . second-highest loss rate of all the foods that the report measures"

Kantor, Linda Scott, Kathryn Lipton, Alden Manchester, and Victor Oliveira. "Estimating and
Addressing America's Food Losses," *FoodReview* 20, 1(January–April 1997), 5, 7

Bloom, Jonathan. *American Wasteland: How America Throws Away Nearly Half of Its Food (and
What We Can Do about It)* (Cambridge, MA: Da Capo Press, 2010), 10

"In her December 2013 editorial . . . '. . . the poster child for unhealthy eating habits'"

Perry, Samantha. "Opinion: Christmas calories: Eating healthy difficult during sweet
season," Bluefield Daily Telegraph. December 23, 2013. http://blog.illumen.org/
healthways/?p=81013

*"As the Dietary Guidelines for Americans have become more detailed . . . applesauce; and lastly, fat-
free milk to whole milk"*

"Dietary Guidelines for Americans, 2010," U.S. Department of Agriculture, Center for
Nutrition Policy and Promotion, xiii, 47. Available for downloading at http://www.cnpp
.usda.gov/dietary-guidelines-2010

"As the introduction explains: 'The ultimate goal . . . become the norm among all individuals'"

"Dietary Guidelines for Americans, 2010," U.S. Department of Agriculture, Center for
Nutrition Policy and Promotion, 1. Available for downloading at http://www.cnpp.usda
.gov/dietary-guidelines-2010

"Just over 70 percent of the milk served in schools is flavored . . . cartons of flavored milk"

Severson, Kim. "A School Fight Over Chocolate Milk," *The New York Times*. Published
August 24, 2010. http://www.nytimes.com/2010/08/25/dining/25Milk.html?_
r=1&

Schultz, Daniel J. "The Sweet Precedent of Flavored Milk," *The Huffington Post*. Last
modified June 23, 2014. http://www.huffingtonpost.com/daniel-j-schultz/diet-and-
nutrition_b_5186892.html?utm_hp_ref=healthy-living

Cruz, Gilbert. "U.S. Schools' War Against Chocolate Milk," *Time*. December 18, 2009. http://content.time.com/time/nation/article/0,8599,1948865,00.html

"Milk chocolate fluid commercial lowfat with added vitamin A and vitamin D," HealthAliciousNess.com. http://www.healthaliciousness.com/nutritionfacts/nutrition_facts.php?id=Milk%20chocolate%20fluid%20commercial%20lowfat%20with%20added%20vitamin%20A%20and%20vitamin%20D&idn=01104; To convert to cups go to: "Nutrition Facts Comparison Tool," HealthAliciousNess.com. http://www.healthaliciousness.com/nutritionfacts/nutrition-facts-compare.php

"Milk whole 3.25% milkfat with added vitamin D," HealthAliciousNess.com. http://www.healthaliciousness.com/nutritionfacts/nutrition_facts.php?id=Milk%20whole%203.25%%20milkfat%20with%20added%20vitamin%20D&idn=01077; To convert to cups go to: "Nutrition Facts Comparison Tool," HealthAliciousNess.com. http://www.healthaliciousness.com/nutritionfacts/nutrition-facts-compare.php

"Coca-Cola Nutrition Information," Coca-Cola Company. http://productnutrition.thecoca-colacompany.com/

"Dr. Walter Willett, who has been called . . . high-fat dairy for high-fructose corn syrup"

"World's most-cited nutritionist debunks dieting myths," CTV News. Published January 27, 2014. http://www.ctvnews.ca/health/world-s-most-cited-nutritionist-debunks-dieting-myths-1.1657609

White, Jon. "Is full-fat milk best? The skinny on the dairy paradox," *New Scientist*. February 21, 2014. http://www.newscientist.com/article/dn25102-is-fullfat-milk-best-the-skinny-on-the-dairy-paradox.html#.U2gIgi-eL4i

"The notification to 'avoid saturated fat' is followed . . . '. . . supply your body's energy needs'"

"Dietary Guidelines for Americans, 1980," U.S. Department of Agriculture, Center for Nutrition Policy and Promotion, 13. Available for downloading at http://www.cnpp.usda.gov/Dietary-Guidelines-1980

"The agency's steadfast adherence to a directive that the current research is proving deeply flawed . . . prone to error"

"Full-fat dairy may reduce obesity risk," Harvard School of Public Health. http://www.hsph.harvard.edu/news/hsph-in-the-news/full-fat-dairy-may-reduce-obesity-risk/

Aubrey, Allison. "The Full-Fat Paradox: Whole Milk May Keep Us Lean," The Salt, National Public Radio. February 12, 2014. http://www.npr.org/blogs/thesalt/2014/02/12/275376259/the-full-fat-paradox-whole-milk-may-keep-us-lean

Bickard, Scott. "Why Whole Fat, Organic Milk Is the Healthiest Choice (But Not the Cheapest!)," University Herald. December 10, 2013. http://www.universityherald.com/articles/6109/20131210/why-whole-fat-organic-milk-is-the-healthiest-choice-but-not-the-cheapest.htm

Kratz, M., T. Baars and S. Guyenet. "The relationship between high-fat dairy consumption and obesity, cardiovascular, and metabolic disease," National Center for Biotechnology Information, PubMed. Published in the *European Journal of Nutrition*, February 2013. http://www.ncbi.nlm.nih.gov/pubmed/22810464

"But that's to be expected given what Dr. Willett is not shy to admit . . . '. . . all the final answers even yet'"

Kirkey, Sharon. "Drinking milk not essential for humans despite belief it prevents osteoporosis, nutritionist says," National Post. January 23, 2014. http://life.nationalpost .com/2014/01/23/drinking-milk-not-essential-for-humans-despite-belief-it-prevents-osteoporosis-nutritionist-says/

"Interview Walter Willett, M.D.," Frontline. Posted April 8, 2004. http://www.pbs.org/ wgbh/pages/frontline/shows/diet/interviews/willett.html

"In March 2009 the International Dairy Foods Association . . . won't choose milk that is marketed as 'reduced calorie'"

"Flavored Milk; Petition to Amend the Standard of Identity for Milk and 17 Additional Dairy Products—A Proposed Rule by the Food and Drug Administration," *Federal Register, The Daily Journal of the United States Government.* February 20, 2013. https://www .federalregister.gov/articles/2013/02/20/2013-03835/flavored-milk-petition-to-amend-the-standard-of-identity-for-milk-and-17-additional-dairy-products#h-4

"The government's sponsorship of milk with more . . . '. . . to greater fat in our bodies'"

White, Jon. "Is full-fat milk best? The skinny on the dairy paradox." *New Scientist.* February 21, 2014. http://www.newscientist.com/article/dn25102-is-fullfat-milk-best-the-skinny-on-the-dairy-paradox.html#.U2gUFS-eL4j

"The solution is especially disagreeable . . . gut health and glucose tolerance"

Vergano, Dan. "Study: Artificial Sweeteners May Trigger Blood Sugar Risks," *National Geographic.* Published September 17, 2014. http://news.nationalgeographic.com/ news/2014/09/140917-sweeteners-artificial-blood-sugar-diabetes-health-ngfood/

"Michael Pollan's book In Defense of Food *. . . '. . . whole fresh foods rather than processed food products'"*

Pollan, Michael. *In Defense of Food: An Eater's Manifesto* (New York: Penguin Press, 2008), 1

"The core of the 2010 edition contains . . . '. . . the refining process'"

"Dietary Guidelines for Americans, 2010," U.S. Department of Agriculture, Center for Nutrition Policy and Promotion, x, 23, 34, 16, 29, 30. Available for downloading at http://www.cnpp.usda.gov/dietary-guidelines-2010

CHAPTER 14: MAKING IT WITHOUT MILK

"'Because 73 percent of the calcium. . . .'. . . has some explaining to do"

Sole, Elise. "Harvard doctor refutes milk recommendations," Yahoo! Lifestyle. July 4, 2013.

https://au.lifestyle.yahoo.com/health/diet-nutrition/article/-/17863803/harvard-doctor-refutes-milk-recommendations/

"Dietary Guidelines for Americans, 2010," U.S. Department of Agriculture, Center for Nutrition Policy and Promotion, 40–1. Available for downloading at http://www.cnpp.usda.gov/DGAs2010-PolicyDocument.htm

"As Joe Satran discovered . . . 'The Dairy Problem'"

Satran, Joe. "My MyPlate Experiment, Day Two: The Dairy Problem," The Huffington Post. Last modified August 4, 2013. http://www.huffingtonpost.com/joe-satran/my-myplate-experiment-day_b_2627648.html#slide=more278777

". . . fiber, another on the 2010 Dietary Guidelines for Americans' list of 'nutrients of concern'"

"Dietary Guidelines for Americans, 2010," U.S. Department of Agriculture, Center for Nutrition Policy and Promotion, 40–41. Available for downloading at http://www.cnpp.usda.gov/DGAs2010-PolicyDocument.htm

"An estimate of the number of calories and milligrams of calcium, magnesium—a mineral that studies show North Americans are low in . . ."

King, DE *et al.* "Dietary magnesium and C-reactive protein levels," National Center for Biotechnology Information, PubMed. Published in the *Journal of the American College of Nutrition*, June 24, 2005. http://www.ncbi.nlm.nih.gov/pubmed/15930481

"The totals are based on online nutrition data sites . . ."

"Nutrition Facts Comparison Tool," HealthAliciousNess.com http://www.healthaliciousness.com/nutritionfacts/nutrition-facts-compare.php

SELF Nutrition Data. http://nutritiondata.self.com/

"As you consider . . . the DV is 1,000 milligrams for calcium and 400 milligrams for magnesium"

"Daily Value (DV) Tables," U.S. Department of Health & Human Services National Institutes of Health. http://ods.od.nih.gov/HealthInformation/dailyvalues.aspx

"For instance, dried figs . . . 12 percent of the DV for calcium, or 120 milligrams"

"Figs dried uncooked," HealthAliciousNess.com. http://www.healthaliciousness.com/nutritionfacts/nutrition_facts.php?id=Figs%20dried%20uncooked&idn=09094; To compare to raisins and dates and convert to cups go to: "Nutrition Facts Comparison Tool," HealthAliciousNess.com. http://www.healthaliciousness.com/nutritionfacts/nutrition-facts-compare.php

"14 Non-Dairy Foods That Are High in Calcium," Health Media Ventures. http://www.health.com/health/gallery/0,,20845429_8,00.html

"While you can buy almond milk . . . before its almond milk is carrageenan-free"

"Carrageenan: Risks and Reality," The Cornucopia Institute. December 20, 2013. http://www.cornucopia.org/2013/12/carrageenan-risks-reality/

Oaklander, Mandy. "The Soy Milk Ingredient That's Getting the Axe," *Time*. August 22, 2014. http://time.com/3162074/carrageenan-whitewave/

"Most store-bought almond milk is also not made from raw almonds . . . ones from Spain"

"Pasteurization," Almond Board of California. http://www.almonds.com/processors/processing-safe-product#tc-pasteurization

7 CFR Part 981, "Almonds Grown in California; Outgoing Quality Control Requirements," Agricultural Marketing Service, U.S. Department of Agriculture. http://www.almonds.com/sites/default/files/content/attachments/pasteurization_federal_register_ruling.pdf

"Chia seeds are a favorite of endurance athletes . . . water to provide them with stamina"

"Can Chia Seeds Help You Run Longer and Faster?" RunnersConnect. http://runnersconnect.net/running-nutrition-articles/chia-seeds-running/

"Most cocoa powder that is not raw has been Dutch-processed . . . cacao the wonder food that it is"

"Update on Chocolate," YouTube video, at 1 minute into the video, posted by "NutritionFacts.org" February 25, 2011. http://nutritionfacts.org/video/update-on-chocolate/

"Remember that cacao contains oxalic acid, which inhibits your body's uptake of calcium . . ."

"Raw cacao vs cocoa," Nourish My Life. Posted April 24, 2013. http://nourishmylife.wordpress.com/2013/04/24/raw-cacao-vs-cocoa/

"Each crispy sage leaf contains about:12 calories . . . "

"Sage Leaves (Fresh)," Daily Burn Tracker. http://tracker.dailyburn.com/nutrition/sage_leaves_fresh_calories

CONCLUSION: UNHOLY HOLSTEIN COW

"A 2013 publication by the Food and Agriculture Organization . . . caused by humans in 2007"

"Milk and Dairy Products in Human Nutrition," Food and Agriculture Organization of the United Nations (Rome: 2013), 342, 346. Available at http://www.fao.org/docrep/018/i3396e/i3396e.pdf

"Methane emissions from 'enteric fermentation' . . . '. . . emissions by 25 percent by 2020'"

"Fact Sheet: Climate Action Plan-Strategy to Cut Methane Emissions," White House Office of the Press Secretary. March 28, 2014. http://www.whitehouse.gov/the-press-office/2014/03/28/fact-sheet-climate-action-plan-strategy-cut-methane-emissions

Bauers, Sandy. "Implementing smarter milk farming in Chesco," Philly.com. Posted September 29, 2014. http://articles.philly.com/2014-09-29/news/54404607_1_methane-emissions-greenhouse-gas-emissions-dairy-cows

"U.S. Greenhouse Gas Inventory Report, 2014, Chapter 6, Agriculture," U.S. Environmental Protection Agency. http://www.epa.gov/climatechange/Downloads/ghgemissions/US-GHG-Inventory-2014-Chapter-6-Agriculture.pdf

"Or maybe you've read that America's livestock are some of the heaviest consumers of GMO crops grown in America"

Chernyshova, Daria. "Green America Urges Starbucks to Use Organic Milk as Chain's Milk Purchases Extremely High," RIA Novosti. Posted October 9, 2014. http://en.ria.ru/ society/20141009/193867014/Green-America-Urges-Starbucks-to-Use-Organic-Milk-as-Chains-Milk.html

The Nation, "Consumers call on Starbucks to stop sourcing milk from cows fed with GMO," *The Nation*. September 7, 2014. http://www.nation.lk/edition/news-features/ item/33041-consumers-call-on-starbucks-to-stop-sourcing-milk-from-cows-fed-with-gmo.html

"Did you know that dairy cows are fed sodium bicarbonate . . . a cow consuming 60 pounds of dry matter"

Block, Elliot. "Increased buffer levels enhanced herd health, productivity," Dairy Herd Management. Last modified March 24, 2014. http://www.dairyherd.com/nutritionist-network/case-study/Increasing-ration-buffer-levels-enhanced-herd-health-251929371 .html?view=all

"In Canada, farmers are permitted to buy over-the-counter antibiotics . . . without a veterinarian's prescription"

Kaye, Marcia . "Superbugs: Drug-resistant Infections Are a Man-made Problem. Is It One We Can Solve?" *University of Toronto Magazine* (Spring 2014): 37. Available at http://www. magazine.utoronto.ca/cover-story/superbugs-bacterial-infection-antibiotics-health-marcia-kaye/

"And in the United States dairy farmers are allowed to give their dairy cows the synthetic . . . boost milk yields"

"Bovine Growth Hormone (rBGH)/Recombinant Bovine Somatotropin (rBST)," Breast Cancer Fund. http://www.breastcancerfund.org/clear-science/radiation-chemicals-and-breast-cancer/bovine-growth-hormone.html

"A 2014 University of Kentucky publication details . . . organophosphates to the mix"

Townsend, Lee. "Insect Control on Dairy Cattle–2014," University of Kentucky College of Agriculture, Food and Environment. http://pest.ca.uky.edu/EXT/Recs/ENT12-Dairy.pdf

"They were on to this fact as far back as the days of Abraham Lincoln . . . then called 'milk sickness'"

Aylor, James. "Plant was at root of Lincoln's mom's death," *The Acorn*. September 25, 2014. http://www.theacorn.com/news/2014-09-25/Health_%2528and%2529_Wellness/

"The insecticides that are the subject . . . kills the maggots before they mature into milking-parlor pests"

Townsend, Lee. "Insect Control on Dairy Cattle–2014," University of Kentucky College of Agriculture, Food and Environment. http://pest.ca.uky.edu/EXT/Recs/ENT12-Dairy.pdf

"Dairies with 1,000 or more cows produce over 50 percent . . . 'a major contributor to contamination of surveyed estuaries and ground water'"

Grossman, Elizabeth. "As Dairy Farms Grow Bigger, New Concerns About Pollution," Yale Environment 360. Last modified May 27, 2014. http://e360.yale.edu/feature/as_dairy_farms_grow_bigger_new_concerns_about_pollution/2768/

"Water: Polluted Runoff," U.S. Environmental Protection Agency. http://water.epa.gov/polwaste/nps/agriculture.cfm

"It all started in 1937 under a different name . . . let out to pasture after a long winter"

Gudex, Brenda. "Farm News & Views column: June Dairy Month kicks off summer, special events," fdlreporter.com. June 7, 2014. http://www.fdlreporter.com/article/20140608/FON03/306080044/Farm-News-Views-column-June-Dairy-Month-kicks-off-summer-special-events?nclick_check=1

"Celebrate Dairy Month with the real deal and the St. Louis Dairy Council," KSDK.com. June 4, 2014. http://www.ksdk.com/story/entertainment/television/show-me-st-louis/2014/06/04/dairy-council/9959645/

"Maybe you can't compare apples to oranges . . . '. . . So she's just going to die quicker' "

Hamilton, Alissa. *Squeezed: What You Don't Know about Orange Juice* (New Haven, CT: Yale University Press, 2009), 147

"As the water workshop wrapped up I was reminded of the Harvard School of Public Health's Healthy Eating Plate. On its plate blue doesn't stand for dairy but water . . ."

"Food Pyramids and Plates: What Should You Really Eat?" Harvard School of Public Health. http://www.hsph.harvard.edu/nutritionsource/pyramid-full-story/

"Making the rounds during 2014's Dairy Month, the St. Louis District Dairy Council joined Missouri's News Channel 5 . . . '. . . a source of essential nutrients'"

"Celebrate Dairy Month with the real deal and the St. Louis Dairy Council," KSDK.com. June 4, 2014. http://www.ksdk.com/story/entertainment/television/show-me-st-louis/2014/06/04/dairy-council/9959645/

"The effects of government and dairy industry efforts . . . Americans are doing the reverse"

"Dietary Guidelines for Americans, 2010," U.S. Department of Agriculture, Center for Nutrition Policy and Promotion, 12. Available for downloading at http://www.cnpp.usda.gov/DGAs2010-PolicyDocument.htm

"Dietary Guidelines for Americans, 1980," U.S. Department of Agriculture, Center for Nutrition Policy and Promotion, 12. Available for downloading at http://www.cnpp.usda.gov/Dietary-Guidelines-1980

"A June 2014 report authored by attorney Michele Simon . . . '. . . unhealthy forms of dairy'"

Simon, Michele. "Whitewashed: How Industry and Government Promote Dairy Junk Foods,"
1, 3, Eat Drink Politics. June 2014. Available for downloading at http://www
.eatdrinkpolitics.com/wp-content/uploads/SimonWhitewashedDairyReport.pdf
"Go ahead, the Dairy Food Group says . . . a total of three and now you have a serving of dairy"
"What Counts as a Cup in the Dairy Group?" U.S. Department of Agriculture,
ChooseMyPlate.gov. http://www.choosemyplate.gov/food-groups/dairy-counts.html

EPILOGUE
"Leave it to my sister . . . '. . . He saw it, he loved it, he ate it' "
"Maurice Sendak," Fresh Air on Tumblr. Posted May 8, 2012. http://nprfreshair.tumblr.com/
post/22652290421/hwentworth-internets-over-people-maurice
"Fresh Air Remembers Author Maurice Sendak," NPR books. May 8, 2012. http://www.npr
.org/2012/05/08/152248901/fresh-air-remembers-author-maurice-sendak

INDEX

Wiley, Andrea, 140
Willett, Walter
    on calcium requirements, 83, 109
    on dairy requirements, 81–82
    on milk requirements, 36
    on vitamin D requirements, 109
    on dietary fat / body fat connection, 175
    on full-fat dairy paradox, 51
    on replacing dairy fat with sugar,
        172–73, 175
    on Healthy Eating Plate
        recommendations, 35–36
    on government to change dairy
        recommendations, 117–18
Williams, Kenneth, 85
Wisconsin, 119–20, 241
World Health Organization (WHO)
    on calcium-bone connection, 99

on calcium-protein connection, 70–71, 99
daily recommendations for calcium, 115
daily recommendations for protein, 65, 67
World Milk Day, 144, 150
World School Milk Day (WSMD), 143, 145,
    146–47, 150

Yogurt
    in Dairy Group, 246
    Greek, protein in, 32
    Greek, USDA classification of, 32
    lactose in, 44
    promoted for weight loss, 47
    sugar-added, 160–61

Za'atar, 192
Zemel, Michael B., 47
Zinc, 113